MW00509504

BARRY WILLIAME MAGLIARDITI

SEX, DRUGS, AND RADICAL SELF-EXPRESSION

THE UNEXPECTED PATH TO FULFILLMENT

LIONCREST
PUBLISHING

Sex, Drugs, and Radical Self-Expression
The Unexpected Path to Fulfillment

ISBN   978-1-5445-2664-5   *Hardcover*
        978-1-5445-2662-1   *Paperback*
        978-1-5445-2663-8   *Ebook*

*This book is dedicated to anyone who
grew up feeling like they didn't belong or weren't enough.
Know that you are unique, beautiful, and powerful beyond
measure and yet only a speck of dust in this existence.
Take this book as your permission slip to become your
most authentic self and all of who you're here to be.
Realise that you are enough and have nothing to prove to
anyone or anything outside yourself. The validation, belonging,
and love you seek will only come from the connection
to your heart and your heart's connection
to the Divine Source.*

CONTENTS

NOTE FROM THE AUTHOR

WHEN I WAS EIGHTEEN YEARS OLD, I WAS AN ABSOLUTE MESS. MY entire life was circling the drain. Drug use, petty crime, depression. I felt completely worthless and alone.

But this book is not a pity party. Far from it.

I start here because I want you to know that no matter how bad you're hurting right now, how much you think you've fucked things up in your life…you can turn it around and start being, feeling, and having everything you need.

If I can go from an eighteen-year-old disaster waiting to happen to where I am now—living my dream lifestyle in Bali, owning multiple multimillion-dollar companies that afford me time to spend my days surfing and enjoying life, working when I want, and feeling pretty fucking amazing and blessed every day—then you can, too.

The truth is that a fulfilling and rich life (in every sense of the word) begins with the relationship you have with yourself.

Years ago, I began healing that relationship, connecting with my heart, and learning to be guided by my intuition. And with each step, my happiness and success grew.

In this book, I share what I learned along the way. I invite you to come along for the journey and find your own path to fulfilment.

WHO THIS BOOK IS FOR

I was a little apprehensive about writing this book. Perhaps you've read my last book, *The Path to Freedom*, and you're expecting something like that. (By the way, if you're an entrepreneur or business owner, you should definitely read it. It's a step-by-step guide to systematising your business to work without you. You can get a free copy at: www.pathtofreedom.com.au/free-book.)

Let me tell you now. This book is quite different.

This book is for anyone wanting to regain authentic control of their life by releasing themselves from the shame, guilt, and perceived judgements they feel for not being enough. Enough of a husband, father, lover, leader, sibling, and all-around human.

I share from the perspective of my eighteen-year-old self, fresh out of the structure and controls of living at home, trying to find his way through life and prove his worthiness to his father and himself.

Throughout the book, I use my own journey to show you core fundamentals I've discovered and spend every day working to master. These fundamentals have helped me to be a happy, successful, and fulfilled human in a very dehumanising world.

This book is also for anyone who knows there can be more to life but isn't sure what steps to take. At this point in my life, I'm living my dream lifestyle. I live in Bali with the time, money, and freedom to do whatever I want. I run multiple multimillion-dollar businesses but only work for a few hours a week. I have an incredible relationship with my partner, my kids, and myself.

If you're reading this now, know that you can have it all, too. Everything you need is already inside of you.

I'm not any smarter or more gifted than you. I wasn't born into privilege; I didn't get any special treatment that elevated me to this level in life. I simply practised what I outlined in this book. I went on a quest to become all of who I am and realise my full potential.

No special tricks, hacks, or connections. What got me here was doing the work on *me*, on who I wanted to be and how I wanted to show up in the world. If you're willing to go within—to navigate and be honest with your own thoughts, feelings, and beliefs—you will find a way to your full potential as well. That's my promise.

WHAT TO EXPECT

This book is divided into three parts, which build on each other. I call the three parts "the holy trinity." They are the heart, the head, and the hand. As you move through the book, you will see how all of these are connected. In order to experience mind, body, and spirit alignment, you can't skip past the heart or only focus on the mind. You need all three.

In Part 1, *The Heart*, we'll explore the spiritual aspects of who we are. We'll talk about the importance of emotions, heart meditations, and more. In Part 2, *The Head*, we'll consider the world of our thoughts and how the ego plays into life. Finally, in Part 3, *The Hand*, we'll learn to actually embody what we desire in the physical world.

Before we dive too far into the book, I also want to offer a couple of disclaimers up front. As you might have guessed from the subtitle of the book, I will be sharing a lot of personal stories. In particular, I will share some of my experiences with drugs.

This book is not about drugs. It's not a druggie book. But it does contain stories of drug use. At various points in my life, I've used drugs to achieve certain outcomes. And for me, a lot of those experiences were defining moments.

Don't get me wrong; I absolutely condemn irresponsible drug use. I'm not trying to glorify drugs in this book, nor am I trying to tell you that they are how *you* should begin exploring your own consciousness. Drugs are simply one of the many methods I have used personally in my own quest for spiritual answers to personal questions. I'll share more specifics about these experiences as we go.

Drugs are substances or compounds that alter the normal state of the body and mind. They are a catalyst that causes the body to behave differently. That's all.

Medicines are drugs. We are conditioned to believe that medicine is good for us and drugs are bad for us. But both alter the normal state of the body and brain in some way. Some create different enzymes and molecules, or more or less of them, to achieve different purposes. Some regulate blood pressure. Some reduce inflammation. Some kill bacteria. Some stimulate our sympathetic nervous system. And some trigger psychological responses.

Of course, the wrong dosage or misuse of *any* compound can do harm. As I share, all I ask is that you suspend judgement and remember that what's 'good' or 'bad' is often in how we use it, not in the thing itself.

Throughout the book, you will also find some ideas that might confront your own views about sex, spirituality, or masculinity and femininity. Some themes in the book might trigger you. Some of the content might seem too "woo-woo." Some of it might seem like absolute bullshit.

That's okay. Because this is *my* experience. I'm sharing it because I know the lessons within my journey so far can help you, too. I don't expect you to agree with everything I say. At the end of the book, you can decide what you choose to keep and what you choose to discard from the lessons, experiences, and ideas I share.

A FINAL NOTE

Remember: this journey starts from within.

So before you put this book down and dismiss it because you're "not a spiritual person" (or whatever your inner voice is telling you right now), remember that you picked it up for a reason. A reason beyond curiosity. I believe you were called to pick it up from the deep wisdom within your heart. So for the next few hundred pages, follow the intuition that led you to pick up this book.

Whether you want to improve your relationship with an intimate partner, experience more love and joy, or start feeling more fulfilled in every area of your life, let this book be your guide.

I'm about to share with you the tried and tested principles that helped me reshape my life—and myself—from the inside out. These fundamentals and the associated practices have worked for me and for hundreds of my coaching clients over the years.

I know they will accelerate you along your path, too.

All I ask is that you read this book with an open mind and open heart. Take off the mask and just be yourself. Remove your preconceptions of what it is to be a man, what it is to be a woman, what it is to live a good life, or what it is to be successful. Take away your perceptions around spirituality. Instead, simply show up as a receptive vessel.

I'll share my lessons and my story as openly as I can. I'll put my niggling fear of judgement (which we *all* have) to the side and show up 100 per cent for you.

When you feel resistance, all I ask is that you explore that feeling. Why are you feeling that way? What are the thoughts behind it?

Chances are your conditioning is kicking in and telling you, *Nope, that's bullshit, it's not the way things work.*

But guess what? The way you currently see and experience the world is not the only way. By picking up this book, your intuition is trying to show you a different way.

Will you listen? I hope so.

PART 1

THE HEART

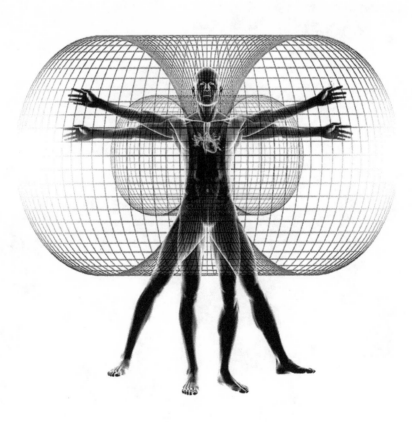

CHAPTER 1

THE AGONY AND
THE ECSTASY

I DON'T LOVE MYSELF.

As I heard my inner voice speak those words so clearly, the impact of my realisation sucked all the breath out of me—just for a second.

Whoa. What a sucker punch to the soul.

After all the years I'd spent on my spiritual journey—practising meditation daily, training in multiple modalities such as reiki, breathwork, neuro-linguistic programming, and more.

After all the workshops. All the shaman circles. All the healing exercises. And I still hadn't landed the most important relationship a human being can have?

Instead of composing a strongly worded letter to the universe asking for my money back, I did the one thing that has always guided me in the direction I needed to go. I asked an exploratory question with an open heart and genuine curiosity.

That question was simple.

Why?

Why don't I love myself?

From there, the other questions followed.

Where did this begin? What are the beliefs and feelings I'm holding onto that have kept me from loving myself? What else do I need to uncover about myself?

Where am I still hiding from myself, deep down inside?

I opened my eyes and started coming out of my meditative state. I felt the warmth on my skin and heard the bugs skittering and birds chirping in the lush green trees surrounding the property. The Balinese humidity was making my singlet stick to my back. I could smell incense burning nearby.

My butt ached on the hard earth. How long had I been sitting here? How long had it been since I'd walked down the path dotted with sound healing bowls up to a beautiful yet weathered old wooden house, past the dragon head altar on the porch, and into this experience?

A man with kind brown eyes was looking at me. His long grey hair, Tree of Life mandala necklace, and hippie clothing made me feel awkward.

Although I had just met him, I felt like he could see a part of me that I wasn't seeing myself. And that made me uneasy.

What was that twinkle in his eye? Was he laughing at me? Was he judging me?

He sat on the ground next to me and smiled a little—a real Mona Lisa type of smile.

"You need to go back in," he gently said.

So I lay back down and closed my eyes.

It was time to let the drugs take me again.

· · ·

THE CURSE OF MODERNITY

Why is it that in these modern times, where we have access to more opportunity, luxury, and freedom of choice than ever before, so many people feel so fucking broken?

Depression and anxiety stats are through the roof. Marriage failure rates are rising every year. Substance abuse and alcoholism are everywhere.

Despite having even more access to each other . . . we feel more alone than ever.

So, we seek comfort. From anywhere and everywhere.

We try to make a million bucks to make our dads proud. We trawl Tinder trying to fuck the pain away. We screw up our relationships. We buy mountains of shit we do not need.

We are constantly striving to fulfil ourselves in the most unresourceful ways. It feels like there's an emptiness inside, so we keep jamming stuff in there to satiate our hunger to feel good.

But no number of sexual partners, career achievements, bottles of Jack Daniels, or fancy bags from Louis Vuitton can fill us up. The buzz fades. And we go seeking the next gratification.

I know what you might be thinking right now. *Geez, why the buzzkill, Barry?*

Look, I don't want you to feel like things are hopeless.

Because they're *not*.

If you're feeling any recognition in my words so far, I've got good news for you.

You're *not* empty. You're *not* broken. You are whole and everything you need to be. You're just looking for fulfilment in the wrong places.

Like a tree that gets watered with Gatorade, you're not able to operate at your best, most fulfilled self because you're getting the wrong nourishment.

It's not your fault. You were taught to value the wrong things by society. By your family. By your friends. And it's not their fault either, because they were taught by the people who influenced *them* growing up. The cycle repeats itself until we each make the conscious effort to break the cycle and experience our lives a different way.

I'd like to show you how to start breaking down the conditioning and biases you've inherited, so you can start to rebuild your relationship with yourself, the people around you, and life itself.

START WITH THE HEART

What I share in this book can help you shift your lens and learn to listen to your heart and soul, instead of the blaring noise from society and the world in general shouting at you about who you should be and what you should want. It can help you change the internal soundtrack that dictates how you show up in life.

And when you shift into this new way of being, the world truly does open up. Success comes easier and greater than you ever imagined. Relationships go from "meh" to "wow." Your sense of self-worth and self-love bloom.

Most importantly, if you choose to read and follow what I outline in this book, it will help strengthen your connection to your intuition and the Divine Source (whatever God is to you—Allah, Jehovah, Gaia).

When I started my journey towards ultimate fulfilment, I had no idea where to start. Then I realised I had to begin at the deepest, most central part: the heart.

As I did, I began to find what I was seeking. I'm not just talking about the material stuff. I'm talking about love of life. A sense of fulfilment that isn't tied to my bank balance. And a relationship with myself that is full of ever-expanding love.

If that sounds like something you want, I invite you to come with me as I share how I got here.

A DIFFERENT KIND OF JOURNEY

When I woke up on the ground in Bali with a kind-eyed hippie dude peering down at me, my mind shot back to a conversation I had with a friend three weeks prior.

We were sitting in a cafe in Canggu, Bali, my newly adopted home. He had just mentioned that a friend of his did DMT.

"DMT? Isn't that the trippy stuff Homer licks off a toad's back in that *Simpsons* episode?" I laughed.

I was mucking around, but I knew what it was. Dimethyltryptamine (DMT) is a simple compound found throughout nature that has a profound psychedelic effect on human consciousness.

DMT is found in all manner of plants, animals, and even us humans. As Joe Rogan once put it, "It's a weird drug to be illegal because everyone's holding."

I'd actually heard a lot of stories about DMT. Some said it evokes a state where you exist in your purest form. Others said they found a new understanding of life and death while using it.

For some people, it unlocks the secrets of the infinite universe. Often it creates a feeling—no, a *knowing*—that you are happy, complete, and sublime.

When people come back from a near-death experience, and report seeing a white light or divine beings, some scientists and medical professionals say this is the result of a release of DMT, which gives the brain a final, all-encompassing hallucination (Bryant 2018).

Among scientists and shamans alike, DMT is fast becoming known as "the God molecule."

I'm always open to experiences that help me understand myself more and strengthen my connection to the divine. So I was curious, though a bit apprehensive.

Flashbacks of acid trippers frantically trying to scratch imagined cockroaches off their skin at raves back in my twenties came back to me.

What if I did it and had a bad trip?

But then again...what if I did it, and it was life-changing?

I put the thought aside then. But over the next week, the possibility tickled the edges of my mind. I kept hearing references to this substance and stories about it, so I decided to listen to the signs that were around me and give it a try.

After researching through my network for a safe and experienced guide to administer the DMT and guide me through my experience, I eventually ended up on the porch of that wooden house in the lush landscape of Bali. There, I met the two people who would facilitate my journey: a forty-something Australian shaman woman, who would initially administer the drug to me, and a gentle hippy dude in his sixties, who would watch over me during my experience.

"It's called the God molecule because it activates the gland that allows us to access ancient wisdom and divine connection with God," the shaman woman explained. "It will give you access to forgotten universal codes that we knew in previous lifetimes but cannot remember in this human experience."

Although in the lead-up to this experience, I was super nervous, I felt in my heart that I just had to let go and surrender to what was there. I'd done my due diligence. I was taking it in a controlled environment. I had to let go.

When I opened my eyes for the first time after taking the DMT, I found myself laying on the grass in the sun, which was above me. I mean, the sun was *directly* above me, right at my third eye. It struck me as wonderfully odd. What was the likelihood of that happening?

The sun was there for me, I thought. I had just had such a beautiful experience where I felt that life and existence and light had been created for me, to support me as a living being. And yet, I realised that I'd spent my whole life resisting. Resisting the challenges, the opportunities, the love...resisting everything that was there in abundance, being given to me. I missed it all in my pursuit to belong and be seen by my father, my mother, and my peers.

I remember sitting up and noticing that my body was covered in ants. Not in the tripped-out raver kind of way, but actual ants were wandering around on my arms, my torso, my legs. Normally, the instinct would be to brush them off, but I felt no such urge.

Instead, I felt a sense of being one with everything. Yes, even the ants. Most living things on this planet are made up of a lot of the same ingredients, after all. Carbon, hydrogen, oxygen, nitrogen, phosphorus, and sulphur. Atoms combine and form these elements in different ways, but at our core, we're all a bundle of stitched-together common elements.

It was around this time that my hippie observer told me to go back in.

"You're not done," he said. "You've had a realisation. Now you have to let go of your need to control."

He was right.

Over the next forty-five minutes of meditation, I started to realise that during my entire life, I had pursued bigger experiences. I'd pursued goals, wealth, status, relationships ... all these external stimuli.

And it was all to make me feel like *I belonged.*

My whole life had been made up of me bouncing from one experience to the next like a junkie, constantly seeking the next thing that would make me feel like I was worthy, accepted, and loved.

As I came back to full consciousness and looked up at my hippie observer, I realised that, in many ways, this guy represented an aspect of myself I'd kept hidden my whole life. I realised why his clothing and long hair had made me feel awkward before. It was because he was a total stereotype ... yet totally cool with himself. He was into some "woo-woo" shit, and he didn't give a damn what I thought of him for it.

For a second, I envied him. Because I'd spent my life trying to be the version of myself I thought I had to be, just to avoid judgement, feel worthy, and belong in the group I was in.

Business Barry. Partner Barry. Father Barry. Friend Barry. Son Barry. Student Barry. Leader Barry.

Each version of me was different depending on who I thought I had to show up as.

But in all of those Barrys, I never showed up fully as *me*. Pieces of me, yes, but never the full deal.

And for the first time, it occurred to me that the only thing that was holding me back from being my fully authentic self was myself.

So why had I suppressed my true self for so long? Why do I still struggle with fear of judgement for being my full self?

EMOTIONAL SUPPRESSION

To reach back to the centre—to who we truly are—we must go all the way back to what blocked us from our own hearts.

We are all born with one core desire that links all the primary and secondary drivers together.

That core desire is *belonging*.

We cannot recognize all our primary and secondary drivers without first recognizing our desire for belonging. Sure, we can fulfil *some* of our core needs without it. But not all. Not totally and holistically.

The need to belong is so ingrained in our human psyche through hundreds of thousands of years of evolution that we'll do anything to fulfil it. We'll deny our true selves and teach our loved ones to do it, too.

From our earliest years, we're taught to stifle our emotions. Babies learn to "self-soothe" (cry their eyes out until they realise that nobody is coming to help them and give up).

Kids are taught to repress their more rowdy or messy emotions in a million ways. The naughty corner. Time-out. Removal of freedoms. Rejection from their immediate family—their tribe. Cast out until they learn to suppress and control themselves.

Yes, children need to learn how to function in society in a productive manner, but the enormous denial we learn in our upbringing has a harmful side effect: it teaches us to hide how we're truly feeling. To push it deep down until we forget it's there. We eventually become so good at doing this that, as adults, we often don't have any connection with our true feelings at all.

As a twenty-year-old man, I had no idea what was going on inside my head or my heart. It was just chaos. It was just urges to party, hook up with women, or achieve recognition. If you'd asked me back then why I wanted any of it, I wouldn't have had a clue. I just *did*. I didn't know why.

Maybe you can relate?

Have you ever felt that you couldn't express how you really felt? When did this begin for you? Did you get sent to your room for "acting out" as a child? Were you told to be quiet when asking to have your needs met? Did you long to just be held and soothed?

I distinctly remember getting in trouble for my emotions. I got sent to my room a lot. I was always "acting out." I wasn't deliberately trying to misbehave; I just had all these emotions and had no idea how to express them. What's more, I was firmly shut down whenever I did express them.

I was—and still am—very empathetic. I feel people's energies. I can look at them and feel their emotional state. To the point where I can feel how people are feeling from inside their houses as I walk down a road. No wonder that, as a child, I sometimes felt like crying for no specific reason.

Now I now know that my sensitive, emotional barometer is a precious gift. It has helped me build a highly successful coaching company by using my intuition to help people get amazing personal outcomes that translate to business successes.

But at six years old, I had no idea how to navigate what was going on in my head and my heart. So, I became the black sheep of the family and the classroom—the "handful." Soon I started identifying *myself* that way, too. I started acting out on purpose with my emotions bubbling away inside of me and no outlet for healthy expression.

Then came rebellion. And lots of it.

Ever wonder why so many teens rebel? So much of it stems back to emotional suppression—especially the suppression of anger.

You see, anger, in particular, gets a bad rap when we're kids. Well, at any age, for that matter. We learn early that it's considered a "bad" emotion, one that is almost universally frowned upon. When, at four years old, we're taught to shut down and repress our feelings of anger or experience the withdrawal of love from a parent or guardian, it's no wonder the effects echo within our hearts into adulthood.

Thankfully, I was able to gain a healthier understanding of anger later in life. Just as I believe drug compounds aren't inherently bad, I believe emotions aren't bad either. Anger isn't bad—it's the *unresourceful expression* of anger that has bad *consequences*.

When we start holding onto "bad" emotions, those emotions still find a way to show up. They bubble to the surface, but instead of being resolved in a healthy way, they push to find a path up through the cracks in our consciousness. Like a tree that's growing in a strange direction because of something inhibiting its natural growth, the energies of unresolved emotions warp the growth of our bodies and minds. They cause mental problems and, I believe, contribute to physical disease as well.

Think of an animal that's experienced trauma. What do they do? They shake their bodies to release it. Birds beat their wings. Dogs shake themselves from head to tail.

What do *we* do when we experience trauma? We go to the doctor and get some form of medication (that's right, a drug) to make us able to function. To make us feel "better," or at least different. But oftentimes, all the drugs do is suppress the emotion that needs to be healthily expressed.

What if, instead, we heard, "You're right to be feeling angry right now because your partner has cheated on you and left. It makes total sense to experience that feeling." Or, "Barry, you've just lost a loved one. You're right to be hurting right now."

Unfortunately, that's not often what we hear when we're angry or upset.

In fact, all most of us know how to say when someone is angry is "Calm down." And what do we typically do when people are hurting? We say, "Don't cry." We try and stop the emotion from happening instead of allowing it to flow naturally through the body, be expressed, and resolved.

No wonder there are so many angry people out there going absolutely troppo at each other over tiny things like a parking spot dispute. We're walking around with all these unexpressed, unresolved, and repressed emotions. And we're boiling over.

Here's the point: emotions *need* to be expressed. Positive emotional resolution is about expressing what you feel in a healthy way, not projecting what you feel onto someone else. In this journey, it will be key to allow yourself to sit in your feelings and let them flow through you. I'll share more of how you can do this in the next few chapters.

When you allow a negative emotion to flow freely, you'll be surprised at how quickly it resolves.

Just the other day, I was pissed off because I'd let someone take advantage of me. I felt angry and frustrated, both with them and myself. My partner, Kate, was in the room with me while I was radiating anger.

"I just need to be angry right now," I told her as I picked up on her concern. "Please just allow me to be in this state right now."

In most relationships, that expression would trigger an adverse response in the other person. They wouldn't want you to be in that state because they're negatively affected by it. That can have a ping pong effect that brings both parties all the way down, down . . . into a fight. Cue someone storming off in a huff, the other person slamming a door, and both parties not really knowing why they are so pissed off with each other.

Fortunately, Kate had a different response.

"Okay," she said.

That's it. She didn't let my anger affect how she was experiencing life in that moment. She didn't make it about her. She didn't demand I calm down or she would leave the room (removal of love).

She simply acknowledged how I was feeling and acknowledged my right to feel that way if I chose. She didn't try to change my state. She allowed me to be fully *me*. What a gift!

The wonderful part was that as soon as she did this, my anger disappeared. Within seconds, I felt lighter in every way. I even started rolling around on the floor, giggling and asking for a hug.

How different do you think your relationships would be if you started approaching negative feelings in this way? If you said, "Okay, I'm just gonna let myself feel this emotion for a while. I'm not going to rant and rave at myself for feeling this way. I'm just going to acknowledge the feeling, sit with it, and let it move through me."

How different do you think the relationship with your *self* would be? Remember, this is an inside-out journey. When you experience change at the heart level, everything else follows.

MY PATH BACK TO ME

After being told to suppress my emotions for so many years, I not only started to identify myself as the troublesome kid but also started to rebel.

Rebellion was the name of the game in my teens, and by my early twenties, I was smoking a lot of pot. The drug of choice helped me suppress my huge fluctuations in emotion and bring me down to a normal level with other people.

When I was stoned, all the anxiety fell away. So did all the sharp pain of not belonging, of wanting to make my dad proud but not knowing how, and of looking at my life around me and feeling so frustrated.

Without it, I was wired. All the time. I easily could have been diagnosed with ADHD if I had been assessed. I couldn't hold a conversation. My eyes would dart off everywhere. I would be talking about six things all at once. My parasympathetic system was on overdrive. I was stuck in the fight or flight response because I had all this emotion built up inside of me that was never allowed to come out or be expressed.

No one had ever held a safe space for me to express my emotions. As a consequence, I was never able to establish really deep relationships—with women or friends. I wondered why I didn't feel anything for anyone. And with those thoughts, I felt more frustrated, more alone.

So I acted out. I did drugs. Petty crime. All that stuff. I feel some resistance admitting it even now, especially in a one-sided relationship such as this, where you're reading my book, and I have no idea how you're reacting. But as I've mentioned, I'm surrendering to the process and showing up 100 per cent.

And besides, I know I'm not the only one. Far from it. Over the years, I hear more and more stories of young men and women, confused and angry, getting caught up in unhelpful coping mechanisms just like I did. You may even be in the grip of an unhealthy habit right now.

Ironically, it was my pot smoking that eventually brought me to the first person to change my life for the better. But the process was painful.

I had been working as a bouncer at a nightclub for a while. I'm not gonna lie; I did it to get chicks. Hey, I was in my twenties, remember?

One Friday night on the job, I ended up injuring my back while breaking up a fight. By Monday, I couldn't get out of bed. I literally couldn't move my legs. Terrified, I called my mum, who proceeded to take me to all the relevant doctors for all the relevant tests.

The news was universally bad. I was told I'd never work in a physically active capacity again. I faced life in a desk job—far from the carpentry career path I had planned.

As you can imagine, hotheaded young Barry gave that news the big two-finger salute. My whole ethos at the time was, "Tell me I can't do something, and I'll show you ten ways I can." Filled with the energy of youth and determined to prove everyone wrong, I started trying every therapy I could.

Despite my predicament (or perhaps because of it), I was still smoking weed. But one night, my stash ran out. Facing the unbearable prospect of a sober weekend, I called a guy I'd been half-friendly with at the gym.

Yeah, he had weed. And yeah, he could come around.

That night was actually the start of a friendship that still exists today. My friendship with Josh is the longest I've ever had and one of the very dearest to me. Aside from the gift of a true brotherhood bond, Josh also introduced me to a path towards spiritual education and awakening.

But before that, he introduced me to ecstasy.

"Let's have a pill and go out on the town," he said one night. This was some months after our first bond over a few cones, and we'd become really close. I was actually living at his house.

I was feeling better and moving again, so, sure. Why not?

And so began my ecstasy phase.

On one of these nights, after dancing our asses off in the city, we were home and having the naturally deep and meaningful conversation that usually occurred when we started coming down. My back pain was starting to kick in again.

"Here, give me your hand," he said.

I put my hand in his, and suddenly, I felt an energy coming from him, directly to my heart. It was unlike anything I'd ever felt, better than any orgasm or the high from some great achievement. Thinking about it now, I can only describe what I felt as a heart orgasm. The energy reached my core and exploded into a feeling of beauty, happiness, and rapture.

"What was that?" I asked, staring at him.

"Reiki."

"How did you learn to do that?"

"I've always been able to do it," said Josh. "I haven't been taught; I just *remembered* how to do it."

What a trip. He remembered? From when? I had no idea about universal energies back then, so it was like my friend was speaking another language.

"I can fix your back, by the way," Josh said casually.

At this point, he could have told me he could fly, and I would have believed him.

"Go on then, give it a go."

For the next half hour, Josh used Reiki on my back. As he did, I could feel the sensation of something being energetically pulled out of me. It was like he took my sore back into himself and processed the pain and trauma for me, a piece at a time.

Over the next month, we had regular Reiki sessions. Each time, Josh took a small piece of the injury away from me and into himself. He actually developed a sore back for a while. Slowly, my own back began to heal. It was incredible.

After a few more months of weekly Reiki sessions with Josh, my back was 100 per cent better. Somehow, I had proved modern medicine wrong. And how? That was the trippiest part...by using a Japanese technique that spiritually guides unseen life force energy! No pills, no operations, no months of rehab. How the hell was that possible? I wanted to find out more.

■ ■ ■

I'd been raised in a minimally religious house, seeing life from a single perspective and thinking there's not much else out there except for the inevitable journey to a house with a white picket fence, mortgage and kids, retirement, and then death. Tick, tick, and tick.

But over the next year, I started having different conversations and experiences, and slowly my resistance to things I couldn't see or touch in the world started to fade.

The more I started to explore these new ideas around energy, the concept of God, the mind and body connection, the more I began to see. My eyes were especially opened while on ecstasy.

I would start to remember things that I had never been taught in this life. I'd blackout in a room, and when I came to, everyone around me would be crying and asking things like, "How did you know that? How do you know what happened to me when I was three years old?" Somehow, I just knew. I could feel it. It was like I was channelling messages about their traumatic experiences and divining how to heal those traumas.

Over about an eighteen-month period, I started to get better at consciously channelling these messages that would come through me. Without fail, the people around me would have these profound healing experiences.

But it wasn't until a devastating breakup left me feeling utterly heartbroken that I truly began pursuing answers to what was going on under the surface.

I'll never forget hearing the news that my girlfriend at the time—who I thought I would end up marrying—had cheated on me with my best friend. I was sitting on a dusty old cream couch in my house in Kings Meadows back in Tasmania. It was a hand-me-down from my parents and well-used in my bachelor pad. Every time someone sat down on this dirty old couch, a faint plume of dust would puff up and out of the back cushion.

I was watching my cat play in the sunlight, batting at a leaf on the Yucca plant that had lived in that loungeroom for as long as I had when the phone rang. It was my friend's dad, Rick, a wise old hippy-type guy who had become a friend and early mentor of mine.

"Hey, Barry," he began. "I've got something to tell you. Kristy spent the night here."

She and I had fought the day before, and she had taken off. I had a feeling she would have crashed at his house.

"Is she alright?" I asked.

"Yeah," Rick replied. "But Jay came over as well, and they smoked a few joints and…well…"

"What? What happened?" I held my breath, expecting the worst. Were they in the hospital? What was going on?

"They slept together."

I couldn't speak.

"Honestly, Barry, I think it's for the best. You two were never going to work out. I just thought you should know."

I felt a sick feeling in my stomach like a hand was reaching up from deep within my gut and choking me.

I threw my phone at the wall. The old Nokia 7110 cracked the plasterboard, then bounced and hit the floor, unharmed. (Those things were unbreakable!)

My first feeling was anger and blame directed at Rick. He was supposed to be a mentor figure to me. How had he allowed this to happen?

My anger then turned to Jay. He was supposed to be my best friend. How could he have done this to me? Then to Kristy. How could *she* have done this to me?

Mixed emotions swirled around me. Rage, anger, blame...and hurt. Incredible, deep hurt.

Every time I pictured Kristy and Jay together, her shining blonde hair mixing with his dirty brown stoner hair as they writhed in bed, it made me feel sick.

After that day, Kristy totally cut me off. She didn't want to speak to me or acknowledge what she'd done. We went from having a fight to never seeing each other again.

I had never felt so lost and alone. My head was spinning with questions. *What if we hadn't had that fight before she did this unforgivable thing? What if I had tried harder to save her from her mental demons? What did it mean about my own worth that this had happened to me?*

How could I ever trust anyone again, lover or friend?

I needed answers, and I had no idea how to find them.

▪ ▪ ▪

That weekend, I wandered around the city, trying to unravel the mess in my head. I ended up standing in front of a wooden door, observing the purple Tree of Life symbol painted above the shop's name, Berkana.

It was one of those New Age shops filled with crystals, draped velvet counters, girls in hemp clothing, and intriguing book covers with pentacles and angels on them.

I felt I should go in, although I had no idea why. This wasn't the usual kind of thing I did. I felt really out of place, but somehow, I knew to trust my instincts.

Inside, the shop was cluttered and bursting with obscure books and mystical paraphernalia. A CD of nature sounds overlaid with the faint harmonies of chanting monks playing from a small boombox on the front counter.

Despite the apparent chaotic nature of its contents, the shop had a beautiful sense of calm and peace. Somehow, it gave me an odd sense of coming home.

I followed the small path between bookshelves and makeshift tables and up a narrow wooden staircase. It creaked and slightly groaned as I ascended the stairs. At the top was another room, smaller than the one below. A makeshift altar had been set up in a cracked and dusty old fireplace in the corner.

On one of the tables against the window, many decks of divination cards were carefully arranged in a display. Tarot cards, Oracle cards, Spirit cards. The cards in each deck were tiny works of art—beautifully painted and painstakingly detailed. I had dabbled in Tarot before but never had the patience to learn all of the spreads and card meanings. Maybe Oracle cards would give me a sense of direction instead?

Fifteen minutes later, I walked out with the smell of Nag Champa incense in my nose and a pack of Archangel Oracle cards in my bag.

Doreen Virtue, who holds BA, MA, and PhD degrees in counselling psychology, designed Oracle cards to give simple answers to your most pressing questions. Unlike a Tarot reading, which requires a long and involved process, using Oracle cards is fast and easy. You just hold a question in your mind and heart and then pick a card from the forty-five-strong deck.

"They work by drawing down guidance and intuitive thoughts from your guardian angel," the cute tattooed and dreadlocked shop assistant had told me." Hmmm, okay. I wasn't sure about the whole archangel thing, but I did know that I believed there was something out there…a Source of energy or a divine being that we humans couldn't explain.

And besides, even if I decided that archangels weren't my thing, each card was beautifully designed with motivational and uplifting words on them. And that was certainly some "food for the soul" that I needed.

As I was exiting the shop, I noticed a sign on the window. It was for Reiki classes. I stopped and looked at it for a second. It occurred to me that recently I'd had all this trauma coming up in my life. My horrendous back injury, my girlfriend cheating on me with my best friend, losing money on a shitty investment…everything seemed to be going phenomenally wrong in my life.

I remembered someone once telling me that we attract severe physical experiences when we're not listening to our divine guidance.

Was that why I felt like my life was falling down around me? Was I somehow attracting this myself by not following the path my instincts were telling me to follow?

On a whim, I went back into the shop and signed up for the Reiki course, too. Why not? I had nothing to lose. And somehow, I just felt I needed to.

A few weeks later, I was sitting on the floor of my Level 1 Reiki workshop. I had been using my Oracle cards daily. I'd stopped being surprised at how damn accurate they were…somehow, they always told me exactly what I needed to hear (even if it wasn't necessarily what I *wanted* to hear).

Whether archangels were guiding me, or the cards were simply helping me unlock my own connection with my subconscious knowledge and universal energy…they really worked.

I'd also been diving into spirituality, devouring every book I could find from authors like Eckhart Tolle, Deepak Chopra, Paulo Coelho, Wayne Dyer, and many more.

I felt pretty confident and maybe even a little bit cocky. After all, I knew I could already channel energy. I had felt people's trauma and shown them how to heal it.

As I sat on a dusty old fake Persian rug in the centre of another room, hidden away up past those rickety stairs, I felt a bit nervous. The people sitting around me were of all ages and types. I saw New Age trendy kids with dreadlocks and piercings right next to a couple of middle-aged women looking like they'd just come from a Pilates class. There was an older gentleman who seemed like he had done these courses many times before and an Indonesian guy who radiated an incredibly grounded energy for his age.

And then there was me. What the hell was I doing here?

The instructor went around the room, asking everyone to introduce themselves. It was already getting muggy inside the small room, and a small fan hummed from somewhere behind me. Soon it was my turn.

"Hi, I'm Barry," I said. But before I could get another word out, I started bawling. I just cried and cried. I didn't know where it came from. Something released in me, and everything else fell away. My next words came from somewhere deep within me, a place I never knew existed.

"I'm Barry," I started again. "And I'm here to remember who I am."

It was the year 2000, and on that day, I felt like I was given a piece of the puzzle I'd been unconsciously searching for. And that was the start of my spiritual journey.

YOUR TURN

Now that you know a little bit about how I got started, it's time to get *you* started. Throughout this book, we'll cover many concepts that are fundamental to finding peace, love, and fulfilment in your life.

But to begin, we'll continue to explore where all life begins: our heart. Over the next few chapters, I'm going to share with you how I developed my relationship with my heart. Not the physical muscle but the energetic Source. I'll invite you to start opening and using your own heart and connect with your intuition in a more meaningful way.

Because from the heart, everything else follows.

As we go, I'll give you some exercises to help you. They're very simple and easy to do (no tribal circle of painted ladies howling under the moon necessary). I hope you give them a try. Because once you start opening your heart connection, you'll begin feeling the beautiful ease of allowing your heart to lead you through life. You'll start feeling a wholeness you haven't experienced before. And you'll start living your life in a more fulfilling and harmonious way.

Is it all woo-woo? Maybe. Whatever you call it, it works. It has for me. It has for hundreds of my coaching clients. And it can work for you, too, because *you are meant to be happy*.

So let's begin, shall we?

CHAPTER 2

SPIRITUALITY

"Spiritual energy is that which comes from pure consciousness.
It's the creative energy of the universe
that gives us vitality and therefore, life."

—*Deepak Chopra*

BACK IN THE '90S, THERE WAS SOMETHING OF AN AWAKENING around spirituality and self-development. In the decades before, going to the self-help section of the bookshop was an embarrassing, almost shameful thing to do.

There was a huge stigma around seeking spiritual guidance (outside of the dominant religious institutions) or exploring areas of thought and study around mysticism, the metaphysical, or esoteric ideas. Doing so somehow made you a weak person, someone who was flailing through life and desperate for something to cling to.

This stereotype was reinforced through movies and TV shows where women with dishevelled hair, bloodshot eyes, a soggy tissue peeking out from their cuff, and a gloomy demeanour would wander self-help aisles in bookstores like lost lambs, clutching books with titles like *Why Doesn't He Love Me?* or *The Emotional Doormat's Guide to Life*.

Even now, I'll occasionally see a movie where the shame of seeking spiritual or emotional answers is reinforced. The cool Kate Hudson type of girl will hide her copy of *Men Are from Mars, Women Are from Venus* under a couch cushion when her date arrives. There'll be a strange woman living down the street from the movie's protagonist who never opens her curtains, wears too much crushed velvet, and celebrates moon cycles.

You've likely seen your share of these characters, who are often portrayed as a bit wacky or loopy. And they're pretty much always women. Why? Because men don't go in for all that spiritual stuff. Men are tough. Right? What a crock of shit.

We are all spiritual beings. We all are made up of the same energies. We all have the same feelings and needs. Why wouldn't men be spiritual, too?

Even after Tony Robbins started bringing self-help concepts off the dusty discount table in the backroom of society to the forefront of our cultural consciousness, men still didn't get a free pass. Because accompanying this awakening came a cultural fad around the "Sensitive New Age Guy."

A Sensitive New Age Guy can roughly be defined as a man who is in touch with his emotional and spiritual side and is unafraid to show it. As we Aussies tend to do, we abbreviated the term to SNAG.

For my friends outside Australia, snag is an abbreviated word for sausages here. (Yes, we abbreviate words a *lot*.) So men who started openly exploring their own spirituality and emotional landscape became aligned with a cooked cocoon of cheap meat we often burn in the company of friends. These men were sneered at by others who were still in a state of resistance about "all this New Age mumbo jumbo."

"Look at that guy with the long hair. What a snaaaaaag," people would drawl nastily. Snags were sooks. They were softies. They were somehow not men because men were expected to never cry, never express their emotions, never complain about working hard...they were stoic. They were rocks. Once again, utter bullshit. But it's what our fathers were taught, and their fathers before them, and so on.

So, whether you're a woman thinking of those stereotypical characters or a man who has been criticized for even thinking about spiritual things, it's likely that you're reading this chapter with a bit of resistance. Perhaps even trepidation. Is Barry going to start talking in tongues and asking me to make a blood sacrifice?

Not today (ha-ha). But in all seriousness, just be aware that you've had a lifetime of gentle reinforcement of the idea that "New Age stuff" is the realm of the cuckoo. It's okay. People tend to ridicule and reject things they don't understand.

WHAT IS SPIRITUALITY *ACTUALLY*?

Spirituality, in the simplest terms, is about connecting with something larger than yourself. It's about being connected to a higher Source. Call it God, Allah, Buddha, Gaia, whatever. The name is irrelevant.

Through spiritual practices, we seek answers about the meaning of life, how people are connected to each other, truths about the universe, and other mysteries of human existence. In order to explore these questions, we must explore something far outside the paradigms of this materialistic world. Something far beyond the constructs of the physical, which over time will age, wear, and collapse.

Spiritually connected people have a deep understanding of who they really are and why they're here on this planet living this life. Because of these deep connections with themselves and the energies of the universe, they are able to see, feel, and take everything in holistically and then make decisions that feel right for them. Not because society tells them that it's the right decision but because they know it's aligned with their true being and purpose.

So, how do we get in touch with our true being and purpose? You'll discover that as you continue to read this book. But for now, know that being in touch with your spiritual self comes from building a deeper connection with your heart. A spiritually connected person is guided by their heart. They're in tune with their intuition. They understand how the energies of life are pushing them and pulling them in the directions they need to go.

Living in a place where you're connected with your spirituality is a beautiful state to be in. It's freeing. You exist in a state of flow. You are happy, at the deepest level. And the more connected you become, the easier—and better—life gets.

Have you ever known a person who seems really lucky? Everything just seems to work out for them? Wealth and abundance come easily? They seem blessed? That is the state spiritually connected people live in. They are aware of who they are and what their purpose is. Most importantly, they listen to their heart's intuition, which is universal energy showing them which way to go.

Now, this view of spirituality is not common. It's not how I was taught to see spiritual life either.

A SEARCH FOR ANSWERS

I grew up in a Christian family. Like many other families in our neighbourhood, we went to church at Christmas and Easter. We went to Christian Christmas concerts. I was sent to Sunday School for a while, which is like an educational boot camp for kids where they get taught stories from the Bible and get introduced to the major themes of Christianity.

One thing I noticed very early on is that I felt a sense of disassociation whenever I heard stories from the Bible or stories about Jesus. It all felt so far away, so separate from me. This feeling of disassociation only grew as I entered my teenage years.

When we're young, we believe whatever is taught to us by the significant people in our lives, usually our parents and teachers. Most researchers agree that by the age of six, a person's belief system is fairly well-formed. Six-year-olds tend to have a pretty solid idea of what they believe to be right and wrong, fair and unfair, good and bad.

But while six-year-old Barry may have accepted that the Christian beliefs he was being taught were "right" from a traditional point of view, there was still something that didn't quite connect in his heart. There was a pretty big cognitive gap between the life of a man who lived centuries ago in the Middle East and his life in 1980s suburban Australia.

In short: I couldn't *feel* Jesus. I couldn't connect with him in my heart.

Although I'd always been around the doctrine of the church, participating as a Christian was more of a hassle than a duty I felt bound to. I didn't want to go to church on Christmas Eve. I wanted to hover around the tree and get excited for the fun of Christmas Day.

When I reached my teens and began questioning everything (which is a teenager's job!), I had a defining moment when I walked into a church in Launceston, where I grew up. They were trying to get people to sign a petition against same-sex marriage.

It didn't feel right. Wasn't God all about love? And isn't that love abundant and all-inclusive? And most importantly, isn't his love unconditional? Surely it doesn't matter if that love is between two men, two women, or two non-binary people. I believed this in my heart then, and I still do today. So how could so many Christians get it so very wrong?

Looking back, I think that was when I started truly questioning the things I'd been taught to believe. If Christianity got it wrong sometimes, surely all religions got it wrong sometimes. And if religion didn't have all the answers, where could I look for the truth behind the big questions bouncing around in my head?

Where did we come from? What was the purpose of life?

Like most people, I had a feeling that there was more to life than what appeared on the surface. Surely, we don't just exist to work and earn money, pay bills, buy a house, and so forth.

All my life up to that point, I'd had overwhelming evidence that life was about advancement. We work to get to a better position than we are now. My parents worked hard to give my brothers and me a nice home, a good education, and the occasional family vacay. But they were always tired. My dad was often absent, working long hours to keep providing for our economic needs.

They advanced their lot in life, but they sacrificed plenty, too. Still, they never stopped and said, "That's it. I've accumulated enough stuff, I've got enough money, I'm done." I doubt many people ever do. Instead, we keep pushing forward. Because we all have this driving feeling that we've just got to get to the next level. But kind of like a video game, there's always another scenario to play after you've beaten every boss.

At some point along this journey of questioning how we live, it struck me that all through our lives, we keep focusing on what comes next instead of being present in the now. We focus on getting through school or university. Or we focus on getting through our apprenticeship. We focus on finding a partner and getting married. We focus on having a child. Then what's next?

We focus on getting promotions and career advancement. We focus on buying nice things that make us feel good about all this work we're doing. To make us feel that it's all for *something*. Then we focus on retiring, hoping we've accumulated enough stuff to keep us comfortable for the next twenty years.

We keep going as though we're really going somewhere...but are we actually getting anywhere? Where is it all leading anyway? We're just climbing a ladder we've created.

Before we know it, life's over. Did you collect all the shiny tokens you could along the way? Did you beat everyone else to the higher levels of the game? And if you did, now what?

If you feel there is "more to life than this" or have a feeling in your gut that is telling you something is not right, chances are your intuition is trying to lead you to the right path.

Our intuition is a gift from the Source, channelled through our heart. It is there to guide us through the chaos of life and keep us aligned with our true self and purpose. But we don't often listen to our intuition. Why? Because we don't develop it. We listen to all outside noise and ignore the quiet voice within.

BARRIERS TO INTUITION

So, there I was in my teens, asking all the questions. Something deep down told me that there *must* be more to life than simply getting from A to Z. But religion didn't have all the answers I was looking for.

Even more than that, I couldn't figure out why my own life was going so wrong. Every day, I was bullied at school. I had very few friends. Kids would beat me up all the time. They would torture and tease me. I was called "big ears" or "wing nut" because my ears stuck out a bit. The bullying was relentless.

But it wasn't just words. It was also "sticks and stones," as the saying goes.

I remember one particular day when I was being picked on for whatever reason by this kid named Martin. He'd broken a branch off a poplar tree and was whipping me with it. Each crack of this branch left a white line on my body and two red marks on either side, almost like a set of lips on my skin.

"Ouch! That hurts! Stop!" I cried out. But Martin wasn't relenting. He was having too much fun. Other boys had formed a circle around us and were cheering him on, smiling and laughing.

"Harder!" they'd yell. "Do it again!"

After the third or fourth whip, I grabbed another branch off the poplar tree and tried to whip him back. But I wasn't fast enough and didn't have his strength. Each whip that hit me was excruciating, and I felt trapped in the pain and fear.

As much as I tried, I couldn't get close enough. Still, he kept slashing at me. No matter how I tried to run and pivot, they came.

Whip... whip... whip.

I can still hear the sound of the poplar branch as it whooshed through the air and the smack as it connected with my bare skin.

By the time a teacher broke it up and sent us home, I was covered in angry red lines that were already bruising.

At home, I bawled my eyes out. My mum saw and was aghast. "What happened?" she asked.

I told her I'd been getting bullied every day by various kids at school.

That night, my father was home early for once. Usually, he came home from work very late, after I was in bed. My mum told him about the bullying, that I was coming home black and blue.

What my dad said to me was unexpected.

"Why haven't you stuck up for yourself?" he asked.

I was hesitant to tell him, because I'd always felt a bit intimidated by him. I didn't want to say the wrong thing and make him angry. But he kept pushing me to say something.

"Because I don't want to get in trouble with you," I eventually replied. My dad was an ex-military man, and he ran an ordered house. I always felt that if I got into fights at school, I would get in big trouble at home. And that was something I wanted to avoid far more than the bullies!

"You'll never get in trouble with me for defending yourself," my dad asserted. That night, he taught me some basic self-defence and fighting tactics. I was so touched that he was taking the time to help me defend myself. I hadn't felt he cared much before then.

There was this deep sense that my dad loved me and wanted me to be okay. I felt like I was getting a piece of myself back, of mateship or camaraderie that I hadn't experienced with him before then. That gave me the courage to fight back.

Soon enough, another bully picked a fight, but instead of letting him beat me, I punched the kid in the face and broke his jaw. He got sent to hospital, and I got suspended for two days.

I'm not glorifying violence here, nor am I saying that it's the way to solve a disagreement. I'm telling you this story because it's the moment when I started to realise how our beliefs and perceptions can create these invisible borders around us.

Nothing had changed from the day I got bullied to the day I defended myself but my own perception of me and what I could do. I wasn't any stronger or smarter or faster. I just had that belief in myself fueled by my dad's approval.

My initial beliefs had caused me to behave a certain way at school. Because of that behaviour, I attracted the bullying. Not consciously, of course. Nobody wants to be bullied. But I had subconsciously created an environment where that could happen to me. When my beliefs changed, my experience did as well.

BEFORE-BELIEFS

Later in my life, when I injured my back, when my girlfriend cheated on me, or when I had shitty experiences during my apprenticeship, I wondered how I was somehow creating the conditions for this stuff to happen.

Why was I struggling in life when many of my peers were thriving? What was different about me? Didn't I have the right beliefs now?

One day, Rick—my friend's dad and my mentor—said something to me that was profound.

"Barry, we attract these big experiences into our life. Big traumas happen when we're not listening to the innate guidance of our heart."

This was a very new concept to me. What on Earth did he mean? It was one thing to see how my thoughts led to a different experience. It was another altogether to tap into intuition.

My whole life, I'd been driven by decisions that came from my mind, not my heart. Through my mind's perceptions and beliefs, I'd created the experiences I had growing up. After all, beliefs create actions, which then create consequences. I wasn't aware of what comes first *before* belief: intuition.

"What I mean," Rick continued, "is that we have the ability to tap into something other than our past experiences. We all have an intuitive knowing, and it becomes an innate knowing once we develop it."

So instead of letting my often-irrational brain drive my behaviours, there was an intuition that could guide my beliefs, actions, and consequences instead?

This idea was kind of revolutionary. All my life, I had seen evidence of men around me repeating their past decisions and getting the same shitty outcomes. Hell, I was doing that myself. But even more than that, I knew that when I was making decisions that weren't ultimately helpful to me or put me in a negative place in life, there was always a little voice whispering to me to go another way.

Can you think of a time when your head told you to do something, but your heart wanted something else? And how many of those times were you really happy with your decision? In retrospect, how many of those times would you have been better off if you had followed your heart from the start?

I'd made so many decisions based on my own biased logic or fleeting desire...and how many of them had actually worked out? Not many.

I stayed in relationships that didn't completely fulfil me. I chose employers who were straight-up tyrants. I neglected friends instead of reaching out. I prioritised work over my mental and physical health.

What would happen if I started listening to my heart's intuition instead of my brain?

I decided to give it a go. As I did, I realised I could change my beliefs and, therefore, my behaviour at any time. I also realised that the majority of what our brain tells us is bullshit.

I'm not good enough. I'm going to fail. I don't deserve success. This is the way life is and always will be. Things like that don't happen for people like me.

Your brain tells you things like that because it's designed to repeat patterns. Your brain is obsessed with patterns. It's how it understands what to do with the trillions of pieces of information it receives each day.

The problem is that patterns keep us stuck. They tell us we're safe and keep us locked in a single way of approaching life. When our brain notices it's survived something before, it steers us towards the same path we've already taken. Of course, we've survived all the experiences we've had up to this point, even the traumatic ones. Does that mean our patterns are the best options? Not necessarily. Still, our brain will keep latching onto those experiences whenever it can and steer us towards them. And in the end, we keep repeating the patterns of the past.

I'll dive deeper into these patterns later in the book. For now, don't be too hard on your brain. After all, it just wants to keep you alive.

But it's time to move past the patterns in your brain because your intuition is a far more wise and helpful compass. The universe wants you to not just survive... *it wants you to thrive.* And when you build your heart-based spiritual connection with God (the Source), you absolutely can.

BUILDING YOUR INTUITIVE MUSCLES

Most of us are never taught how to listen to our intuition. Our days are filled with instructions, lessons, and learning all the unwritten rules of life. Along the way, we never slow down to learn how to tap into our innate knowing.

Certainly, nowhere in my experience of growing up was I taught to use my intuition or to use my heart and my instinct, which I now believe is the way to tap into a universal consciousness, which is tapped into God (whatever your version of God happens to be).

And the more our inner guidance gets drowned out by the cacophony of modern life, the less we can tap into it. It's a tiny voice, a tiny feeling that gets drowned out. But that doesn't mean it's not there or that your connection cannot be revived and strengthened.

Building a spiritual connection to your Source is kind of like going to the gym. You've got to work at it. And the first few times you try, it's hard. It hurts. It's a lot of effort, and you feel a long, long way from the eventual reward.

But the rewards will come.

Looking back over the last fifteen years of my life, I can see how following my heart-based intuition has always served me well.

It hasn't always been easy. There have been plenty of things that haven't worked out the way I wanted. But I have slowly learned to surrender to my deeper consciousness that guides my way. I've had the intuition to break up with partners whom I loved very deeply, and while it was so painful at the time, I'm now so thankful that I did. Because the relationship wasn't right for them, and especially wasn't right for me.

In business, it's been the same. I've learned some hard lessons and had to deal with failure many times throughout my journey. But the more I listen to my intuition and let it guide my decisions, the more my business thrives.

I wonder how many people are stuck in jobs they hate or relationships that ultimately don't fulfil them, just because they believe it's better to stay for whatever reason. All the while, they've got this heavy feeling deep inside because they know they should get the hell out.

We all have that spark of knowing inside us. You might not be able to see it, touch it, or really even comprehend it, but it's there, even if you've pushed it way down. It's that little voice that says to leave that relationship. To start your own business. To reach out to a friend. We innately know what to do in our heart, but our head is filled with so much junk that it distorts our efforts.

Think about it. If nothing was in your way, you'd have everything you want right now. But what's in your way is largely *you*. Your own beliefs, feelings of inadequacy, shame, or fear. We hold ourselves back by letting our brains dictate our decisions and actions.

We push our real feelings down and suppress them because our brain is so addicted to comfort and safety. So we do what we think is expected. We do what we think will keep us accepted in our tribe. But those decisions aren't always serving us at the highest level spiritually. On the other hand, the heart doesn't have all that distortion from a lifetime of pattern-making. It is pure love.

So it's time to learn how to let it show you the way.

I invite you to make a little commitment to yourself. Pledge just five minutes a day to start building your spiritual muscles. You don't have to do anything yet. Just accept my invitation to spend some time each day doing one of the exercises I'm going to show you a bit later in this book.

Everybody can find five minutes for this. It's a really small commitment to make. When I started learning to play the guitar, I practised for five minutes a day at first. A year later, I could play complete songs. The point is, a small effort can reap very big rewards over time.

While I can show you the door, I can't make you walk through it. I can ask you questions and challenge your way of thinking, but the final decision is up to you.

On that note…

YOUR JOURNEY, YOUR PATH

I'm not here to preach to you what to believe or what spirituality should mean to you. I'm simply here to ask questions and challenge your beliefs and assumptions and allow you to potentially open up to a new experience.

I'm not saying my way is the only way. I can tell you that if you try to walk my exact path, you'll get lost because it's *my* path. You need to find your own. I will share the tools and teachings that helped me find my way, and I hope they help you find yours, too. But only you can find your path through your connection to the higher Source, whatever or whoever that is for you.

The first step is to be willing to challenge the paradigms and perceptions you've had to this point because your life can be *anything* you want it to be. I don't care how old or disadvantaged you are; there is always a path available to you. The only thing stopping you from going down it is your own brain telling you it's not possible.

■ ■ ■

My mum made a comment the other day that made me quite sad. She and my dad got home from another long day at work, completely exhausted. "When I got home, I opened your Instagram," she told me. "You'd posted a photo of yourself lying by the pool in Bali."

I remembered posting that photo. I'd captioned it, "I love Tuesdays."

"You looked so happy and relaxed," said my mum. "I'm so glad one of us has made it."

It really struck me. Yes, I'm really happy with my life right now. I've worked hard and made some good decisions that have shaped my life and brought me to this place.

But do I believe that can't be possible for them? For *you*?

Of course not. You can decide what you choose to accept about your life and what you choose to let go. At any time, you're one decision away from a happier and more fulfilled existence. You can decide to be happy. You can decide to leave a bad situation. You can decide to do something different. I'm not saying it's always easy, but it is entirely possible.

Spirituality is about learning to make decisions that are not guided by the past wounds and traumas you've endured but, instead, exploring something beyond the paradigms of your known world.

And the more you choose that path, the closer you get to the life you actually want for yourself.

CHAPTER 3

THE BRAIN VERSUS
THE HEART

"It is only with the heart that one can see rightly
what is invisible to the naked eye."

—*Helen Keller*

"I THINK YOU'RE GOING TOO FAST, MAN."

The yellow Volkswagen Beetle zipped through the Friday night traffic like it was in a real-life game of *Mario Cart*.

From the radio came the whirling energy of Roxy Music's latest single, *Virginia Plain*. Bryan Ferry drawled his vocals and tapped the piano as the band kept a rapturous pace around him, almost like a carnival ride in reverse.

The year was 1972, and Ed Rubenstein was on his way into New York City with a friend. Like pretty much every twenty-year-old in modern history, Ed felt invincible. He was in college and throwing himself into his life's mission: *have a good time, all the time.*

The city was close by, and Ed felt a rush of adrenaline in anticipation of the wild night ahead. He was dressed up, primed, and ready for whatever was in store for him.

Suddenly, Ed saw a bright light in the corner of his eye. He turned his head to look out the passenger window just in time to see two headlights staring him down.

In a split second, Ed realised his friend hadn't yielded at a crossing, and a car was about to hit Ed's passenger door head-on at 60 kph.

And he wasn't wearing a seatbelt.

The next thing Ed knew, he was flung up and into the driver's seat. The car took a few spins and tumbles, and it tossed Ed around like he was in a washing machine.

But instead of plummeting into the dark unconsciousness that one might expect with such violent trauma, something different happened to Ed.

He felt himself get catapulted out of his body. And he had a kind of "life review." Everything that had ever happened to him in his twenty years played for him like a video on four-times speed.

As he was on his way to the hospital, Ed tried to make sense of the experience he'd just had. Not so much the car crash itself, but the life review that followed.

Ed knew that although near-death experiences (NDEs) are well documented, science still hasn't uncovered the mysteries of what happens within the brain during these experiences. Far from being fancy flights of the imagination, NDEs share broad commonalities such as visual phenomena, out-of-body experiences, and even remembering past lives (Koch 2020).

"Did I see any angels?" Ed asked himself. "No. A light? No. Did I see a tunnel? Heaven or hell? No to all."

But Ed knew that he'd definitely had a NDE, and it scared the hell out of him. Ed's twenty-year-old bravado shattered into dust as he realised just how close he'd come to dying. In the hospital, during the long recovery period after his multiple surgeries, Ed started to ask himself some pretty big questions.

Where did I go when my mind left my body? Why was my life played back to me during the crash? What is life all about, anyway? What is the purpose of my own life?

Ed began to realise that he spent the majority of his time in his conscious mind, preoccupied with nonsense that didn't really matter. His "monkey mind" jumped from branch to branch, constantly skittering about, taking Ed's emotional state with it.

He realised that all the worries, jealousies, desires, fears, and other mental junk banging around his head wasn't what "normal" is supposed to be. So, Ed started inspecting his own mind, taking apart his thoughts and examining them as though *they* were on the operating table.

What makes me believe this thought? Where did it come from? What purpose does it have in my life? Do I need it, or should I replace it with something better or kinder?

Ed started to realise that his thoughts weren't his whole being; they were just voices. What's more, some of those voices were helpful. Others were not. Some were kind. Others were not. But most of the time, he'd let himself be completely guided by his internal monologue. Whichever voice was speaking at the time was driving the bus. But were these voices really leading him the right way? And just who was in charge of this internal monologue, anyway?

Ed started to seek out new information about the brain, how thoughts and emotions work, and the relationship between the mind, body, and spirit.

Today, Ed Rubenstein, PhD, is a licensed psychologist and Director of Education for the Heart Based Institute, where he researches and trains in heart-based therapeutics.

He's also one of the incredible mentors who taught me what you're going to learn about in this chapter: the heart.

A WAKE-UP CALL

That night when the yellow Bug raced towards good times in the city, Ed's life was violently interrupted. It was Ed's wake-up call—a chance to reassess how he was showing up and start living purposefully instead of letting life happen to him.

Can you remember a time in your life when you've had a wake-up call?

Hopefully, yours didn't come in the form of a traumatic car crash. It could have been any event that truly caught your attention. In some way, it turned your life upside down.

My wake-up call came in a series of stages. The back injury, my girlfriend cheating on me, feeling like I was simply moving through life instead of really living it...the culmination of a lot of things going wrong.

Whether you've had a near-death experience like Ed, or you're just noticing that your life seems way too bloody hard for some reason (like bad luck just keeps happening to you...something is trying to *wake you up*.

We keep repeating life's lessons until we learn what they are teaching us. Even the really shitty lessons. Even the ones that hurt.

So why don't we learn them quickly?

Why do we keep getting into bad relationships? Bad situations? Bad habits?

Because we're listening to our *mind*, not our heart. We're doing what we *think* we should do...so we get what we *think* we deserve.

And after twenty years of coaching, I've learned that, sadly, not too many people out there really believe they deserve the best things life has to offer. Instead, they believe all the crap that their mind has accumulated throughout their lives about who they are and what they deserve.

If you're reading this right now and don't believe, deep down in your heart, that you deserve love and abundance in every way, you're wrong. Because you do. We all do.

YOUR MIND IS LYING TO YOU

For a long time, I thought that I was the only one with an inner voice. It took a long time for me to realise that everyone has an internal soundtrack playing in their head, talking to them all the time.

That breakthrough was eclipsed by the one I had when I realised that *I was not my thoughts*. Instead, my thoughts were just reflections of various beliefs, patterns, and neuroses that my brain developed in reaction to my experiences growing up. And one bad experience can potentially lead you down a different path for the rest of your life.

A child who grows up with a beloved pet dog will have great bonds with dogs throughout their lives, whereas a child who has a bad experience with a dog will likely always be suspicious of dogs, if not downright afraid of them. That doesn't mean that all dogs are good or bad. The mind puts meaning on the experiences we have in order to make sense of the chaos of life.

In short, your mind tricks you. It's *not* out to get you. It's just functioning on autopilot. Throughout your whole life, your mind has been conditioned by your parents, your peers, society, and especially yourself to believe the things you do about the world and, most importantly, about yourself.

These beliefs aren't facts. They're just biased interpretations of your experiences. They're biased because reality is subjective. It's pretty dangerous to base your actions on that inner voice because it's kind of like an incorrectly programmed GPS.

Eckhart Tolle puts it beautifully:

> "The mind is a superb instrument if used rightly.
> Used wrongly, however, it becomes very destructive.
> To put it more accurately, it is not so much that you use your
> mind wrongly—you usually don't use it at all. It uses you.
> That is the disease. You believe that you are your mind.
> This is the delusion. The instrument has taken you over."

Your beliefs dictate your actions, and your actions dictate your results. If you believe you don't deserve love, you'll keep attracting shitty relationships. If you believe people with money are absolute jerks, you'll never break through to the next income level. If you believe working hard is the only noble way to live, you'll always find a way to be busy even if you never actually get anywhere.

What we think, we become.

In today's busy modern world that's obsessed with shiny things, living our lives from a mind-based approach leads to accumulation of stuff... but little that's nourishing to our heart.

You think you need to work hard, make money, get the house with the picket fence, and so on. But when you reach the end of your life, I can guarantee you that you won't be thanking yourself for working all that overtime.

You'll be thinking about memories with your loved ones. Watching your kids grow up. Having adventures. Christmas with your family. That wild European trip you did in your twenties with your mates. Meaningful experiences where you connected with others.

That's the stuff that makes up a life. Not the amount of shit you accumulate.

Sure, things can add a bit of happiness to life, but they'll never make you *fulfilled*.

Don't get me wrong, I understand that money is important for living. Our society is built around money as the key form of currency for everything material that we need to live comfortably. Shelter. Food. Even sexual companionship (nobody's attracted to broke guys!). But the problem is that we become obsessed with money in and of itself.

Money is just a tool for enabling us to live the lifestyle we want. Somehow, we mess up what this means and just want more, more, more. We're never happy with what we've got.

What's interesting is that we innately know that what the heart is telling us is our truth, but busyness makes us forget. We swipe our heart's gentle voice away to listen to the raucous yelling from our mind. And that can lead us on a wild goose chase, where we spend our life fighting to get things we don't even want…until one day, we wake up and are sick of it all.

People call it a mid-life crisis, but I think that's the wrong way to frame it. People don't have mid-life crises. They have a *spiritual* crisis where, all of a sudden, they realise they have no idea who they are, what they really want, or why they even exist. That crisis typically translates into Porches, bikini models, and seeking more of the external gratification that they think will fill them up.

I once heard a parable that helped me realise how much our brains can lie to us. Here's how it goes:

An American investment banker was at the pier of a small coastal Mexican village when a small boat with just one fisherman docked. Inside the boat were several large fish. The American complimented the Mexican on the quality of his fish and asked how long it took to catch them.

The Mexican replied, "Only a little while." The American then asked why he didn't stay out longer and catch more fish? The Mexican said he had enough to support his family's immediate needs.

The American then asked, "But what do you do with the rest of your time?"

The Mexican fisherman said, "I sleep late, play with my children, take siestas with my wife, stroll into the village each evening where I sip wine and play guitar with my amigos. I have a full life."

The American scoffed, "I'm a Harvard MBA and could help you. You should spend more time fishing and with the proceeds, buy a bigger boat. With the proceeds from the bigger boat, you could buy several boats. Eventually, you would have a fleet of fishing boats. Instead of selling your catch to a middleman, you would sell directly to the processor, eventually opening your own cannery. You would control the product, processing, and distribution. You would need to leave this small coastal fishing village and move to Mexico City, then LA, and eventually New York City, where you could run your expanding enterprise."

The Mexican fisherman asked, "But how long will this all take?"

To which the American replied, "Fifteen to twenty years."

"But what then?" asked the Mexican.

The American laughed and said, "That's the best part. When the time is right, you would announce an IPO and sell your company stock to the public and become very rich. You would make millions!"

"Millions—then what?"

The American said, "Then you would retire. Move to a small coastal fishing village where you would sleep late, play with your kids, take siestas with your wife, stroll to the village in the evenings where you could sip wine and play guitar with your amigos."

The Mexican man gave the investment banker a curious look and said, "I'll pass."

Pretty eye-opening, right?

Now, I'm not suggesting that you throw away all your worldly goods and become a fisherman. I'm not suggesting you abandon your ambitions, your passions, your dreams. Not at all.

What I am suggesting is that you become more aware of your highly biased programming. It's easy to get swept up in what our mind tells us to want. What society tells us to want. But it's not necessarily the path to fulfilment.

· · ·

So what *is* the path to fulfilment?

It's different for everyone, and you can only find it by following your heart.

We like to think that our mind and heart are connected. But the mind and the heart are actually thinking about completely different things. Don't get me wrong; it is possible to connect the mind and heart. And when they're both pulling in the same direction, life becomes pretty amazing! But chances are you've got a few different voices inside of you vying for your attention. And they're on very different tracks.

The mind: *Am I good enough? I'm going to fail. I'm a loser. My dad doesn't love me. I'm sick of this shit happening to me.*

The heart: *Knock knock . . . you're not going in the direction you need to be. Your spiritual compass is off . . . go this way and you'll get the experiences you need to grow and thrive . . . I'm here with you. I love you.*

Which one do you think is going to give you a better experience of life? (Hint: it's the heart, unless you're some kind of spiritual sadist).

There is an innate longing in the core of every being. It's a longing to feel profoundly safe and unconditionally loved. Parents often provide this safety when bonding with their babies. Babies don't wonder if they deserve to be loved. They don't soil their nappy and think, *Oh, well, I don't deserve love anymore because I have messed myself.* Instead, they live in a state of love and wonder. That's how we all begin our lives, and then we lose our way.

We grow up and realise we aren't always loved no matter what. So, we seek acceptance and unconditional love in unhelpful places: drugs, alcohol, sex, money, shiny toys. We look for completion.

And when our heart opens, the connection becomes clear. The deeper purpose of our life is not about accumulating stuff. It's still about unconditional love.

So then, how do we start opening our heart to love?

Well, first, let's define what we mean by the heart (no scalpel necessary).

THE ENERGETIC HEART

The heart is our true centre. Both spiritually and physically. You can be brain dead but still alive if your heart is beating. But you cannot be alive if your heart is dead.

The heart is also the first part to develop when we're a fetus. The heart and circulatory system are up and running before the brain even begins to develop. In fact, the ultra-magnetic field from our physical heart is sixty times greater than the amplitude of the brain. That's right, the biggest electromagnetic generator in our physical system is our *heart* (The HeartMath Institute).

Our mind gets a lot of attention, especially these days when mindfulness and various cognitive therapies are becoming more and more commonplace. Don't get me wrong, our mind is pretty important...but are we looking in the wrong place for many of the answers?

All through time in cultures around the world, the spiritual consciousness of the heart has been given special significance. On Valentine's Day, do people send their lovers a picture of a kidney? Or a liver? Or a brain? No, they send a heart. Not the visceral physical version but a representation of it just the same.

When someone feels something deeply, do they say they feel it in their mind? No, they say they feel it in their "heart of hearts." When we are really touched by a kind gesture, where do we put our hand? Not on our head but over our *heart*. When we want to tell someone we love them, do we say, "I love you with all my mind"? No, it's the heart.

The heart is more than a physical thing inside of us. There's also a spiritual heart that is tapped into a much higher knowing than we can understand. Our spirit—our true self—is within our heart. The True Source, whatever you want to call It, is a spirit, and therefore, our true self is also a spirit. It's a spark of the True Source. Through our heart, we have a beautiful connection with the True Source: God, Allah, Nature...

Why do you think we say "follow your heart" when trying to make important decisions? It's because the heart has a consciousness that's more evolved than our brain's consciousness and knows the real truth—what is best for us.

If that's a concept you feel resistance around, let me propose the following. Prove to me that your mind is real. Show it to me under an MRI. Show me your thoughts. Your brain will show up, just like your physical heart does. I could see the quality of your thoughts in terms of biochemical changes and your hormones. Maybe you have heightened cortisol if you're feeling threatened or on edge. But you cannot show me your mind...yet, it exists. So why not the energetic heart?

When I talk about the heart, I'm talking about an innate wisdom, a guiding force that we are somehow connected to. And when you get the right connection with your heart, the brain comes into alignment. Most people think they need to control their heart's feelings with their brain. Not true. In fact, it's the other way around.

Our brain is there to help us run our bodies and lives and to learn the lessons from our experiences. But the heart is the special tool with which we can improve our connection with the Source. While the spiritual heart is not physical, it's just as easy to use once you practice opening your heart for some time.

You actually need to use your *heart* to get your mind in proper alignment. Think of it like this: the heart is your device, and you're trying to get your brain to pick up a Bluetooth connection to it. When that connection happens, the mind comes under the influence of the wisdom of the heart. You know which way to go.

Having the heart and mind working together as a team is the natural configuration that allows us to function at our highest good.

What I'm sharing may be difficult to comprehend if you've solely been living in your mind, as you've always been taught to do. The mind is the CEO of your life. It's all you've ever known.

But your non-physical heart, your spiritual heart...that's special. It's something that's much more than can be fully explained. And the more that you connect with it, the more you're able to live in a predominant space of peace, calm, joy, love, and gratitude. You gain a new operating system.

Sure, sometimes you'll still get pulled out and let emotions like hate, anger, and so on overrule your life. You're only human! But the more you build that heart connection, the less this happens. And when it does happen, you don't stay gone for a long time. You can come back to your new normal state of peace, calm, joy, and love quickly.

When I am with my kids, and they have a tantrum or express an emotion such as anger, I don't tell them to stop it. I don't tell them to calm down. I don't threaten to leave the situation. I sit there and let them express what they're feeling, holding the space of love. I look at them lovingly and tell them, "I love you. I'm not going anywhere. I'm here for you. I love you."

And do you know what? That always brings the situation to a beautiful conclusion. The anger fades, the tears dry, and a smile breaks out. Then it's time for a hug. The more I do this with my boys, the less they act out with me.

What do you think would happen if you started taking this approach with *yourself*? If you replaced your self-hate talk with love? Why not give it a try and see?

GRATITUDE:
AKA, HAPPINESS ON COMMAND

Gratitude is a pretty hot subject right now, in self-development circles at least.

"Make a gratitude list."

"Write in a gratitude journal morning and night."

"Think about what you're grateful for three times a day."

This makes sense on one level. After all, it's hard to be happy and ungrateful at the same time! It just doesn't work. As soon as you start focusing on what you're grateful for, you start to feel a softness inside, right? The edges start becoming less sharp. If you want to be happier in life, gratefulness is certainly one key.

But when we talk about gratitude, it's important to go one level deeper. Where does gratitude come from? When was the last time you felt gratitude in your brain? It's not a coincidence that we use the phrase "heartfelt gratitude."

So why aren't all the people journaling and creating lists walking around like lightbulbs of joy all the time? The problem is that they are attempting to listen to and follow their heart from the level of their mind. If you're actively thinking about what you're grateful for, it's brain-based gratitude. It's not *heartfelt* gratitude.

When gratitude is cultivated at the heart level, not the thinking level, you ultimately become grateful for the connection that exists at the Source of your being. That's the deepest gratitude, the deepest fulfilment.

If you're a parent, you know what it's like to hold your baby in your arms. How they are perfectly content with being held and attended to. What babies teach us is how they accept unconditional love, as we have unconditional love for them. This is pure gratitude. They're role modelling for us what we're supposed to be doing on a macro-cosmic level.

Real happiness comes from our heart's connection to the Source of our being. And the key to that connection is unconditional love. When you're open to that condition of loving and being loved, it radiates from you. You are becoming a role model on Earth. You are showing others how to fulfil their innate longing for love.

And in that role modelling, by learning to be loved, accept love, and let your heart open, you become an instrument. Energy radiates from you, which has a positive influence on everyone around you and the world itself.

Because we are all energetic beings, we are all connected.

HOW TO BEGIN BUILDING YOUR HEART CONNECTION

You already have a connection with your energetic heart. We all do. But for many people, that connection is as thin as a fishing line. That doesn't mean it's not still working for you.

Think about experiences you've had where you followed your heart and things worked out. Or the opposite: you followed your logical brain, and things went to shit. Maybe you've had a wake-up call like Dr. Ed where you just feel that things aren't right in your life … that there is something more to life. But you just don't know how to access it.

I believe we all have a deep connection to the Source, a deep knowing, but we need to learn how to listen to It. In Chapter 6, I'm going to share with you some practical exercises that will help you strengthen your connection.

When I started doing these exercises and consciously listening to my heart-based intuition, things started to shift. No, my whole life wasn't immediately rosy. But I did start having experiences that allowed me to grow.

These experiences weren't always pleasant or what I thought I wanted. On a couple of occasions, I broke up with wonderful partners and felt a lot of pain in doing so. But looking back, I know it was the best thing to do because it opened the doors for me to find more suitable partners and to have wonderful new life experiences that I wouldn't have had otherwise.

Thinking that listening to your heart will automatically make your life amazing is just going to lead to disappointment. You won't always get the result you want, but you will get what you need. Your heart always knows what you need...it just doesn't always look how you want it to.

Sometimes, to go forward, you've got to take a step or two back. There might be some truths about your life, your relationships, or your career that you know deep down but have been ignoring. You let your brain stay in control because it's keeping you on the known track, the easier track. But life is an adventure. It's not always meant to be easy.

You can't build an amazing life without careful selection of what you want to put in it. Think of your life as a house right now. It's as old as you are. It's filled with the things, people, thoughts, and feelings that you've collected as you've grown up.

Which rooms don't you like going into? Which walls need to be knocked down? Which objects need to be thrown out? And yes, which people don't belong anymore?

At the end of the day, we're just energy, and energy is attracted to other like energy. There's a reason millionaires hang out with each other and druggies hang out with each other. We attract the same energy we're projecting into the world.

If you can feel in your heart that you're on the wrong track, it's time to give some conscious thought and take responsibility for your path. Look at your friendships. Look at your intimate relationships. Look at your career. Look at what you're experiencing on a daily basis. Give yourself an honest appraisal of where you're at. Don't beat yourself up over it. That will only keep you in your mind's endless loops. Instead, feel it in your heart and accept it.

How is your life's house holding up? Is a little demolition needed? Sometimes, to build something wonderful, you need to knock some stuff down. Deconstruct so you can build something different. In the next few chapters, I'm going to ask you to peel back the layers and see what's really there.

I invite you to check out your foundation and assess whether it's one for building your fulfilling and prosperous life, or whether you've got a bit of mold hanging around, or some beams that aren't up to building standards to give you the life you've always dreamed about.

Every experience brings you closer or farther away from where you need to be. Your heart tells you where you need to go. You just need to start listening.

CHAPTER 4

EMOTIONS

"If you don't manage your emotions,
your emotions will manage you."

—*Deborah Rozman, PhD*

"BARRY! WHAT HAVE YOU *DONE*?"

My mother stared down at me, eyes wide and mouth agape. Her face was full of anguish, and I saw something I hadn't seen in her before—*rage*.

She surveyed the scene before her: a bright red Ferrari splayed on its side with its roof crushed inwards. Beside it was a deep blue Chrysler that had hit it moments before. It had finally come to rest after spinning out a few times after the accident. Paint was chipped off its side, and one tyre was bent inwards.

Other cars had skidded off the concrete driveway and into the grassy bushland next to my childhood home. They lay there in various states of disarray, reflecting the severity of the crash that had happened just moments before as I had smashed the toy cars together with all the ferocious intent of a six-year-old boy.

It was my masterpiece: a car crash in miniature, played out by my toy cars at the top of the driveway. I painstakingly created this scene for hours, lost in creative delight as I invented backstories for the cars and placed carefully selected rocks and twigs around the scene to represent a tiny intersection.

It was my birthday, and that morning I'd received a gift from Mum and Dad—a brand new red toy Ferrari. I was obsessed with Ferraris at the time, so naturally, it was the star of the show.

To give the crash scene ultimate realism, I used a rock from the garden to crush the Ferrari's roof in. Delighted by my own creativity, I couldn't wait to show Mum this ingenious scenario I'd pieced together—a miniaturised snapshot of a major life event.

As the cloudy afternoon turned into the twilight of early evening, the light outside started to dim. Soon, Dad would be home to join us for my birthday celebration dinner. This was a real treat, given he usually didn't make it home from work before eight o'clock in the evening.

But when Mum came outside to tell me to get off the driveway and make way for Dad's approaching car, things didn't go as I had planned.

"Mum, look what I made!" I beamed at her. I started excitedly talking her through the scene, giving her a blow-by-blow account of how the scenario played out. Surely, she would be caught up in the same joy of pure imagination that I had been basking in all afternoon, right?

No, she wouldn't.

My elation and pride curdled in my stomach as I realised that Mum didn't see the scene as the creative masterpiece that I did.

All she saw was destruction. And I was in big, big trouble.

At first, Mum gaped at me in disbelief. I watched as emotion visibly grew within her, eventually spilling out in the form of angry words.

"Barry, look at what you've done!" she yelled. "We don't give you things just so you can destroy them!" She kept yelling as tears began to tickle my eyes. How had things turned from delight into despair so quickly?

As an adult today, I understand that money was tight in my family growing up. She and Dad worked hard for every penny and had especially saved up for my new present. Seeing it wilfully damaged was, in Mum's mind, the ultimate insult.

But my six-year-old self didn't understand the concept of money. I thought I had done something great, only to abruptly find that my form of expression was very wrong. I didn't understand why.

Mum eventually gathered herself. Slowly wiping her hands on the front of her daisy-dotted apron, she growled at me to get inside, go to my room, and said, "Wait 'till your father comes home."

I burst into tears and sprung into the house, skittering up the hallway and into the relative safety of my room. Sitting on my bed, I blinked tears away while trying to process the emotional rollercoaster of what had just happened.

I had expected to receive my mother's love and admiration at the creativity of my miniature car crash scene. But I found myself experiencing quite the opposite: I had been shunned and sent away. To my developing mind, it was a rejection. A removal of love and belonging. I was cast out of my family, my tribe.

Up until that point, I'd managed to live my young life, having always done the "right" thing and experiencing love and belonging as a reward. So this experience was something new and very unpleasant.

Not only that, but my form of play had also been rejected as "wrong." Did that mean something was wrong with *me*? It surely felt so.

Although I didn't realise it at the time, I created a lot of meaning around this experience. My ego flew into protection mode, designing new rules to keep me safe from ever feeling like that again.

It wasn't safe for me to be different. It wasn't safe for me to create. It wasn't safe for me to expand beyond what was previously marked as "good."

Like many rules the ego creates to keep us safe in childhood, these rules actually hindered my efforts to grow and thrive as an adult. They shaped how I showed up in life and in business. I spent years trying to create but always struggled because I was afraid of getting it wrong.

I spent 80 per cent of my time second-guessing what I was planning to do or what I had done. I agonised over the "right" course of action. I never wanted to experience the feeling of being shunned, rejected, or thrown out of my tribe again.

My six-year-old self still existed inside of me, desperately not wanting to get into trouble.

Knowing what I do now about how emotions, thoughts, beliefs, and actions all interplay, I completely understand why Mum reacted the way she did. She was just trying to keep me safe. She was trying to teach me to respect my belongings and look after things.

But in processing the emotional fallout of the experience, I created the belief that I wasn't good enough. That I couldn't create. That I couldn't express myself.

So that was the reality I created.

I sometimes wonder how different my life would have turned out if I had learned some different lessons from that day. How would my personality be different if I had placed another meaning on my mum's emotional reaction? I also wonder what emotional patterns my mum was following to have the reaction she did.

Who knows?

What I *do* know is that in life, people aren't always going to see the same thing you do. They will respond and react according to their own patterning and past woundings. Sometimes, they might even get triggered. And that's okay.

But how we respond and behave is on us. Whether that response leads our life in a positive or negative direction is entirely up to us as well.

When we understand how our emotions work, we can consciously choose the direction in which we go. We can empower ourselves to choose how we show up and respond to things that happen around us. Most importantly, we can begin to guide our life's journey in a beneficial way.

• • •

UNDERSTANDING EMOTIONS

Our true guideposts in life come from the heart. But our emotions often scramble the message. That's why it's so important to understand how emotions work.

Emotions influence everything we do in life. Yet few of us really understand what they are, where they come from, and how they really influence us.

And the consequence of this is that we spend our lives as puppets ruled by our emotions, swinging this way and that, often leaving some form of destruction in our wake.

The problem is that most of us have been brought up to follow the mind. To think about things and make decisions from a place of logic. But what we don't realise is that everything we think, feel, and believe is derived from our emotions.

Our emotions are raw data that get interpreted by our brains to become feelings, which become actions, which bring our results.

Emotion > Thought > Feeling > Action = Result

Logic doesn't come first—emotions do. We often feel we are being completely logical when we are, in fact, just at the mercy of our emotions without even realising it.

When the heart and the mind are in alignment, the way we respond to our environment and the nature of our thoughts change completely—as do our actions and, therefore, our results.

But the first step is understanding the relationship between emotions, thoughts, and feelings. Only when we understand what's really driving our actions and beliefs can we influence them for better results in our life.

EMOTIONS, FEELINGS, AND MOODS

Emotions and feelings are often used interchangeably, but they really aren't the same thing.

Emotions come first. Emotions cause the release of chemicals in our brain in response to our interpretation of a specific trigger. Their purpose is primarily to help us survive. To take action. To avoid danger.

When the electrical current of an emotion travels along our neural pathways, it triggers a release of chemical proteins called neuropeptides. Neuropeptides communicate chemical messages throughout the body, creating physiological responses. Adrenaline, hormones, oxytocin, and endorphins are all examples of these chemicals (Russo 2018).

Emotions happen fast, putting our minds in a state of catch-up. It takes our brains about a quarter of a second to identify the trigger and about another quarter of a second to produce the chemicals needed for a flight-or-fight response.

While emotions are associated with bodily reactions that are activated through neuropeptides and hormones released by the brain, feelings are the conscious experience of emotional reactions.

Here's where it gets tricky.

Feelings are created by unconscious patterning shaped by personal experiences, memories, and previous outcomes linked to that particular stimulus and emotion.

Because the brain processes millions of pieces of data each day and needs to assign meaning quickly (in case the emotion is indicating something life-threatening), it attaches a belief to this threat based on our past experiences and what we made those mean—our unconscious patterning.

But the thing is, everything we believe is made up. Our reality is subjective. And our feelings fuel our interpretation of the world around us.

It's not much of a surprise then that we develop moods from our feelings. Moods are more generalized. They're not always tied to a specific incident but can arise from a collection of several factors such as the environment (weather, lighting, people around us), our physiology (our diet, exercise habits, our general health), and finally, our mental state (where we're focusing attention).

Where focus goes, energy flows.

The good news is that moods are the most easily adaptable parts of the emotion-to-behaviour chain that governs what we think, triggers what we do, and drives the results that we get.

We can choose to put ourselves in a different mood if we influence the factors that lead to our mood. We can reframe our thoughts more positively. We can change what's going on with us physiologically by exercising, practising breathwork, or meditating.

And we can explore the emotion and feeling that is contributing to our mood, find the belief that is fueling that mood, deconstruct it, and reconstruct it into a more empowering belief. Hence improving our mood.

The bottom line is our emotions are essential to our functioning. They are an essential part that provides us raw data about the world around us.

But our feelings (how we interpret that data) and mood (the mix of feelings and emotions we choose to prolong) can be altered if we are willing to do a little self-exploration.

The great thing is that when you practice emotional awareness and do the inner work needed to regain control, negative emotions occur less and less. Because like attracts like. When your outlook is more positive, and you are vibrating in a higher state (we'll cover this in a minute), you will attract higher quality emotions, relationships, and experiences into your life.

I'm not saying that life becomes rainbows and fairy-floss...but you certainly feel and function a hell of a lot better.

EMOTIONAL ADDICTIONS

Happiness, joy, laughter, and orgasms cause the release of natural opiates called endorphins. These powerful opiates make us feel good. They boost our immune system, relax our muscles, elevate our mood, and dampen pain.

On the flipside, adrenaline and cortisol are triggered by fear, anxiety, or stress. They cause our heart to beat faster and blood vessels to dilate, making our skin flush. We might then have rapid, shallow breathing. Our muscles tighten, especially around the stomach and shoulder area. A slight sweat may break out.

The purpose of adrenaline is to place our body in a rapid-response fight-or-flight state. In emergencies, this is beneficial as it aids escape. But over a long period, adrenaline can be very damaging to the body. It suppresses our immune system, impairs digestion, causes pain and stiffness, makes our body acidic (resulting in inflammation), and drains our vitality (American Psychological Association 2018; Hormone Health Network 2018).

All of which have a direct effect on our feelings and moods. Which in turn have a direct effect on how we interact with others and how they interact with us. Our mood might trigger feelings in the people around us, feelings that are linked to their own triggers, experiences, and beliefs.

Left unresolved, regular clashes of feelings such as anger or frustration erode everything good with friends, family, or romantic partners. That's how relationships deteriorate and begin to circle the drain.

Addiction to feeling good is also a well-known problem. Aside from drugs, alcohol, or sex addiction, it's easy to become addicted to feelings that trigger a soothing chemical payoff, even if we don't enjoy it on the surface.

As an example, when we cause conflict with our partners because we're not getting one of our needs met, but we don't know how to ask for it in a resourceful way, we poke and prod to get a reaction, and then there's a blowup, followed by a tension release.

You might work overtime because the recognition from your boss for sacrificing your weekend soothes your unconscious fear of not being good enough.

The thing is, many neuropeptides such as adrenaline are highly addictive. Our body can become accustomed to over-stimulation over time and eventually need those chemical reactions to maintain higher energy levels.

The over-stimulation becomes "the new normal" as we regularly readjust to our emotional and physiological state. Think about this common analogy:

if you drop a frog in a pot of hot water, it will immediately detect the change in environment and jump out. But if you sit a frog in a pot of warm water and gradually turn the heat up, it will recalibrate its body temperature until it overheats and dies.

We can be just like those boiling frogs.

As an example, people who have experienced extended periods of adrenal overload, especially from childhood, will often unconsciously attract dramas or crises in their lives to feed their adrenaline dependence. Even overwork can be a sign of adrenaline dependence.

We can become addicted to feeling stressed. Feeling tired. Feeling anything that gives us some type of payoff, whether it's the high from getting people's attention, proving yourself right, or a range of other ultimately negative payoffs that keep us stuck in patterns.

If any of this is hitting home for you, know that it's not entirely your fault. At least, not consciously. We have been taught to believe the things that shape our feelings by society, our parents, teachers, and other influential factors. And we repeat patterns of stimulus-response that we have learned from them.

Beginning when we are children, our rational mind makes judgements about our emotional experiences based on our perception of pain or pleasure. That's how we decide what is good or bad and how we create beliefs. These beliefs influence our thoughts, actions, and results.

By the age of five, we have already decided how we must show up in life to survive. From these decisions—these "beliefs" about how the world is— most of our fears, inhibitions, and self-limitations grow. We learn to settle for less than we really want, to make choices that fall short of happiness, and to accept not having our needs met.

We often mistakenly believe that's just how life is. In reality, what we have learned, what we choose to believe, and the response patterns we continue to perpetuate are exactly what hold us back from the love and belonging that we crave.

EMOTIONAL REPRESSION

Many years ago, I went to my spiritual teacher for advice on dealing with my anger. This was shortly after coming out of the period of my life where I had been cheated on, lost a friend, hated my business, and was feeling so incredibly lost in life.

He said to me, "You have a lot of anger," which I already knew.

"Yeah," I replied. "It just doesn't end."

What he said to me next took some time for me to really understand.

"The issue is not actually the anger. The issue is what happens when you get angry. Imagine for a moment that all the negative emotions from this life and past lives are stored in a safe. And that only you have the combination to that safe."

I didn't know where he was going with this, but I continued listening.

"The True Source is constantly wanting to help remove all that negativity. God wants to dissolve those emotions that don't make you feel good. Yet the Source's love cannot access the safe because it doesn't have the code."

It took a while to understand this, but eventually, I came to this realisation.

Life has a way of pressing us, of challenging us. When you squeeze an orange, what happens? You get orange juice. Life has a way of squeezing us, too. And what comes out is what's inside. If pure love is what's inside, that's what will come out.

But the reality is that we get squeezed, and we have these negative emotions. Situations happen, and we choose to see them negatively. We choose to take on negative emotions.

When we create these emotions, and they get trapped around our heart, only we can take them on, but only love can help to remove them. So what happens is life squeezes us, the safe gets unlocked, and out comes these negative emotions. If, at that point in time, we choose love, compassion, and belongingness—when we choose to surrender to the fact that we're not perfect beings—love can enter the safe of negative emotion because the door is open. It can enter and cleanse the root cause.

But what often happens is that the safe opens, and we get angry. Then we judge ourselves for getting angry. I used to do it all the time; I'd get angry with myself for getting angry! I'd get more pissed off and beat myself up even more.

It was like I was driving down the road, and I'd get a flat tyre (get angry), but instead of getting out and changing that flat, I'd puncture holes in the other three good tires (get angry that I got angry about being angry).

Doesn't make sense, right?

The emotion would build and build into a flurry whizzing around me...and then, I'd shut the safe closed while it was still filled with anger. And the next time life squeezed me, there it was, ready to come rushing out again.

For me, this realisation was massively impactful. I started looking differently at how I engaged with myself emotionally. I'd recognise when I was starting to feel angry, and instead of kicking myself in the guts for it, I allowed myself to be okay with it. I started realising that it was there for a reason. Most importantly, I started realising that the anger wasn't something new that I was creating...rather, it was something that had been inside me and was being released.

And I chose to be grateful for the anger. I chose not to judge it. And over time, I started experiencing anger and other emotions that I didn't enjoy less and less.

As I've said many times in this book, what we suppress gets expressed. The pressure builds. And the more that I was shamed or told that my negative emotions were not welcome, the more I tried to ignore them, the more they built up like a pressure cooker inside of me. And they had to come out.

Now, I'm not saying it's time to take out your anger in a hurtful or destructive way. I'm not talking about taking your anger out on somebody else. It's your emotion, and you are the one who should be dealing with it.

There are plenty of resourceful ways of dealing with anger. One of my favourites is exercising. It's nearly impossible to feel angry after a good workout or a run through nature. Just let it flow out of you while your endorphins fill you up with the good stuff.

Or I might sit with the anger and just let myself feel it. Just let it move through me and accept that at this current time, I am angry. I don't need to yell, scream, rant, or rave for it to flow out of me. I just need to let myself feel it and understand that it needs to flow out of me, almost like a ghost leaving someone's body in an old cartoon.

When I started letting myself become okay with feeling my negative emotions, a weird thing started happening. The people around me started to reflect that. They stopped reacting to my reactions. They kind of became okay with it, too. They took my lead and went, "Well, Barry is experiencing anger right now. It has nothing to do with me. I'm just going to let him feel it and let it release."

It didn't take long after I started dealing with my negative emotions in this way that my anger no longer had a hold on me.

Think about what happens when kids do the wrong thing. They try and hide it. Adults do it, too. Often, we feel so guilty that we do it again. But the second or third time, it's often because we unconsciously want to beat ourselves up because of the guilt we still carry from the first time.

The moment we give a voice to this, the moment we allow it to be fully expressed, it no longer has a hold on us. But if we ignore it, it just gets louder and louder. Like a kid that nags you for a chocolate in the supermarket, it will not stop until you address it.

One thing you will find if you decide to start practising some of the concepts in this book is that you might get triggered more often than you did in the past—at least at first—as everything in your life begins realigning itself with your new path.

That's not a bad thing. The whole reason that trigger is happening is because there's something within you that needs to come out. It needs to be expressed. It needs to be resolved.

If you have an interaction with someone and they piss you off, that emotion is not created instantly. It already existed within you. And something that person has done or said has unlocked the door for it to come out.

It's important that you actually allow those emotions to come out.

Again, don't just start projecting your shit onto other people. That's not what I'm saying. But if you need to take yourself away to shake or dance or kick and scream or throw your hands around to deal with your emotions, that's your responsibility.

The first step is to accept that other people don't "make" you do anything. Not a damn thing. They've simply reminded you of some part of you where there's still some trapped emotion. And it's your responsibility to deal with it. Or it will keep coming up again and again.

It's easy to blame others. But that doesn't give us what we want. It moves us further away from being in truth and of being in connection with our self. And the further away we go from that connection with self, the less balanced, happy, and fulfilled our life becomes.

So don't be afraid to *feel*. It's the best part of being alive.

RAISING YOUR EMOTIONAL VIBRATION

We've spoken about how emotions trigger chemical reactions in our bodies to make us react to the data our brains are detecting. For example, we get a fright when we think a snake is near because they are dangerous.

What do chemical reactions do? They create *energy*.

Everything in the universe is made up of molecules vibrating at different speeds. This includes plants, bodies, animals, thoughts, and emotions. Emotions are simply a form of energy that runs through your body like an electrical current.

Emotional energy, just like any other form of energy, moves and vibrates. Like everything and everyone else in the universe, we are constantly vibrating and creating energy. Think about it; the very word emotion is based on the word "motion."

Using atomic force microscopes, researchers have detected vibrations on the nanoscale—much smaller than 1/1000th the diameter of a single human hair. These vibrations generate electromagnetic energy waves. By measuring these nano vibrations in a series of tests using emotional stimuli, they can detect the physical vibration of an emotion (Stanborough 2020).

The vibrations and the electromagnetic energy associated with emotions actually cause changes in our cells, which can then affect how our body functions at every level. Different molecules vibrate at different rates—and those rates can speed up or slow down if conditions around the molecules change (Stanborough).

Those conditions can be composed of everything from our physical environment to the thoughts we think. You've probably heard about the experiment where students directed anger at one plant and love at another? They essentially praised one plant every day and yelled hateful things at the other.

As you've probably guessed, the plant with unpleasant emotions directed at it withered and died, while the positively reinforced plant thrived. Now, there are a number of other factors that may have contributed to the health of one plant over the other. Minute differences in soil quality, for example. Nevertheless, the correlation between energetic vibration and physical and emotional state certainly exists.

Just start taking notice of how you feel in your body when you're in a high-vibe state in comparison with when you're in a really low mood. Researchers are regularly finding evidence that the mind-body connection is more tightly correlated than we previously imagined.

Thinking back to energetic vibrations and how they relate to our emotional state, take a look at the chart below. We can see that feelings like shame, guilt, and apathy vibrate at very low levels. But peace, joy, and enlightenment vibrate quite high.

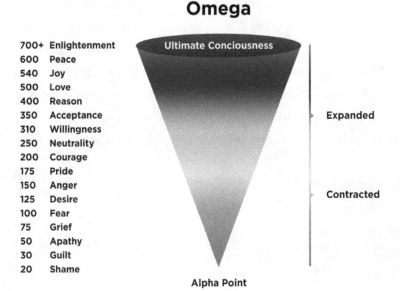

Omega

		Ultimate Conciousness
700+	Enlightenment	
600	Peace	
540	Joy	
500	Love	
400	Reason	
350	Acceptance	Expanded
310	Willingness	
250	Neutrality	
200	Courage	
175	Pride	
150	Anger	
125	Desire	Contracted
100	Fear	
75	Grief	
50	Apathy	
30	Guilt	
20	Shame	

Alpha Point

Source: David R. Hawkins, *Power vs. Force: The Hidden Determinants of Human Behavior.*

When we are vibrating at a higher level, we feel lighter, happier, and more at ease, whereas lower vibrations make us feel heavy and unhappy.

It's no surprise then that we classify some emotions as "negative." Like I have said previously, emotions themselves aren't inherently good or bad; they are simply states of feeling. But low-vibe emotions certainly can cause a lot of reactions that have a negative effect on your own wellbeing and those around you.

In short bursts, negative emotions can prompt us to take action to get our needs met. But, over a long time, neuropeptides prompted by these emotions can cause health issues, as well as impact our relationships and daily life (Reichmann and Holzer 2016).

Emotions in the upper frequencies are beneficial for our health and our well-being. They flow through us and radiate into the people around us, which means they are beneficial both for ourselves and for the world in general.

So, it makes sense then to try and spend as much time as you can in a high-vibe state. That's not to say that life should be nothing but rainbows—there are two sides to any coin, after all. But the more you work at what you're reading in this book, the less you'll find that you experience low states of feeling. And when you do, you can process it much more resourcefully.

There are many ways to raise our vibration and experience a high-vibe state. It comes down to trying them and seeing what feels best for you.

- Breathwork
- Meditation
- Outdoor immersion
- Reiki
- Generosity
- Gratitude
- Diet
- Yoga

All of these techniques have not only been shown to have psychological benefits but also physical ones, thanks to the mind-body connection.

Simply put, they raise your vibrational state. So not only do you start experiencing more high-vibe feelings such as peace, joy, and love, but you also spread them to the people around you. And then they experience, attract, and spread high-vibe feelings, too . . . and so it goes on and on in a ripple effect that quietly changes the world, one person at a time.

CHAPTER 5

DECISION-MAKING

"Once you make a decision,
the universe conspires to make it happen."

—*Ralph Waldo Emerson*

"BARRY, YOU OWE $1.3 MILLION. IT'S TIME TO MAKE THE CALL FOR bankruptcy."

Have you ever been on an amusement ride that takes you up... up... and then drops you from a great height, pushing your guts into your mouth and making your blood run backwards?

That's kind of the feeling that came over me when I heard those words. The ground was dropping out beneath me. I was free-falling. I felt sick.

I blinked back tears and prepared myself to say the next words, trying to overcome the massive knot that was choking my throat, as my identity as a successful guy who had it "all" crumbled into pieces.

"Okay. I'm making the call," I croaked. "When can I come in and take care of the paperwork?"

It was 2012, and my first business, a kitchen renovation and installation company, had just spectacularly imploded. I'd built the business fresh out of my apprenticeship, employing a team of nineteen tradespeople and turning over multiple seven figures annually, all within just four years.

Suffice to say, I moved fast and worked hard. But somewhere along the way, the business took over. Instead of me controlling it, it controlled me. Like a greedy monster, it always wanted more. More of my time, money, and sanity. I was like a kid running down a steep hill, barely remaining upright while picking up speed. It was only a matter of time until I stumbled and fell, taking everything down with me.

I know now (and I knew then, but by the time I realised, it was too late) that I was doing business the wrong way. I was sitting at the top of the decision-making chain, and everything depended on me. I'd been working eighteen-hour days for as long as I could remember. My phone rang at night and on weekends. In the precious time I had away from work, my head was back at the office, organising jobs, planning Monday's to-dos, and obsessing about making enough money to keep up with this monstrous machine I'd built around me.

My heartbreak was compounded by the fact that earlier that day, my partner had rung me. She was leaving me. And taking our kids. She was tired of not having her needs met because I was always absent, always stressed about the business, and never focused on her needs.

How had what started as a normal day turned into the worst day of my life?

I drove to a nearby beach lookout and sat in the car looking out at the ocean. Tears pricked my eyes as I thought of my staff, a pang of fear surging through me at the thought of having to tell them their jobs were gone. These people relied on me for their income.

What about them? What about their families?

I had let *everyone* down.

For a minute, I felt like I might throw up. I tried to sit through the sickening falling sensation that had overtaken me as my nervous system pumped adrenaline and cortisol into my body. I fixed my eyes on the sparkling azure water in front of me and focused on my breathing.

Eventually, I was ready to do a mental recon. It was time to face some shit through my tears. In a short month, I'd gone from running a multiple seven-figure business, living in a family home with my partner and sons, to literally having nothing.

Where did it go wrong? Was there one single point where I doomed everything? One moment where I fucked everything up? No, I realised, life isn't that black and white. There was no major moment where I made the single wrong turn that took me down this path. Rather, it was a smaller series of decisions, every day, that got me further and further in the shit.

There had been a tiny voice deep inside telling me that my micro-decisions were leading me to a major crash. But I hadn't listened because there was a much louder voice in my head, constantly shouting at me that the only direction was *forward*. And forward meant more work, more hours away from my partner and kids, more stress, more bills…until ultimately my sandcastle toppled over.

I had to face up to the fact that this was *my* doing. I'd created this situation, and it was my responsibility to clean it up. I reflected on every decision I'd made that had gotten me to this point. Every time I chose to say "yes" to a job while I knew we were at capacity with our workload. Every time I picked up the phone from a client when I was supposed to be present with my partner. Every time I sat at the park with my kids checking emails instead of making memories with them.

There were plenty of outside pressures that led me to make those decisions, sure. My business had snowballed into an enterprise that was broken, and the only way I knew how to fix it was to pick up speed and do more, faster.

(Since then, I've recreated the way I do business and have built several wildly successful businesses that operate largely without me or any other single point of failure. You can find out the exact formula I use in my book *The Path to Freedom*. Get it at: www.pathtofreedom.com.au/free-book)

. . .

Two weeks later, I found myself sitting in a small, drab office with chipped chairs and a faded motivational picture on the wall. The papers were signed, and I was starting over with absolutely nothing. In fact, less than nothing.

The one thing I knew was this: I wasn't going to sit on my arse and wallow for the rest of my life. I was going to pick myself up and try again. But I was going to do things differently next time. I was going to start by making different decisions about how I ran my business and my life.

. . .

MAKING GOOD DECISIONS

We all understand the importance of decision-making…at least on the surface. Morpheus asks Neo if he wants the red pill or the blue pill, with one option having the power to change his life forever. In *Sliding Doors*, Gwyneth Paltrow takes the Tube home at a slightly different time and opens up a new story arc that leads to a snappier hairstyle and happier life. Donnie Darko makes the decision to get out of bed before a plane engine hits his house and opens up a wormhole into a parallel world that threatens to destroy the universe.

We tend to focus on the big decisions that mark our lives. But while the "big life decisions" certainly deserve the airtime they get, it's actually the smaller decisions we make every single day that matter the most.

Like an ocean wave is just a collection of billions of tiny particles of water all moving together in a similar direction at once, where you are in your life right now is a combination of small decisions that have gotten you where you are. Whether those decisions were good or bad…where you are right now is the successful outcome of all the decisions and actions (or inactions) you've taken in your life so far.

The thing is, while we understand the importance of big decisions, and perhaps even smaller ones…we are pretty rubbish at making them. Some people make a list of pros and cons, trying to use logic to solve the decision like a puzzle. Others make decisions fast, using more "flip of a coin" type of thinking. Some people try to predict a stream of future outcomes. And some people spend so much time agonizing over every tiny detail that they make no decision at all and, instead, just fall in line with whatever is going on around them.

Like many people, you might have had the experience of finishing school and just picking a career path that seemed okay simply because you needed to do *something*. You didn't know what you really wanted to do in life, but you felt an urgency to just get on with things.

I remember the pressure of career days at school where a bunch of kids were basically supposed to figure out what we'd spend the next ten, twenty, forty years of our life doing. How the hell were we to know?

These days, many young people take a gap year to just travel and explore the world and experience life. During this time, supposedly, they'll pick up sparks of ideas that resonate with them about how they want to spend their time on this planet.

But back when I finished school, there was no gap year. I remember agonizing over my career decision because I didn't know which decision to make…yet I was sure I needed to get it perfect. I knew I liked making things with my hands, so I went straight into an apprenticeship. And I felt that once I made that decision, it was final. That was my life's career path locked in (or so I thought back then).

A lot of people do the same thing. They choose a path and then think, *I've made my bed; now, I've gotta lie in it*. Once we're pointed in one direction, we let ourselves believe that we can't switch paths…even if the road we're headed down is not the right one for us. *Better the devil you know*, we think.

And so, we stay in bad jobs, in bad relationships, in bad housing situations, in bad friendship circles. Why? Our head fills us with fear about what's going to happen if we make a different decision…the decision to change, to do something *different*.

My boss will yell at me if I leave. My girlfriend will not know how to cope without me. My housemate will not be able to pay the bills. I'll be alone and won't find new friends... These are all imaginary outcomes that your brain tells you on repeat. Because the brain doesn't want you to change things. Change is the unknown. And the brain likes familiarity. That's why so many of us spend our lives repeating the same patterns. Patterns of abuse (of ourselves and from others), patterns of struggle, patterns of sadness.

Yet life is not fixed; it is forever moving and changing. In fact, if something stops moving, it's dead. Plants, animals, fish, even smaller organisms like fungi, moss, bacteria... all move. Movement is the single characteristic of being alive that we all share.

With this movement comes change. Some changes inevitably happen to us as we age, but most changes are the ones we make ourselves, either passively or on purpose. Either way, we are always going somewhere. Time passes, no matter what we choose to do with it.

At any given moment, we have the ability to change our decisions and change our lives. Decisions aren't always easy, but we *always* have a choice.

I can hear you questioning me at this point: "So Barry, you're saying that I can just choose to leave my crappy job if I decide to? Then who's going to pay my bills, huh? Huh?"

Look, I'm not saying that you should walk out on your responsibilities because you simply decided to one day. But you *can* decide to leave that job and then make a series of smaller decisions that will create a supportive environment for you to take action on that decision. You can get your résumé updated and start looking for another job. You can explore new business opportunities available to you. There are hundreds of small decisions you can act on to facilitate *any* big decision you choose to make.

But unfortunately, a lot of the time, we ignore this and choose to see life as black and white. "I can't do that because..." I get it; making some decisions seems hard. Emotionally turbulent even. And it involves stepping into uncertainty, which can be scary.

But what would you rather? A life spent trudging through various daily miseries, or the life you dream of having? Either option is 100 per cent available to you, whether you think it is or not.

So, what's really stopping us?

If we're making decisions all the time, how do we make sure those decisions are the right ones? The best ones? The ones that will result in a fulfilling life?

As with most things in life worth having, it's a question of *quality* over quantity.

The one thing that's stopping us from achieving whatever we want in life is the quality of the decisions we make. But making good decisions isn't always as easy as it should be. Because...

YOUR DECISION-MAKING IS FLAWED

Most of us grow up making decisions on the fly, doing whatever we think is a good idea at the time. But since our brains are on perpetual loops, trying to keep us stuck in the same "safe" holding pattern ... how do we know if we're actually making a good decision? The right decision?

Many people try to solve this conundrum by putting criteria around what a good decision looks like.

In Navy SEAL Teams, for example, there are three criteria upon which decisions are made: The mission, the team, the individual. Namely, who does the decision serve? Hint: The individual comes last. These criteria serve the higher purpose of the team: mission success.

You might try and create your own criteria around what a good decision looks like. You might do this by considering the following questions:

What is "mission success" for me? Does it foster opportunity? Does it positively impact others? Does it lead me closer to my goals?

This is all well and good. After all, it's good to have goals, right? Then all you've got to do is reverse-engineer your way towards them.

But here's the problem: most people's life goals aren't actually things that will make them ultimately happy. As I've already said, we often base our goals on things we think we want because, on some level, we'll achieve a sense of status or belonging. Or a sense of achievement. Or we'll make our dad proud. Or our partner will finally be happy with us. Or whatever else.

But these goals are all focusing on status and material things... stuff that happens outside of us. When the buzz of achieving those things fades, we seek new things to give us the same sense of accomplishment, connection, status, or whatever high we're chasing. And so the cycle continues.

So, if we end up making decisions based on goals that aren't going to ultimately fulfil us, or the criteria we put around what makes a "good" decision is flawed, or we keep repeating cycles that didn't work for us before, what else can we do?

The answer lies not in our head... but in our *heart*.

Have you ever been absent-minded when driving your car and ended up on your route back to your old job? Or your old house? Our brain makes so many micro-decisions every day that it cannot possibly keep up with every decision consciously. So, it runs our previous patterns in the background while our conscious mind is dealing with other stuff. That's why when our head drives our decisions, we slip back into old habits.

When you let your mind take over on autopilot, it will only take you where you've already been... not the new place you want to go.

The truth is that if there was truly nothing stopping you from having what you wanted, you'd already have it. You'd do the things needed to make it work. But our mind mucks it all up. It focuses on the wrong goals, uses our old patterns of behaviour (even if they didn't work), and fills us with roadblocks grown from our biases and fears.

The key to making good decisions that *stick* is to make them with your *heart*.

When you start making decisions from heart-based guidance, at first, the results you get might not be what you want. But that's the perfect opportunity to keep trusting and developing your "heart intuition" muscle. Like going to the gym, you're not going to get the body of your dreams after three sessions. But if you discipline yourself to keep going, eventually, you can transform your life completely.

HARD DECISIONS

Just because some decisions are the right ones doesn't mean they're the easy ones.

Making decisions that aren't going to be somebody else's cup of tea is never easy. We don't want to hurt anyone. We don't want to put anybody out.

Besides, it's painful to break up with a partner, leave a job, or leave your business. And it takes a lot of work, too. You need to move out of your home and find a new one. You need to find a new job and dive into the unknown of a new position in a new company. It's challenging. It's difficult. So, although we may know in our hearts what we need to do, taking that step can seem an insurmountable task.

But think about this. When we are kids, we make decisions from our heart. We are impulsive. We are pure. We know what we want and what we don't want, and we aren't afraid to tell our caregivers! But like most living creatures on the planet, we live in groups. Throughout our evolutionary history, we've needed to rely on the shared knowledge and resources from a tribe of peers for our survival. With that comes a dizzying network of social rules and customs that have evolved so that we can maintain our social groups and, therefore, our survival.

The downside of this is that as we learn many of the rules of how to be a good member of our family and tribe, sometimes we experience what it's like to have our "membership" in our tribe temporarily removed. Our hand gets slapped away at the dinner table. Our parents send us to our room if we break a rule.

Given that our truest desire is to belong—a desire that's cemented by millions of years of evolution—when we experience loss of belonging as a kid, it can be downright traumatic.

And then, as we grow up, our need for belonging often turns into fear of judgement, fear of abandonment, fear of being shut out, fear of loss of status.

We want to belong, so we become afraid to say no. We put off making decisions that might impinge on somebody else's comfort or plans. We don't want to be cast out of our tribe. We want to belong, and we want to be loved.

But every time we make a decision that doesn't honour who we are and reflect healthy boundaries, we teach others that our needs are not important. The ancient part of our brain that desperately wants to keep us in the "gang" has taken over. But the brain doesn't always know what's right for us. Maybe we're better off without that tribe and should really go and find a new one?

Recently, I remembered times when I literally spent years going along with what someone else wanted…simply because I never consciously realised I had a choice. My desire to please others and put the needs of people I care about before my own is so entrenched within me that I didn't even realise I was sacrificing my own needs for theirs.

I'm sure that you can relate because everybody on the planet does this to some degree. (We'll unpack healthy ways to say no later in Chapter 9.)

For now, think about this: *A no to someone else is a yes to you.*

Where are you not making a decision you should make because you are afraid of upsetting someone else?

Where are you saying that their priority is more important than yours?

Where are you not honouring yourself because you're afraid of some form of rejection or removal of love or esteem?

DECISION-MAKING FROM THE HEART

Some people seem lucky in life…but that's not because they've been touched by some mystical fairy magic. It's because the decisions that they make are more aligned with their true path and purpose than those who choose unhelpful paths of action. Simply put: they're making decisions from their heart.

We are all connected to the innate knowing of our heart. We all have access to it. But it takes time to remember how to use it and rebuild the relationship we have with it.

When we have access to the heart, we are tapped into a consciousness far greater and far smarter than our mind. And if we listen to that, we'll always arrive at a life that fulfils our needs more than we could ever imagine.

I'm not talking about material riches, although that can certainly come along with your spiritual fulfilment. We were born into a society of greed and of status. And that's the paradigm we now need to start to shift. We need to stop focusing on shit that doesn't serve us and allow ourselves to open up to our highest purpose.

Stop and think about your life right now. Are you happy? Are you truly fulfilled?

The truth is that wherever you are right now, at some point in the past, you wished to be here. At some point, you wanted to be with that partner. At some point, you wanted to have that job. At some point, you wanted to run your own business. Sure, you want other things, too, and sure, you probably wanted the things you have now without the stress and worry that you may be experiencing in your situation right now. You didn't know that X, Y, Z would be part of the equation.

But at some point, we all wished we were where we are. The level at which we feel fulfilled and happy in that choice reflects the level at which we actually chose to trust our heart in making that decision.

When I declared bankruptcy, it was the hardest decision of my life. My whole identity as a man was ripped apart. I was no longer a successful businessman. I was no longer a provider for my family. I was no longer someone I felt my dad would be proud of. But looking back on it now, declaring bankruptcy was the best decision I ever made. And I'm so grateful for that experience because it led me to where I ultimately needed to go.

I'll never forget, shortly after my life imploding, I decided to drive to Perth to try and salvage what I could from my relationship with my ex, the mother of my kids. I remember driving across the Nullabor in my busted-up, old ute with a thousand bucks to my name, my dog sitting beside me, and all my belongings in the back. I was bankrupt, and I had no idea how I'd messed things up so bad.

Despite spending most of the twenty-hour drive crying as I processed my emotions, something deep in my heart felt right. That, in itself, messed me up. How could I be so conflicted? How could I be so messed up, yet somewhere deep inside of me, so calm and almost happy I had shed the old layers of my life?

I'd been exploring meditation and heart connection for a while before this. In the months before the business broke down, I'd had an intuition that I needed to cut ties and get out, that the horse had bolted, and it was taking me with it. My whole life and identity were wrapped up in that business and that feeling of being a successful, busy guy. I didn't want to let my family down. I didn't want to let my parents down. I didn't want people in my social circles to laugh behind my back because I'd failed. So I kept pushing against that intuition, that quiet voice that was trying to tell me to wind things up.

Essentially, I was trying to swim against the current, and you can only do that for so long until you drown. If I had listened to my heart earlier, I could've saved myself and my family six months of pain as I raced towards the inevitable conclusion of my well-intentioned but fundamentally flawed business model.

Looking back now, I absolutely know it had to happen, and I'm so grateful for the experience because every single aspect of my life today has grown from that adversity. And my life today is pretty fucking spectacular. I live in paradise, am at the head of several wildly successful businesses, have an incredible relationship with my partner...and most of all, I have positively changed thousands of lives—the people my company and I have coached over the years.

And I've been able to make this progress not just because I'm listening more to my heart but because I'm not letting my emotions mess up my progress. When things get challenging, it's easy to blame others, get pissed off, and so on. And sometimes I still do. But not for long. Because ultimately, that's all just noise that distracts me from my true purpose. The truth is, I'm responsible for everything I put into the world and everything that I get back in return. And so are you. The only way you can progress is if you take responsibility for it and move on with love.

TAKING RADICAL RESPONSIBILITY

My experience of bankruptcy nine years ago helped me start making better decisions to get better outcomes. The first choice meant getting back up and trying again. I could just as easily have given up and declared myself a failed businessman. I could've decided that I should "stay in my lane" and go back to being a carpenter.

The decision was mine. And whatever is going on in your life, the decision is also yours. Even the hard decisions. Your life—and what you do with it—is your own responsibility. You can blame your parents, society, God, or any other thing in this world for your circumstances. But at the end of the day, you're responsible for where you are and where you're going.

Am I saying that if you're in a shitty situation right now, that it's completely your fault? No, we can't always control the things that happen to us in life. I can't control whether I might get hit by a bus when I walk across the street tomorrow. But I can do certain things to make sure I get the outcome I want. I can cross at the lights. I can look both ways first. I can walk without music blaring through my headphones. Does that completely negate the risk of something going wrong? No, but it certainly reduces it a hell of a lot.

The things that happen to us aren't necessarily our fault, but they're our responsibility. Whether you're happy right now or not, you have the opportunity to live a fulfilling life. Every person on this planet deserves to live the best version of themselves. But we get caught in our patterns; we keep believing our well-intentioned but misinformed brains telling us, "You can't do that, because…"

It's time to start questioning the decisions that come from your brain. Ask yourself, "Why am I choosing to do this? To what end?" Take your brain's decisions with a grain of salt. Then meditate on them before acting. (I'll teach you some simple yet powerful meditations later in this book.)

Let me state the obvious here: I'm not advising you to disbelieve everything your brain says you should do and start walking out in front of traffic or running around without your clothes on. Obviously, there is a range of unconscious practical decisions that we make every day to keep us safe.

But I want you to start analysing why you do what you do. Are you making these decisions because you saw others on social media doing it? Are you doing things because you think your partner expects you to? Are you doing things because you believe that they make you a good parent?

Question them and ask, *Is doing this actually making me happy? Or do I absolutely hate it? And if I hate it,* why *am I doing it?* You'll find a lot of insight in your answers. And that will, in turn, help you start creating the blueprint for your new life.

Remember our house analogy from Chapter 3? Earmark the shit you want to get rid of. That mouldy old cupboard in the kitchen. The green pool that's a bitch to maintain, and you never swim in it. The more you earmark what needs to go, the more you'll start to understand what you want to keep.

But the first step is taking radical responsibility for where you are now. What aren't you happy with? Where aren't you fulfilled? What have you fucked up completely? Remove the emotion you've tied to the decision or its outcome. Straighten up and look it in the eye. You are not your fuckups. Your fuckups are the result of your decisions. That's all. And do you know what the wonderful thing about that is? It's that you can make *new* decisions to change the trajectory of your life. And you can start right *now*.

But first, you have to acknowledge what you've created. You may not have created the external stuff that others have done to you, but on some level, you *have* created an environment that has allowed that to happen. It's not your fault, but it's your responsibility. And nobody can change it for you but you.

YOUR NEW OPPORTUNITY

We tend to suppress our fuckups, our failures, our shame. But that's denying us from learning what those experiences can teach us. And when you don't learn the lessons the universe is teaching you, you're going to repeat the same mistakes again and again.

And as we touched on in the previous chapter, what's repressed gets expressed. Things bubble to the surface one way or another. When we push it all down, hoping it will all go away, we're not allowing that energy to be transformed into inspiration for a better way in the future.

If you're feeling resistance when thinking about the areas in your life where you're not happy or fulfilled, recognise that you're attaching negative emotions to the thought. You're attaching regret, shame, embarrassment, whatever. Strip the emotion away. The result you're getting is not the issue. It's not a reflection of the person you are deep down. It's just the successful result of the system you've been using to govern how you live your life.

Everything we do runs on a system. Driving a car. Making coffee. Going to shops. We have a series of things we do each time that remains largely the same. If you make a crappy tasting cup of coffee, the coffee's not the issue. Your system for creating it is.

Our decisions are the same. We typically make our decisions based on what we did in the past, what we see others doing, or based on a set of rules society has imposed on us (or what we've imposed on ourselves). Change the system, change the result.

Say to yourself, "Wow, look at what I created! Okay, I did that. Now, what do I have to do to create something different? What input do I need to listen to? My head got me here…where can my heart take me?"

The wisdom in your heart came first. Just like it was the first organ to form in your body. Your heart's intuition isn't muddied by past experience, by your upbringing, by your social circle, by the gurus you listen to, by society, or anything else. Our most powerful intelligence is the direct guidance from our heart, our intuition, and our connection with the Source.

Before my bankruptcy, I spent years listening to my brain instead of my heart. I did what I thought I should do, the way I thought I should do it. And I just dug myself into a deeper and deeper hole.

Maybe you can relate?

Where you're at right now, for better or worse, is because you've been listening to your brain. You've used logic and reason, and that's brought you disconnection from what you really want and who you really are.

In the next chapter, I'm going to share with you the exact exercises I did (and still do today) to build my heart connection. Doing these exercises changed everything for me...not overnight, but I wouldn't have achieved the growth, success, and fulfilment I have over the past ten years without them.

CHAPTER 6

THE JOURNEY WITHIN

"If we neglect our heart,
we may attain success and material goods, but
serenity and happiness will always still be
in front of us, just out of reach."

—*Irmansyah Effendi*

"BERSANTAI...TERSENYUM...LEPASKAN HATIMU...."

"Relax...smile...let go of your heart...."

I was at my first open-heart Reiki workshop with someone who was to become an important spiritual mentor to me, Irmansyah Effendi. And I was having my first experience of deeply feeling what my heart connection could do.

On the first day of the workshop, we'd been asked to pair up with a more experienced guide who would take us through an open-heart meditation.

I looked around the small workshop room and surveyed the mix of people around me, hoping to catch the eye of someone willing to partner with me. A slight feeling of trepidation came over me that reminded me of being at school and waiting to be picked for a team in Phys Ed.

Eventually, I locked eyes with a tall and slender Indonesian man, who began to approach me. He had grey hair and a stern-looking face. His name was Willy, and he offered to be my partner for the exercise in halting English. At first, I felt a bit intimidated by him, but I accepted his invitation regardless.

Yes, I nodded; let's pair up.

We each gathered one of the colourful pillows that were scattered around the bare wood-panelled room and sat crossed-legged across from each other.

Willy guided me to close my eyes and touch my heart.

"Bersantai ... tersenyum ... lepaskan hatimu ...," he chanted softly.

As he started to guide me into meditation, I began to block out all other sounds and sensations: the gentle hum of others chanting around the room, the smell of old wood polish mixed with incense and dust, the faint itching of my bottom against the sequined elephant stitched onto my pillow, an occasional scuffing noise as someone moved around. And the stuffiness created by twenty bodies filling the small room in the tropical Indonesian humidity.

As I sunk deeper into a trance-like state, the craziest experience happened.

My body started to move into a state of orgasmic pleasure. And it kept growing as my heart opened more, and more, and more.

Soon after, Willy got up and walked away, having guided me to the point where I didn't need him anymore. But I didn't even realise it at the time ... all I knew at that point was that my heart just kept opening, and I felt increasingly elated.

I was elated beyond anything I'd ever experienced before.

It was similar to the euphoric feeling of peaking on ecstasy, yet it encompassed not just my body and my mind but somehow my *spirit* as well. Or some deep part of me that I hadn't fully realised had existed before then.

An almost overwhelming sense of pleasure, of remembering, of *home,* just poured over me. It was like a heart orgasm that just kept growing and growing until I felt a profound connection with the core of who I was.

As I sat there mesmerised and in a state of orgasmic pleasure, I slowly and gently opened my eyes with love, tenderness, and gratitude.

When I noticed that Willy was no longer sitting in front of me, I realised that he had lit the spark of my heart's opening, and once it had started, and I was connected in that space, there was no limit to my feelings of euphoric knowing, understanding, and the sense of coming home.

And I realised that my true home, where my greatest joy, happiness, and potential lives, is inside of me. Not only that, but I could access it at any time I chose to.

Just like you can, too.

. . .

CONNECTING TO YOUR HEART

At this point in the book, we've spoken a lot about the heart. We've spoken about the heart versus the brain. Where emotions fit in. How decisions are made. All sorts of important stuff.

Within this chapter, I want to take things from a theoretical level and bring them to an energetic level. In short: I want you to have the experience of the connection I've been talking about.

Because up until now, all you've got is an intellectual experience of what the heart does and how it feels when you open your connection to the True Source (God, Allah, Spirit, Gaia). But the experience of actually *feeling it* goes far beyond intellect.

Try to explain what it feels like to be in love, and you'll only scratch the surface. Try to explain what it's like to feel the joy of looking at your new-born's face, and you're at a loss to find the right words, right?

Some things just can't be explained . . . they need to be experienced. They need to be *felt*.

Think about it this way: I could describe the taste of a bubblegum Paddle Pop ice cream, but unless you've physically tasted it yourself, it's just an explanation. Sure, you can use your previous references of what bubble gum tastes like and create a kind of intellectual flavour-palate in your mind . . . but you don't really know for sure until you've actually tasted it.

And so, in this chapter, I invite you to take what you've learned intellectually and create the experience of it because that's where learning is really cemented—by *doing*.

So far, I hope I've helped you disarm at least some of the constraints, beliefs, and biases that we all take onboard growing up. I hope you've thought about what I'm sharing with you and have started asking some deeper questions within yourself. I want you to be open at least enough to give the exercises in this chapter a proper go. After all, you've got nothing to lose . . . and a lot to gain.

Because as we covered back in Chapter 2, the heart is where our highest and best feelings live. The lower emotions, such as anger, frustration, overwhelm, they live in the mind. They are produced in the mind. The high-vibe emotions such as love, joy, happiness, fulfilment, they come from the heart.

We tend to think that when external things happen to us, that triggers our feelings of happiness, joy, and fulfilment. But the truth is that those feelings are already inside of us all the time—and you can feel them whenever you choose to . . . even on the shittiest of days.

And do you know what? The more you choose to feel these feelings every day, the more better things will happen to you, which, in turn, will give you more opportunities to feel these feelings. Because positive energy attracts positive energy. Like attracts like.

So while you read this chapter, I want you to consciously nurture your connection with feelings of happiness, joy, and fulfilment, and the Divine Source of energy that they—and all life—spark from.

THE POWER OF HEART MEDITATIONS

It's no secret that we're getting busier and busier. Technology gives us the amazing ability to connect to things and people wherever, whenever. You can send emails for work while lying on your couch. You can watch a stream of funny cat videos on the train. You can FaceTime friends anywhere in the world with a couple of taps on your phone.

But it's a double-edged sword because we can't unplug. We're always "on." Work doesn't necessarily occur in a nine-to-five office anymore... it happens everywhere, at any time. Emails ping us at ten o'clock in the evening. We log in to check something on Saturday because we can't resist.

Our lives are hopelessly unbalanced; they disassociate us from others, from nature, from ourselves. We feel we have to act a certain way to belong or fit in... when, in fact, if we are connected to our heart, we would experience a sense of home. Of belonging. Of connectedness. And that helps us be clearer and more intentional with the decisions we make and improves the quality of what we put out into the world. Most importantly, it helps us to create a life we choose, not a life where we're trying to fit in with somebody else's idea of who we should be.

It's no coincidence that more and more people are looking into the power of meditation to help facilitate their own journey within. We are only just starting to understand the power of meditation, the power of going inside ourselves to find stillness and peace and answers.

Have you ever noticed that when you're on holiday, or on the toilet, or in the shower, you tend to have really great ideas? That's because when we quieten the background noise of life, our brain finally has the space to operate on a different level. There's room for inspiration to come in. In normal daily life, it's just too damn noisy.

A friend of mine and a fellow entrepreneur, Carissa Hill, actually considers her holidays the most important part of running her business. Because when she unplugs and relaxes, she has the best ideas for new products and other business innovations. Some of her most incredible successes have been born from a spark of inspiration that came through when she was relaxing on a beach. And she's certainly not the only one.

While meditation certainly has amazing neurological effects, in the following exercises, we're going to focus on your heart, not your head. Naturally, your brain will definitely play a part—especially when it's trying to take over! At first, it will fight hard to stay busy. But in time, it will learn to quieten so you can stop thinking—and start *feeling*.

BUILDING YOUR HEART CONNECTION

I find that doing heart-centred meditation for half an hour in the morning allows me to enter my workspace with incredible clarity of what needs to be done. It also helps me to become more focused, more outcome-driven, more productive, and most importantly, more connected with what I'm sharing.

Let's be honest, if you're having a conversation with someone and they're not fully present, you can feel it. You know that although they're looking at you, their mind is elsewhere. That can lead to frustration. Maybe you'd feel disrespected. Maybe you wouldn't feel heard. It might trigger all sorts of low-vibe emotions for you.

Now think about that in your own life. If you're showing up to do your own life's work and you're not present, what message are you giving? What is the quality of the energy you're sending out into whatever it is you're doing or creating? People can feel it. Your partner feels it. Your work colleagues feel it. Your kids feel it. Are you present? Are you focused? Are you there at all?

This brings me to a very important point that ties back to a question I presented earlier in the book: Why are we so unhappy when we've got more opportunity than ever, we've got access to more shiny toys and fun stuff to do? The world is more open than it has ever been. Yet, we feel more alone than we ever have.

The key to that is *connection*. And the key to *connection* is being *present*. You can't connect if you're not feeling present. It just doesn't happen. Think about areas of your life where you don't feel you're present. *I'm not a present partner. I'm not a present mother. I'm not a present father. I'm not present with what I'm doing.*

In the exercises that follow, you'll start the journey within to learn how to be present. You'll begin to learn how to connect from the inside. And you'll start building your connection with your own feelings of happiness and joy that you can access and project outwards into the world, whenever you choose.

BEFORE YOU START: PUTTING YOUR BRAIN IN THE PASSENGER SEAT

When we were kids, we knew how to live in joy, curiosity, freedom and peace. But growing up, we learned to use our brain more than our heart. Reason, logic, and other rule-based systems began to shape our growth and development.

The brain grew stronger…and our heart grew weaker. So, in these exercises, there's going to be a bit of a struggle to make your stronger muscle, the brain, sit down and shut up for a while, letting the heart come through.

Try not to let your brain block your heart. Like a spoiled younger sibling that got all the attention, it's going to want to be the star of the party. It will bombard you with thoughts and compulsions, and at first, you'll have little ability to control that. After all, the brain has had free rein most of your life!

If you find yourself following a thought, realise it's just your brain doing its thing. Just let the thought pass by. Let thoughts come and go. As you keep practising, you'll get better at putting your brain in the passenger seat, I promise.

EXERCISE 1:
STRENGTHENING OF THE HEART

Note: This exercise, as with the ones that follow, are a gift from one of my spiritual teachers, Irmansyah Effendi. They are taken from his highly impactful book, *Smile to Your Heart Meditations*. I highly recommend you read it. Go to this link to get your copy: https://www.amazon.com/Smile-Your-Heart -Meditations-Practices/dp/1569758158.

Exercise 1 is the fundamental exercise that forms the base of the others that follow. It will help build your ability to focus more on your heart, lessen your brain's domination, and strengthen your heart connection and feelings.

As with every exercise that follows, begin by finding a quiet spot where you won't be distracted. Sit comfortably, making sure your spine is straight. Don't dip your head. Look forward. And relax.

Then, when you're ready:

1. Close your eyes to reduce the activities of your brain.
2. Completely relax your body and mind.
3. Breathe in deeply through your nose, and exhale through your mouth several times to help you relax even more.
4. Touch your heart with one or more fingers.
5. Smile freely to your heart without thinking how.
6. With your eyes still closed and staying relaxed, smile to your heart for about one minute. When you find yourself thinking, don't follow your thoughts. Just relax and allow them to pass easily through your head.
7. Gradually, you should start experiencing an expansion in your chest area, along with feelings of calmness, peacefulness, lightness, or joy.
8. When you feel any of these feelings, it's a wonderful indication that your heart is starting to work. Just follow the pleasant feelings to let your heart and feelings become even stronger.

9. If you're not feeling anything yet, don't put in any effort whatsoever. Simply stay relaxed and keep on smiling. The moment your brain stops trying and looking for sensations, you'll be ready and able to feel.

10. Relax even more and smile more freely.

11. Once you start experiencing feelings of calmness, lightness, or joy, follow your feelings while continuing to relax, and smile for two minutes or more.

As you can see, this exercise is simple and straightforward. But don't be fooled by its simplicity. It's also a very deep and important exercise that will help you strengthen your heart and your connection to it.

Keep doing this exercise daily (or many times a day if you're able) until you start experiencing calmness, lightness, or joy with ease. It's important that you don't rush into the other exercises until you become well practised at this one. You've got to learn to walk before you can run!

If you don't feel anything:

Chances are you'll try so hard to feel something that your brain will block your heart. Trying harder is an intellectual exercise, and intellect is not what's needed here. This exercise isn't about thinking; it's about feeling. It's the heart's domain, not the brain's.

It can be difficult to switch from the head to the heart at first. But as difficult as it may seem, try to let go of any effort in wanting to feel something. Just surrender to the process, and let it come through naturally. It will happen when you're relaxed enough and when you stop trying to control the situation with your mind. The brain's just a passenger for this, remember?

So don't rush, don't force, don't focus on what you think the end goal should be. Just surrender. Relax. Breathe. And be curious about what's happening within you.

EXERCISE 2:
STRENGTHENING OF THE HEART—
RELAXING VERSUS NOT RELAXING VARIATION

The next few exercises use the fundamental framework you've just learned and add some variations to help you build your heart muscle stronger.

Like a gymnast stretching different parts of their body to achieve peak readiness, these exercises will help you stretch a few heart muscles (not the real ones, don't worry), so you get better at the skill of heart meditation.

Once you begin to do each key step better, the overall quality of your exercises will improve, and your heart and feeling will grow even stronger.

As before, find a quiet spot where you won't be disturbed or distracted. Sit in a comfortable position while keeping your spine straight. Relax. Then when you're ready, complete steps one to eleven of the previous meditation.

Then, do these next steps with your eyes closed but still touching your heart and smiling freely to your heart.

1. Now stiffen your body.
2. If you're sensitive, you will feel how your heart and chest are pressured, or at the very least, that the expanding, peaceful, joyful feeling diminishes considerably.
3. Now relax your whole body.
4. If you continue to follow your feeling, you will experience relief the instant you relax your body. Feel how your heart is free from pressure and heaviness as soon as your body is no longer stressed.
5. Stiffen your body again.
6. Feel the pressure on your heart and the lessening of the expanding, calm, happy feeling.
7. Now relax your whole body once more.
8. Feel how your heart feels free from the pressure or heaviness.
9. By stiffening and relaxing your body and noting the differences in

feeling, you should be able to better identify the remaining tension in your body. Once you do, completely relax those parts.

10. As soon as your feeling is free from the pressure or heaviness, follow the changes or progress in your heart and feeling. In doing so, your heart and feeling will be even freer from the limitations that your brain has imposed all this time.

11. When this exercise is done properly, you will be able to feel how your heart and feeling have become stronger, deeper, and more enjoyable.

Do this strengthening of the heart exercise with the key step of relaxing or not relaxing once or twice a day until you are able to relax your whole body and you feel completely calm, peaceful, and free from any tension. Follow the changes that your heart and feeling experience as they become free from the limitations of your brain.

EXERCISE 3:
STRENGTHENING OF THE HEART—
CLOSING VERSUS NOT CLOSING THE EYES

You would think that closing your eyes for a period of time is easy. You just close them, and that's it, right? Well, from an evolutionary perspective, when your eyes are closed, you're more vulnerable. While you're no longer in danger of being eaten by a wild tiger or falling off a cliff (unless you're taking a selfie), the ancient part of your brain remembers this danger. And it will fight to open your eyes constantly to check what's out there...just in case.

Not only does this clearly prevent you from relaxing, but it also activates the brain, which further blocks your heart. This variation of the heart exercise will help you to learn to close your eyes while staying even more relaxed.

As before, get quiet, get comfy, get relaxed. Then, do steps one through eleven of the original strengthening of the heart exercise (Exercise 1).

Perform the next steps while staying relaxed, touching your heart, and smiling freely to your heart.

1. Follow that nice, pleasant feeling to let your heart and feeling become stronger (for one minute or longer).
2. Now open your eyes.
3. You should feel that your attention has moved upward from your heart into your chest area, towards your eyes and your brain. Your heart and feeling are not as strong as before you opened your eyes.
4. Close your eyes again.
5. You will feel that your attention gradually returns to your heart and that the nice feelings grow stronger.
6. Now close your eyes and focus on how they feel. You will feel pressure not only on both of your eyes but also on your forehead area—because your brain is also working harder. Instances like these are moments when your brain is limiting your heart and feeling.
7. Knowing this, now close your eyes and relax them completely. Feel that the pressures on your forehead lessen and slowly disappear quite naturally. The feeling from your heart is becoming stronger and stronger.

Get good at this exercise, and you'll be able to relax and connect with your heart without your brain screaming at you: "Open your eyes, you damn fool! There could be a tiger out there!" In short: you'll have one less distraction and a clearer path to your heart.

EXERCISE 4:
STRENGTHENING OF THE HEART: TOUCHING YOUR HEART VERSUS NOT TOUCHING YOUR HEART

This one is designed to pump your energetic heart muscle via touch.

When you're somewhere quiet, relaxed, with a straight spine, and ready:

Complete steps one through eleven of the original strengthening of the heart exercise (Exercise 1).

Then, do these next steps while staying relaxed, with your eyes closed and smiling freely to your heart.

1. Now remove your fingers from the centre of your chest.
2. Feel how your feeling is diminishing or is not as clear as it was before removing your fingers.
3. Touch your heart again.
4. Feel how your attention is directed towards your heart and that your heart and feeling are becoming noticeably stronger.
5. Stop touching your heart again.
6. Realise your feeling is fading once more.
7. Return your fingers to your heart.
8. As soon as your fingers touch your heart, feel clearly how your heart and feeling become deeper and more expansive.
9. Follow the changes from the moment your heart and feeling were not as strong to the moment they become stronger. By following the changes, you are letting your heart and feeling become stronger in the best way.

EXERCISE 5:
STRENGTHENING OF THE HEART:
SMILING VERSUS NOT SMILING TO YOUR HEART

In this final variation of the fundamental strengthening of the heart exercise, you might feel silly at first, sitting in an empty room and smiling. That's okay! Don't worry about feeling silly! Besides, nobody can see you.

People tend to think that a smile is another thing that is triggered by an outside influence, but we actually have the power to smile genuinely and freely whenever we choose. Smiling is scientifically proven to boost our mood, reduce blood pressure and stress, and strengthen the immune system. It's good for you, so just do it!

First, get into a place and space where you're ready to begin. When you're ready, complete steps one through eleven of the original strengthening of the heart exercise (Exercise 1).

Then, do these additional next steps while staying relaxed, with your eyes closed and touching your heart.

1. Now stop smiling to your heart.
2. Realise that the feeling you're experiencing in your heart is diminishing or is disappearing completely.
3. Smile to your heart once more.
4. Feel how your heart and feeling become stronger, and you are able to feel the expanding light and happy feeling you felt before.
5. Stop smiling to your heart.
6. Notice how the feeling in your heart lessens or disappears again. Realise that your chest is not as full and light as it was.
7. Smile to your heart again.
8. Feel that your heart and feeling are becoming stronger once again. Notice how the wonderful feelings grow, expand, and radiate.
9. Now smile even more freely to your heart following your smile and feeling.
10. Feel how by smiling more freely, your heart and feeling are becoming even stronger and more enjoyable.
11. Follow the changes from the moment your heart and feeling were not as strong to the moment they become stronger. Following the changes as you switch back and forth between smiling and not smiling is the best way to let your heart and feeling become stronger.

Don't try to widen or force your smile. That will only activate your brain (which is itching to get back in control.) Smiling freely just means letting the happy feelings from the heart grow stronger while effortlessly enjoying the moment—something we don't do often enough—or at all!

EXERCISE 6:
OPEN-HEART MEDITATION

The previous exercises are designed to improve the quality of your strengthening of the heart exercise. Much like how we focus on different muscles for a better body at the gym, the variations you've just read work on a different part of your technique for a better overall outcome. Done together, this workout program for your heart will result in a tangible improvement.

As an addition, this open-heart meditation can begin to cleanse your heart from all the negativity that has been sitting in there for so many years. Remember, there is energy attached to each emotion, so the longer you've been holding negative energy in your heart, the more it can seep into every area of your life like rot seeps through the walls, roof, and floor of a house.

Now, although this is called open-heart meditation, this type of meditation is different from the commonly known concept in the case that we are not trying to empty ourselves. We want to be more relaxed but never vacant. Also, we don't visualise anything, focus on our breathing, chant mantras, or bend into twiggly sticks.

We're simply connecting to the True Source—whatever you name It.

Do this meditation twice a day if you can. Once in the morning, then again before you go to bed. You'll find that your days are clearer and lighter, and your sleep is deeper and more restful…and that's just the beginning!

Below are the instructions for the open-heart meditation. But as you'll discover as you read them, it's best to listen to a voice recording that can guide you through. I have created one that is available for you at: https://soundcloud.com/user-865171340/sets/open-heart-meditation.

1. Find a peaceful, quiet place to do this meditation so you won't be distracted or interrupted.
2. Sit down and relax, keeping your spine straight without becoming tense.

3. Place both palms on your lap, with both palms facing upward.

4. Close your eyes so that your brain is not active.

5. Relax and smile. To do this open-heart meditation the best way, let your whole self be here and now completely.

6. While relaxing and smiling, inhale deeply without forcing yourself, and then exhale from your mouth. Let all the burdens on your mind be expelled as you exhale. Feel and enjoy this moment when your thoughts are becoming more relaxed as you continue to smile more freely.

7. Inhale deeply and exhale through your mouth, letting all the tension in your body be removed as you exhale. Feel your whole body as it becomes more relaxed. Enjoy the moment when your whole self is relaxed, and let yourself smile even more freely.

8. Inhale deeply and exhale through the mouth, allowing all remaining thoughts and tension in your body to be removed.

9. Your body and mind are now very relaxed.

10. Smile, enjoying this moment when you are completely relaxed, body and mind.

11. From now on, breathe normally, inhaling and exhaling through the nose.

12. Now, place your fingers or one or both palms on the centre of your chest where your heart is located, and smile to your heart. Do not think or try to find the exact location of your heart; just smile freely while listening to the instructions.

13. Keep on smiling freely to your heart with all of your feelings. Realise that you are becoming calmer. Enjoy continuing to smile. This is the moment when you are letting your heart become stronger.

14. Keeping your palms on your chest while smiling freely to your heart and enjoying the calmness from your heart, let us now pray for the True Source's blessing, asking that the emotions in your heart be cleansed so that it can open even more to the True Source.

15. While praying, simply let your heart pray:

> *True Source, please bless our heart so that all arrogance*
> *is replaced with Your blessings.*

> *True Source, please bless our heart so that all anger*
> *is replaced with Your blessings.*

> *True Source, please bless our heart so that all selfishness*
> *is replaced with Your blessings.*

> *True Source, please bless our heart so that all envy and*
> *jealousy are replaced with Your blessings.*

> *True Source, please bless our heart so that all cunningness*
> *and greediness are replaced with Your blessings.*

> *True Source, please help us to realise that our heart is*
> *the key to our connection to You. That we must keep our heart clean*
> *because our connection to You is the most important thing.*
> *Please bless us and help us to sincerely forgive others.*

16. Now, for one minute, forgive those who have done you wrong, even if they're still hurting you. Remember that your connection to the True Source is the most important thing.

> *True Source, by forgiving those who have done us wrong,*
> *please bless our heart so that all hatred, grudges, resentment, dissatisfaction,*
> *and all other negative emotions are removed from our heart*
> *to be replaced with Your blessings.*

> *True Source, please bless and help us to realise all of our mistakes to You and to*
> *others. Help us so we can regret them and ask for forgiveness sincerely.*

17. Now, for one minute, realise all of your mistakes to the True Source and to others. Acknowledge them and ask for forgiveness.

> *True Source, please forgive all of our mistakes to You and to others.*

Having been forgiven, let all burdens, fear, worries, and all other
negative emotions caused by those mistakes be cleansed from our whole
heart and our whole self to be replaced with Your blessings.

True Source, please bless our heart, so all worries and fears caused by the
lack of trust in You be cleansed and replaced with Your blessings.

True Source, with the negative emotions removed from our heart,
please bless our heart to open better to You and also to be directed even
better to You. Let Your blessings flow more abundantly into our heart,
so our feeling becomes stronger, so we can feel the calmness,
the peace, and the beauty of Your blessings even better.

True Source, let Your blessings fill our whole heart and our whole self,
so that our whole heart and our whole self are filled with kindness and peace,
so we can rely more on Your blessings, so we are always
within our hearts and within Your blessings.

True Source, thank You for Your love that has
removed the negative emotions from our heart and our whole self.
Thank you for opening and directing a heart even better to
You so that our whole heart and our whole self is filled with Your blessings
even more so that we can feel and enjoy the calmness, the peace,
and the beauty of Your blessings even better.

Thank you, True Source. Amen.

18. Keeping one or both of your palms on your chest while smiling, feel
    that your heart and your whole self are becoming lighter. Enjoy it. Stay
    within this peace and calmness. This is the moment you are within
    your heart. Keep on smiling and enjoying.

19. While smiling and enjoying, let yourself be pulled even deeper into the
    peace and calmness of the blessings, and dissolve even more within
    this peace and calmness. The more dissolved you are in this peace and
    calmness, the lighter and more beautiful your feeling is. Enjoy.

20. Continuing to smile while enjoying the peace, the calmness, and the beauty of the True Source's love, slowly move your fingers and open your eyes with a happy smile.
21. Live your daily life, staying within your heart, the peace, and the calmness from the True Source's blessings.

After you practice these exercises for some time, you will be able to simply close your eyes, touch your heart, smile freely to your heart, and connect with the calm, peaceful, happy, feeling radiating from your heart at any time.

When you're ready, feel free to try these more advanced heart exercises.

EXERCISE 7:
LETTING YOUR HEART AND FEELING BECOME STRONGER

This next set of exercises builds on the foundational exercise, the strengthening of the heart. When you start doing these next three exercises, you should be at a place where you can do the strengthening of the heart and feel the pulling without effort. It should be a natural process that comes easy to you.

If it's not yet, that's okay. Just keep practising until you can experience joy, calmness, and happiness with ease.

Then when you're ready, begin adding the next steps you'll learn in the next three exercises.

I'll repeat the beginning here for you.

1. Close your eyes to reduce the activities of your brain.
2. Completely relax your body and mind.
3. Breathe in deeply through your nose, and exhale through your mouth several times to help you relax even more.
4. Touch your heart with one or more fingers.
5. Smile freely to your heart without thinking how.

6. Staying relaxed with your eyes still closed, smile to your heart for about one minute. When you find yourself thinking, don't follow your thoughts. Just relax and allow them to pass easily through your head.

7. Gradually, you will start experiencing an expansion in your chest area along with feelings of calm, peace, lightness, or joy.

8. As your heart continues to expand and grow, keep on following the pleasant feeling for one more minute to let your heart and feeling become stronger and deeper.

The next step must be done with your eyes closed while staying relaxed, smiling, and touching your heart.

9. Now, let your whole feeling and your whole self be pulled into this expanding light, calm, and peaceful feeling. Realise that the more you follow and allow the pulling into the wonderful sensation of your heart, your feeling becomes stronger and deeper. Continue this process without stopping for two to three minutes.

EXERCISE 8:
REALISING THE PRESENCE OF THE TRUE SOURCE'S BLESSING WITHIN YOUR HEART

As with every exercise, begin with the basic steps to strengthen your heart. Complete steps one through nine of the previous exercise.

Then, when you're ready:

10. Now, realise that the joyful, expanding, light, and peaceful feeling you are experiencing is from the True Source's blessing within your heart. Feel how your heart and feeling react as soon as you realise this. Keep on following the shifts you're feeling, which will strengthen your heart even more.

11. Now for understanding, stop realising that the joyful feeling is from the presence of the True Source's blessing within your heart. Regard this beautiful sensation as just a feeling from your heart instead of from the True Source's blessing. Recognise how the radiating feeling from your heart is diminishing.

12. Realise again that the joyful feeling from your heart is from the True Source's blessing. Feel changes in your heart and feeling, and follow the changes as they grow and expand.

13. Repeat steps eleven and twelve three times, recognising the shifts in your feeling as you complete the final step. Follow the changes in your feeling even further and deeper. You should experience a radiating, more joyful and beautiful feeling within your heart. Stay relaxed and keep on smiling sweetly and freely to your heart for another two to three minutes.

EXERCISE 9:
REALISING THE TRUE SOURCE'S
BLESSING IS WORKING

The last in this set of three additional exercises that complement the foundational strengthening of the heart exercise, Exercise 9 is designed to help expand the high-vibe feelings that flow out from your heart, through your body and soul, and into the world around you.

To begin, get comfortable and relax. Make sure you're sitting with a straight spine. Make sure there are no distractions. Complete steps one through nine of Exercise 7.

Then, when you're ready:

1. Now, realise that the joyful, expanding, light, and peaceful feeling you are experiencing is from the True Source's blessing within your heart. Feel how your heart and feeling react as soon as you realise this.

Keep on following the shifts you're feeling, which will strengthen your heart even more.

2. Realise that the joyful, expanding, light, and peaceful feeling you're experiencing is from the True Source's blessing within your heart. Feel how your heart and feeling react as soon as you realise this. Keep following the shifts in your feeling to strengthen your heart even more.

3. Also, realise that the True Source's blessing within your heart is helping you in so many ways. Feel clearly how your strength of feeling is becoming even deeper and more beautiful.

4. For understanding, stop acknowledging the True Source's blessing is working within your heart. Recognise how your feeling is becoming strong again and begins to radiate so wonderfully. Follow the changes in your feeling to allow it to grow and strengthen further.

5. Realise again how the True Source's blessing within your heart is helping your heart in everything. Recognise how your feeling is becoming strong again and begins to radiate so wonderfully. Follow the changes in your feeling to allow it to grow and strengthen further.

6. Repeat steps twelve and thirteen several times until your feeling is strong and free. Continue following the changes in your feeling while staying relaxed and smiling sweetly and freely to your heart for another two to three minutes.

This variation helps you understand and follow your feeling more naturally. You'll find the more you do it, the more the feeling stays with you long after you're back into your normal daily life.

EXERCISE 10:
LETTING TRUE SOURCE'S BLESSING WORK

This final heart exercise is a more complete meditation that includes Exercises 6, 7, 8, and 9.

1. Close your eyes to reduce the activities of your brain.
2. Completely relax your body and mind.
3. Breathe in deeply through your nose, and exhale through your mouth several times to help you relax even more.
4. Touch your heart with one or more fingers.
5. Smile freely to your heart without thinking how.
6. Staying relaxed with your eyes still closed, smile to your heart for about one minute. When you find yourself thinking, don't follow your thoughts. Just relax and allow them to pass easily through your head.
7. Gradually, you will start experiencing an expansion in your chest area along with feelings of calm, peace, lightness or joy.
8. As your heart continues to expand and grow, keep on following the pleasant feeling for one more minute to let your heart and feeling become stronger and deeper.

The next steps must be done with your eyes closed while staying relaxed, smiling, and touching your heart.

9. Now, let your whole feeling and your whole self be pulled into this expanding light, calm, and peaceful feeling. Realise how the more you follow and allow the pulling into the wonderful sensation, your heart and feeling become stronger and deeper. Continue this process without stopping for two to three minutes.
10. Realise that the joyful, expanding, light, and peaceful feeling you're experiencing is from the True Source's blessing within your heart. Feel how your heart and feeling react as soon as you realise this. Keep following the shifts in your feeling to strengthen your heart even more.
11. Also, realise that the True Source's blessing within your heart is helping you in so many ways. Feel clearly how your strength and feeling are becoming even deeper and more beautiful.

12. Let the True Source's blessing work. Realise how the joyful feelings within your heart, which is from the Trues Source's blessing, radiates farther, stronger, and freer.

13. Now, for understanding, do not let the True Source's blessing work for a moment. Recognise how the radiating feeling is blocked.

14. Let the True Source's blessing work again. As soon as you feel the True Source's blessing radiate far and free, let it radiate even further, more beautifully and expansively, while continuing to smile sweetly and freely.

15. Repeat steps thirteen and fourteen two to three times. Then keep letting the True Source's blessing radiate far and free, without any limit, while staying relaxed and smiling sweetly and freely.

When you can feel the changes in your feeling as you do the exercises presented in this chapter, it means your heart connection has become stronger.

And a strong heart connection means better relationships, opportunities, decisions, outcomes, connections, and overall, a better life.

NEXT STEPS

Remember the emotional frequency chart I shared in Chapter 2? When you start practising these meditations, you'll probably feel pretty neutral. It can take a while to start opening the connection, especially if you haven't done anything like this before.

Maybe you'll even feel frustrated or angry...where's my Nirvana?

We want things to be different. We want to get where we want to go. But right now, it's important to remember that you're moving into a space of courage—courage for things to change.

But reaching neutrality is a big achievement when you consider that you've been living in this space of guilt, fear, shame, and anger for so long.

Neutrality is your turning point because, at that stage, you can start to experience a sense of willingness and acceptance for the fact you've created these experiences.

Not feeling the burden of those negative emotions you've associated with various experiences in your life is quite a relief, I can tell you that!

The thing is, we can't transcend to love, joy, peace, or enlightenment while denying shame, guilt, apathy, greed, or desire. They all exist inside of us. Denying the things we want to change isn't going to help us resolve them and move past them. How can we overcome these feelings if we don't accept that they are there and that we're responsible for them?

It's only by first moving to a place of acceptance that you can begin the process of change, and start feeling the courage to do things differently, make better decisions, and not repeat past unhelpful patterns.

In short: do these exercises to start to move towards *love*. Love for yourself and love for life itself. From that love, you can start to experience more *joy*. Joy for the ups and the downs, the ins and the outs…you'll exist in a place of more peace and calm. What's more, you'll exist with a sense of knowing that regardless of what you're faced with in life, whatever shows up for you, no matter how challenging, you have the capability to move past it.

The more you tap into your heart's energy and wisdom, the more you start to experience a sense of enlightenment. Because you are no longer trying to deny the pride, the anger, the desire to belong in the group, and whatever else is currently holding you back from living the life you dream of.

Instead, you see that all spectrums of the rainbow exist inside of you right now. And you can start to use your heart's intuition to better navigate through those spaces in life. It's all inside of you already. No matter what you've gone through up until now, no matter how shitty your outlook on life has been, you can recalibrate yourself to journey through your own life on the highest path: the path of love, joy, and fulfilment.

You just have to choose: Do you want to keep living your life as you are right now? Or will you choose a different path?

The exercises in this chapter are the key to everything you always wanted but never thought you could have. Use them—for a week at least. Then hit me up on social media and tell me the changes in how you're feeling and how you're showing up in life. I want to hear from you!

PART 2

THE HEAD

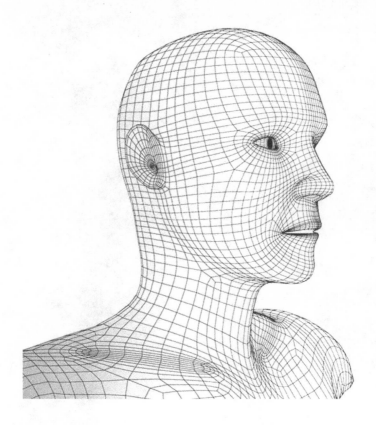

CHAPTER 7

EGO

**"The ego is the single biggest obstruction
to the achievement of anything."**

—*Richard Rose*

"How *dare* you do this to me! Pack your bags and get *out*!"

My skin tingled, and my blood boiled as I looked at my friend. Ben was standing in front of me with a shocked look on his face, as though he had no idea where my rage was coming from. His innocent expression made me even angrier.

I wanted to punch him. I wanted to tear him to pieces. But deep down inside, I wanted to drop to my knees and cry.

I was about to destroy one of the most beautiful friendships I'd ever had. And it was all for a *lie*.

Back when I was in my late teens, Ben and I had been as close as brothers. A young, sweet boy from Scamander in the east coast of Tasmania, Ben hung around at my friend Josh's, the Reiki master, house a lot. We would smoke weed and talk about life. I had immediately connected with him because, like me, Ben was a bit lost and needed some guidance.

Gentle, quiet, and thoughtful, he was truly one of the most beautiful guys I have ever met in my life. We quickly developed a really strong friendship. Ben, Josh, and I were a tight trio. We would hang out all the time. We grew weed on Ben's mother's property. I even bought my first property primarily because he needed a place to stay. "I can buy a house, and you can rent a room off me," I'd told him.

I loved Ben to bits. He was one of the most amazing people I'd ever met.

So how did it come to this? How did I end up screaming in his face that cold autumn night so long ago?

Naturally, it all started with a girl.

Shortly after I bought the house and rented the room to Ben, I met Kristy (yes, *that* Kristy, from Chapter 1). Kristy was a hot blonde with curly hair and a gym-toned body. I fell for her quickly and hard. I was eighteen years old, and she was my first big love. In my mind, our future was set; I'd marry her, and we'd have kids and live together happily forever. That's what people did, right?

But Kristy had different ideas. Like many people, she had some mental health issues. She struggled. She needed professional help and medication. So unsurprisingly (although I didn't realise it at the time), she didn't share my rose-coloured vision for her future. She didn't want to sail off into the sunset together. She was just trying to make it through each day.

My relationship with her began at the same time I was also starting my spiritual journey and realising how powerful my intuitive abilities were. Back when I was the guy at parties who would "read" people and leave them gobsmacked at how accurate I was.

I'm not gonna lie; all the attention and validation really fed my ego.

So when I saw Kristy struggling, my over-confident young self decided that I was the answer to her problems. I had these spiritual superpowers, right? I knew what to do. I knew how to save her.

Without me consciously realising it at the time, I built my self-image around that belief. My ego blew up … and the more Kristy resisted my "help," the more frustrated I became. With all my eighteen-year-old superego bravado, I didn't see the truth: she wasn't getting on board with my advice and guidance because she bloody well hadn't asked for it, nor did she want it, thank you very much! Still, I pushed on. And on.

Long story short, the bigger my "super guru" self-identity grew, the more of a pain in the ass I became. I was controlling. I was jealous. Eventually, I started feeling like Ben had been making moves on her.

And I allowed that story to grow in my brain, becoming bigger and nastier, consuming my thoughts and driving me wild inside.

Until, one day, I came home from work to find Kristy and Ben sitting on the dusty old couch in my house smoking a joint. They were stoned, chatting and laughing. And in my mind, they were almost a bit flirty with each other.

I'd already been carrying around a lot of burden in this relationship. Beyond the jealousy. Beyond the bravado of my newfound intuitive abilities. Perhaps they were amplified by the deep gut feeling that Kristy was somebody I couldn't completely trust.

Seeing them so close and giggly that day was the straw that broke the camel's back.

I started yelling and screaming, accusing Ben of having a relationship with Kristy behind my back.

They looked at me like I was crazy.

But the more they tried to reassure me nothing was going on, the more I felt they were lying to me, and the angrier I became.

I screamed at Kristy to get out, and then I turned on Ben.

I still remember the shocked look on his face as I blew up at him that night. I was enraged. I was shaking and heaving. My whole being at that moment was raw, unfiltered, and unhinged anger.

"Get *out*!" I screamed. "Get the *fuck* out of my house! Take your shit and leave!"

Ben had pleaded with me to believe him. He had done nothing wrong. What the hell was wrong with me? His eyes shone with tears as I brutally unleashed upon him all my ego-driven anger and arrogance.

An hour later, I was standing at the back door of my old weatherboard house, with my arms outstretched, hands on each side of the doorframe. Beyond the door were several steps down to the concrete where Ben's panel van was parked.

As I clutched the door frame, I felt an overwhelming flurry of emotion: anger, betrayal, hurt, loss, and despair.

How could Ben have done this to me? After everything that I had done for him?

It was a wintry day in Tasmania, and the cool, crisp breeze stung my face. I could almost see the heat of my words as I continued to yell at Ben as he packed his panel van with a washing basket full of his clothes.

He shook his head at me one last time, then got in his car and drove away.

Shortly after, I realised that my intuition had been right…Kristy *had* cheated on me. But not with Ben. With another of my best friends, Jay. As I tried to deal with that fresh wound of betrayal, my heart ached over what I'd done to Ben.

Ben was gone. Ben, my gentle, caring, loyal friend. What had I done? How was I so blind?

I know now that if I had had a connection with my heart, I would have seen the truth and sincerity in Ben's pleading that he had done nothing wrong. But back then, I couldn't see past my own arrogance as I tried desperately to control my relationship with Kristy so I would feel the love and belongingness that I so craved.

I don't really regret anything in life. I don't regret relationship breakups. Business decisions. Stupid things I have done. I don't even regret the bankruptcy. But the one thing I regret is losing that friendship with Ben.

There's something special about the friendships we form when we're young. You can make friendships all through your life, but they'll never feel quite the same as your mates from back in the day. You can tell someone the crazy stories from your youth, but it's not the same as reminiscing with the people who were actually there.

Destroying my friendship with Ben is my biggest fuckup in my entire life. And it was fuelled by ego-driven bullshit. I wasn't even right about my suspicions. And look what it cost me.

I'm still friends with Josh. We catch up. Nothing's changed. I'd still do anything for him, and he'd still do anything for me. If it wasn't for my meltdown, Ben would still be in our circle. We'd have another rock-solid friendship enriching our lives, a years-long and miles-deep friendship.

I often ask myself how things could have played out differently if I hadn't let my raging ego drive my actions. And I wonder how many other people out there have destroyed something precious in their lives because they let the story they told themselves distort the truth.

Can you think of an example in your own life?

Was it worth it?

■   ■   ■

YOU ARE EXACTLY WHAT YOU THINK

What if I told you that the only thing stopping you from having, doing, or becoming anything you want is yourself? Your education, upbringing, location, even your intelligence...it all doesn't matter.

Whatever roadblocks you're facing, there are solutions for every single one of them. The problem is that we don't see the solution, we don't believe we can execute it, or we don't actually want to solve the problem in the first place.

If Oprah Winfrey can overcome extreme poverty, racism, and sexism to become one of the most successful women in the world, who says you can't achieve *your* goals? If Elon Musk can reinvent the rocket and create the first private company to put people into orbit, you can do whatever the hell you want with your feet on the damn ground, don't you think?

Hell, I was ridiculed by my teachers at school for my grammar and spelling abilities. Yet here I am, writing my second book.

Whatever is holding you back from getting any result you want, I can guarantee it's not a resource problem. Achieving anything in life depends on how well you can continually use the resources available to you until you get the results you want. The only thing that is stopping you is you. Or rather, what you think you can (or can't) achieve.

I've coached over 2,000 people over the last ten years, and many of them believed they were facing an insurmountable problem. I've heard "I can't..." from them a hundred thousand times. But when I helped them make shifts to their beliefs about the world and themselves, doors opened up, wings appeared, and they flew past their previous roadblocks.

In my business coaching company, The Game Changers, we don't even touch the business owner's marketing or sales strategies during their first three months with us. All we do is work on their mindset, on how they're showing up in their business and their life. And it works. Usually, they'll add another 50–150 per cent to their monthly revenue without even touching the "bells and whistles" of business. Most importantly, they start to create a new self-identity that is more capable, confident, and content.

So, what gives?

If we can have anything we want, overcome any obstacle in our way, and design our own life as we choose...why don't we? What keeps getting in our way?

One thing: our *ego*.

The ego is the part of the mind that is responsible for our sense of personal identity. Your ego is how you see yourself. It's the end of the "I am" statement.

- "I am brave."
- "I am funny."

- "I am a mother."
- "I am an underdog."

The ego is made up of many different beliefs that we acquire over our lives and is characterized by labels, masks, and judgements. Each person's ego is made from the thoughts and emotions that they identify with and the beliefs that they think are rock solid and completely true. In that sense, our ego is a reality filter, presenting the world as we each believe it to be.

Whenever you have thoughts about yourself that you agree with, it becomes another "fact" that forms part of your identity and your reality.

When you're unaware of your ego, it's easy to believe that your ego is you. "I did a dumb thing" becomes "I am dumb." "I overspent last month" becomes "I am terrible with money." But it's important to remember the ego is our self-image, not our true self. The ego comes from the mind and lives in the mind. It is the mind's identity of our own construction.

You could say that the ego operates in a space of judgement (good and bad), while the heart operates in a space of love.

Although it's an artificial construct that we make for ourselves, the ego is a very strong driving force across both the unconscious and conscious mind. It's an active and dynamic part of our personalities, playing an immense role in creating emotional drama in our lives.

Think about any fight you've had, and I'll bet it was fuelled by ego. You felt wronged somehow and felt angry or pissed off, which caused conflict, right?

Just like my perception of Kristy and Ben's friendship was warped by my ego, our ego can keep us stuck when we're too heavily invested in what we perceive as our reality. Since childhood, our ego has applied so many biases and filters to the way we see the world that it hides the magic that is actually available to us.

But ego isn't a bad thing. Everybody has one. Developing a self-image is a normal part of socialisation as we grow up. It's just that some people's egos are defined by different dominant characteristics.

Every time we have a thought that we agree with, we contribute to our ego's structure. But problems arise when that self-image is negative, inaccurate, or even overly positive (arrogance).

- "I'm not good at spelling."
- "My freckles make me ugly."
- "Nobody likes me."
- "I am better than you."
- "That was stupid of me."

When we have such thoughts and agree with even the slightest conviction that these ideas define us, then we are building or reinforcing our ego. And like any construction, the overall result is determined by the quality of the stuff you've built it with.

Unfortunately, many of us build our ego using the wrong materials. We listen to the negative crap in our head and let it define who we see ourselves as. And our self-image drives how we show up in life and the results that we get.

Ego is the reason for pretty much any problem you're having difficulty overcoming. Relationship fracturing? Can't lose weight? Not advancing professionally? Your ego—your own self-image—is holding you back, I guarantee it.

IDENTITY AND REACTIONS

Everybody has an ego or personal identity. Actually, most people have multiple perspectives and possess a number of different self-identities.

Have you ever noticed how you act differently around different groups of people? Sometimes you're a father. Sometimes you're a party animal. Sometimes you're a serious professional. In each scenario, there's a slightly different set of beliefs and behaviours that define each version of you.

You might even *feel* like a different person depending on your external environment, too. This doesn't mean you have some kind of personality disorder; it just means that you're human!

The ego is large and complex, just like our personalities. But its foundations can be broken down into nine general areas:

1. Abilities (funny, smart, shy, introverted, extroverted, etc.)
2. Affiliations (football fan, club/society membership, etc.)
3. Attributes (reliable, hard-working, good-looking, dishonest, lazy, etc.)
4. Family relationships (parent, sibling, child, etc.)
5. Hobbies (athlete, collector, gamer, musician, singer, etc.)
6. Occupation(s) (doctor, lawyer, plumber, electrician, white-collar, blue-collar, etc.)
7. Quasi-occupation(s) (helper, volunteer, part-time teacher, etc.)
8. Religion (Buddhist, Catholic/Christian, Hindu, etc.)
9. Social relationships (colleague, friend, spouse, mentor, etc.)

The ego is difficult to see because it hides behind opinions that appear true (our attachment to our identity). It's also difficult to see simply because we haven't practised looking!

The easiest way to spot the ego is by the trail of emotional reactions it leaves behind: anger at a loved one, a need to be right, a feeling of insecurity in certain situations, feelings of jealousy that are unexplained, the need to impress someone, and so on.

It's the voice that says, "How dare they push in front of *me*?" at the supermarket.

It's the rage that builds when someone wrongs you.

It's the reason why you cannot escape the patterns in life that you're desperately trying to change.

One thing's for sure: when you're feeling low-frequency emotions such as anger, self-righteousness, or jealousy, just know that your ego is running the show.

WHERE DOES THE EGO COME FROM?

Our personal identity is built through many years of growing up as we try to work out where we fit in with our wider social and physical environment.

As children, we enter this world with an intuitive nature. Our level of consciousness is pure awareness. We have no filter. We play, imagine, and create. We are not self-aware in the sense that we aren't yet tied to an identity of who we are.

Our first ego-forming thoughts occurred when we were kids, perhaps when we were teased on the playground or when reprimanded or praised by a teacher or parent. Because we don't know much about life, we're learning at a rapid pace. Every experience we have, and every feeling that experience gives us, gets mentally processed pretty quickly. Like sorting through a mountain of paperwork, we delete, distort, and generalize information according to the "rules" we've created about the world so far.

Was it a good experience? Was it bad? Do we want to do it again? Did it make us feel terrible? We quickly sort all data into the appropriate mental pile and move on. But as we do, we keep making more rules. *This* means *that*. A snapping dog means dogs are bad. Praise from the teacher means speaking up in class is good. Crying means I'll be sent to my room, which is bad.

Childhood wounds are particularly impactful in this period because it's not until our teenage years that we develop abstract thinking—the ability to observe outside of our own perspective. As kids, we take everything to heart.

For example, if a parent is constantly absent, the kid doesn't understand the worldly reasons why their parent may need to be away. But they need to come to an understanding of what the situation means regardless. There's a lot more incoming information to sort through!

So the kid makes an assumption about why their parent is away. Being self-centric by nature, the reason is always related back to themself. This is where kids may form the belief that they are unworthy of love or that people they care about will always abandon them. That story becomes part of their ego—their self-image and beliefs—which in turn causes problems in adulthood as they create scenarios that validate that deeply embedded "fact."

At the same time, we're forming our own beliefs about what things mean; we are also taught (mostly unconsciously) our tribe's values around things like intelligence, achievement, preferred emotional states, relationships, and other people. Remember that our greatest need is to receive love. We want to be part of our tribe. So to fit in, we learn to identify with these values *even if they are not positive.*

As we grow up, all of our experiences and lessons keep getting poured into our brain to be processed. They get sorted one way or another. We delete some, keep others, and the stuff that really makes sense to us based on the rules we've already created gets sent deep into our unconsciousness and tacked onto our ego. Layer by layer, it builds up every day, every year.

In our teenage years, the ego we've developed so far goes through a bit of an overhaul. We might rebel. We might seem to change quite a lot. Some kids get louder, some get quieter. Some start sneaking out and getting in trouble at school. Others might become a bit narcissistic and spend all their time posting on Instagram. Some bullied kids might become the bully. Or not. It depends on what's going on deep within.

If you are currently being driven crazy by your teenage child, take a minute to remember that they're doing a lot of very important self-development work, even if they're not fully aware of it.

They're navigating all sorts of social minefields, forming the next stage of their own identity, coming to grips with the pressures of young adulthood, and going through some pretty hectic neurological changes. It's a lot to handle…especially when you're not equipped with the wisdom, experience, and hindsight that we later enjoy in adulthood!

The teenage years are where stronger personality traits are defined, and the ego is set in another layer of bedrock. It's where we start really finding our groove in life, where (and how) we fit in with our tribe and the wider world around us. We're the jokester. The one with a shoulder to lean on. The tough guy. The go-getter. The battler. The bimbo. The hustler. The loser. All these self-imposed labels are kind of like signposts that indicate who we are and what we're about in this world.

Does that mean that by the time we reach adulthood, our ego is set in stone? Unchangeable and immoveable? Fortunately, no. The ego is always developing and changing in accordance with the meaning you place on things. Simply put, your ego will become whatever beliefs you feed it, whether positive or negative.

THE PROBLEM WITH EGO

Your ego is kind of like a security guard you didn't ask for. It's very rigid. It has to be. It's spent decades creating a whole set of beliefs, patterns, and ideas that make up your personality. It's been doing this since you were little to keep you safe from experiences that hurt you.

But here's where things get tricky. Your ego is very defensive about your identity. It's worked hard to keep you safe through your life so far. And it's not giving up on protecting you, no way. Remember, the brain loves patterns, and the ego is part of the brain. So it rejects anything outside of its confirmed thoughts, beliefs, and behaviours.

You've probably had this experience a few times throughout this book when you've read about ideas I've expressed that have challenged the way you see the world. It shows up as a feeling of resistance.

Resistance isn't dangerous as long as you're aware that it's just your ego behind the wheel, trying to keep you on known roads, and you don't let that resistance stop you from going to new places. But when you stop listening to new ideas and opinions, that's dangerous territory because you are becoming as rigid and stale as your ego!

Conflicting opinions or concepts often bring people to a place of anger, too, because the ego feels the most out of control when it's challenged. This leads to a lot of insecurity and low self-worth. When we're in this fragile state, the ego works overtime to "defend" us. But its protection is actually far from helpful…it can be downright destructive.

A few ways the threatened ego will overcompensate:

- Strong emotional reactivity
- False confidence (bravado)
- "Black and white" rigid thinking
- Rejection of any idea that conflicts with the ego's beliefs
- Extreme competition
- Constant comparison to others
- Judgement of others
- Analytical paralysis (obsessive thoughts that stop you from completing any action)

When you experience these reactions, your ego is trying to keep you safe. But these behaviours aren't useful or helpful. And some of them can turn you into a bit of an asshole.

Considering that we develop our concept of "self" as children, it is inevitable that our self-image doesn't map to reality as adults. And so, we create patterns of self-sabotage on a grand scale—economically, romantically, socially…you name it.

But what the ego is protecting is *not* reality. It's often just protecting your wounds, ones you received a long, long time ago.

FIGHTING WITH YOUR EGO

Have you ever fought with yourself after overreacting to something? Maybe you lashed out with anger at something trivial.

One of the most deceptive aspects of the ego is that it generates powerful emotional reactions and then blames us for how it made us feel. The anger we feel comes from ego-based beliefs of being right and "knowing better" than someone else. Perhaps there is also a victim-centred interpretation of betrayal or injustice like I felt about Ben all those years ago.

After you overreact with anger, you probably feel bad about what you expressed. You might wonder, *What came over me that I reacted that way? What the hell is wrong with me?* That's your ego taking the identity of the "stupid idiot" that takes the blame for overreacting.

The funny thing is that what's really happening here is that the ego has not only triggered an emotional response, it's hijacked the analysis of your response and turned it into a self-criticism/blame process.

And so, the cycle repeats itself, as you lash out at others, then lash out at yourself for doing so. A cycle of victimisation. When the ego controls the self-reflection process, you have no chance of seeing the root cause of your emotional dramas because the ego reaffirms itself and hides in self-criticism.

Clever little bugger, isn't it?

THE TRIGGERED EGO

What do I mean by triggered? Getting triggered is having an emotional response that's not equal to the event that's happened.

For example, your brother says, "You look tired" at a family dinner. You respond sarcastically, "Of course I look tired. I've been working sixty hours a week and raising two kids. Must be nice to have tons of free time."

What your brother said, objectively, "You look tired."

What your ego heard, "He's always so rude and condescending to you. It's because he's been jealous of you your whole life. Now he thinks he's some kind of hotshot."

The ego is a master storyteller. It has thousands and thousands of emotional events and experiences logged that you can't even consciously remember. These stories serve to protect you, *but they always keep you tied to your past experiences.*

That's why we often find it so hard doing something new. We struggle to break through invisible barriers. We find reasons to fail. Because our ego is telling us all the stories of what we've survived before…it cannot tell us stories about what we want to do next because we haven't done it yet!

TRUSTING INTUITION OVER EGO

Most people's ego would fight to the death over something that they would later find out was not important or that they were wrong.

As an example, a while ago, I let go of an employee of mine from The Game Changers because he wasn't a good culture fit for that business. But he is exceptionally good at what he does. So, when he told me he wanted to go out on his own and start his own business, it was a no-brainer for me to invest. I went in on 25 per cent with no money down; instead, I would give coaching, access to my high-level contacts, and access to my own business' intellectual property to help him scale fast.

In less than a year, the business blew up and was doing $250k+ a month. Profits were increasing rapidly and will continue to do so because it's a great offer, and the guys running it are highly skilled at delivering the goods.

But for some time, my intuition was telling me that something was happening between the scenes that wasn't quite right. I remember telling my partner I had a feeling that I needed to exit. The new business was consuming a lot of my energy at a time when I wanted to consolidate. Plus, I had my funny feeling playing in the back of my mind that something just wasn't right.

I felt like they were paying themselves more than what we agreed upon in our contract, and in doing so, reducing my dividends. Sure enough, when I got access to the business's books, my suspicions were confirmed.

I brought it up with my former employee, and we got into a bit of a back-and-forth about whether what he was doing was justified. We both thought that we were in the right. The next day, I got a call to tell me the company's best employee wanted to buy a large percentage of my shares.

Suddenly, I was getting what I originally wanted—to remove myself and free up my time and energy for other projects.

Isn't that interesting? What happens when we trust our intuition and align our desires in the space of divine wisdom?

Most people in this situation would have reacted through ego. They would have fought tooth and nail about the dividend discrepancy, taken it as an insult or whatever, and brought up a whole lot of conflict. And probably parted on bad terms feeling like they'd been screwed, whether they actually had been or not.

But I didn't have that reaction. Because I was in tune with my intuition and aligned with my heart. Instead of going down the road of conflict, I instead manifested the exact outcome I wanted—to exit the company. And not only that, but I exited on good terms and got a very nice payday to boot. It's been a positive experience for everyone. Had I reacted out of my ego, it would have been messy and painful.

So often, our ego can block us from really tapping into the path that we really want and getting the outcomes that we really desire. Is your ego tricking you into fighting for something you don't actually want right now?

KILLING YOUR EGO

Our ego defines who we are and how we connect with others. And for the most part, it's useful. It gives and receives important social cues and helps us navigate life easier. But ego becomes an issue when it becomes overpowering.

In the personal development space, there's a lot of talk about killing your ego. Over the years, various teachers have told me I should kill my ego, or I should rip out my limiting beliefs.

How do I kill my ego?

What an awful thought to want to murder a part of yourself!

Think about it like this. Killing an integral part of yourself is like trying to run away from your shadow. It's impossible. And the more that you focus on trying to remove it or to kill it, the stronger it becomes. *What we resist persists.*

You are not looking to "kill" your ego or deny its existence. The ego is your protector and has been a part of you since you were a small child, helping you cope. Remember, the ego is protecting aspects of us that have been wounded. It's not until we resolve those wounds through love, appreciation, and acceptance that the ego can then help us to have a healthy sense of self.

Remember that, in many ways, the ego is intrinsically linked to the "I am" statement. We say, "I am a father," and that creates a certain context and frame in which we live. It defines how we act, how we speak, how we show up in the world. "I am broke." Again, it carries a certain connotation around who you are and how you show up in the world.

"I am ugly." "I am loved."

The moment that we move into a sense of "I am," we separate our *self.*

We are not our ego. We are not any one belief about who we are. We wear different caps at different times. But all we are at our core is pure love. All there has been, all there is, and all that will ever be is love. Our ego is just the different hats we wear.

In our energetic form, we're nothing more than a speck of dust, created into this meat suit that we call human beings, having a human experience. The ego is like an identity suit. It's not who you are deep down, but it's all the different faces that you wear in society, in your relationships, in the different facets of life.

So the way that you start to evolve and to transcend is to actually learn and understand and befriend your ego. You know that saying, "Keep your friends close, keep your enemies closer."?

If you're befriending your ego and taking the time to understand it as an aspect of you, you're actually allowing it to merge with the pure love that you are in the first place.

But when you're trying to run away from it, what you're actually doing is keeping a part of you separate and in the shadows. You can't erase the ego by denying it and keeping it out of your awareness. You'll only end up giving it more strength.

And if we give it more strength, we're limiting ourselves. By its very nature, the ego defines a limited set of variables within which we operate. So, if we're not also nurturing our heart and our spirit, we'll create things in our lives that ultimately don't fulfil us. Because we're focusing on the things our ego thinks we want. Things that give us a sense of self-importance and self-worth, but at the detriment of our relationship with our partner or kids.

When we befriend and learn to understand our ego, we can actually use it to empower us, to develop healthy self-esteem and get a handle on our triggers.

In the end, you must address the root cause of your ego's beliefs, which is the separation of love. Every problematic belief in your ego is from a separation of love. Choosing something other than love has created these limitations and beliefs. It's as simple as that.

"Win at all costs" can give you a great buzz when you're operating in a purely egocentric state. It fuels the ego and your sense of self-importance, but you can't ever fulfil the ego. Operating only out of the ego equals an endless pursuit of goals and outcomes.

On the other hand, when you're connected to your heart, you'll have this energy coming down from the universe, coming into your heart and flowing into your whole being. When you're connected with your heart, you're connected to your true purpose, and because you're listening to your heart's intuition, you stay on track of where you *truly* want to go.

So before continuing to the next chapter, I want you to spend some time getting a clearer vision of your ego. Get to know it as a separate thing from your real self.

Some good questions to start you off:

- Who am I?
- Who do others see me as?

- Who am I pretending to be?
- What am I most comfortable sharing with others about myself?
- What part am I least comfortable sharing with others?
- What part of me am I most proud of?
- What are my values? Am I living according to them?
- What kind of things does my inner critic tell me?

As you answer the above questions, where is your ego trying to protect your wounds?

Getting to know your ego through these self-identity exercises will help you define the different aspects of yourself that guide everything you do.

Remember, your mind is in the control seat for much of your daily life, so the more you get to know its characteristics, the better you can navigate life's roads together.

And the next time you feel your ego at work, treat it as a well-meaning friend whose advice you're rejecting with love. Thank it for trying to protect you and then reconnect to your heart.

CHAPTER 8

VULNERABILITY

"Vulnerability is not weakness;
it's our greatest measure of courage."

—Dr. Brené Brown, PhD

"Now it's time for everyone to take their clothes off."

The room stopped buzzing with chatter and went dead silent. *What did he just say?* One hundred strangers looked around at the people to their left and then to their right. We caught each other's eyes, looking for what? Fear? Nervousness? Excitement?

It only took a few seconds for a collective laugh of relief to ripple around the room as they realised the same thing I was realizing...

I wasn't scared. I was ready to do this. I was going to get naked in front of one hundred people. Not only that—I was going to then walk into the centre of our circle and share something about myself that I'd never shared with anyone else before. Something that made me feel vulnerable.

And I was totally okay with it.

My mind flew back to the first time I got naked in front of a bunch of strangers a few years prior. I had been in Munich with my girlfriend, and we were attending a thermal sauna. The Germans, I was finding out rather abruptly, prefer to sauna nude.

I started freaking out. The place was huge, with different areas including a bar and even a restaurant. There were naked people everywhere, walking around like it was no big deal. "But where do we put our clothes?" I chattered. "Do you just walk out there naked? Do you put on a wearable like they do in the movies?"

I knew that my never-ending questions were just me trying to gain control over a situation where I felt pretty far out of my comfort zone. Because even though I'd had plenty of sexual partners who had told me it was just fine, like many men, I felt kind of insecure about the size of my penis deep down.

Like many boys growing up, I had nothing to compare my penis size to, so I really had no idea how I actually measured up against my peers. I hadn't been part of a football team or done sports where all the boys would shower together. I hadn't been to camp or changed clothes around other kids in dorms. All I had to compare myself to was porn…and that was terrifying.

What if those guys with the massive dicks that I saw in porn movies were actually the standard…and I just had no idea all this time? What if mine was actually really small…and this was the moment where I would finally get found out?

Would the Germans laugh me out of the sauna? Would my girlfriend decide to dump me? Would I ever be able to have sex again?

No matter how much my partners had assured me over the years that my sexual performance was great and that I satisfied them, I still had this worry about it deep down inside. What if they were just being nice? And if it turned out that I did have a little dick, what did that mean? How was I going to process that and decide to be okay with that? We didn't talk about body positivity for men back then, and we still don't really talk about it today.

I was spiralling.

So, I decided to own it. I turned to my girlfriend and told her, "You know, I'm feeling super vulnerable right now. I've never been around other naked men before." Then I told her about my fears about my penis size. Thankfully, she was gentle and reassuring and helped me feel comfortable enough to get naked and get out there.

That day ended up becoming one of the most liberating experiences of my life. Because once I got over my ego screaming at me not to go ahead with it, and I stripped off my clothes and went out, do you know what happened?

Nothing. Nobody pointed and laughed. Nobody shielded their eyes in horror. I looked around and saw that my penis fears were unfounded—I was doing just fine size-wise, as my partners had been telling me all along.

But a funny thing started to happen in the days afterwards. My girlfriend started to gently tease me about my fear from that day. She'd joke around about how I handled things and laugh at me for it.

When I showed my discomfort at her teasing, she'd just say, "I'm only doing it because it's not an issue anymore." But it still *was* an issue. My vulnerability didn't magically disappear—it doesn't work like that. I was still raw. I'd just opened my heart and shared something that's so close to me, something that's so deeply fearful, and I hadn't even had a chance to process it. And she was already giving me shit about it.

Whether she was consciously aware of what she was doing or not, I don't know. It doesn't really matter because that relationship is in the past. What I do know is that was the first experience I had around being vulnerable and having it thrown back in my face.

And you know what?

I'm so grateful for the experience. Because it gave me the gift of being vulnerable and having the worst happen . . . and I survived it. The ground didn't open and swallow me up. The stinging pain of my girlfriend's jibes in the following days didn't send me to my knees, unable to ever get up again. The fallout from being vulnerable wasn't nearly as bad as my mind had made it out to be when I stood in that sauna, clutching my towel and afraid to let go.

I was able to use that experience of her teasing as a reference point to help me whenever I felt hesitant about sharing my vulnerability again. Because now I knew that I could survive the worst. So what was there to be afraid of?

Around three years after that day, there I was, standing in a room full of people and taking my clothes off. Two days earlier, I had walked into this self-discovery workshop with an open mind and a willingness to participate, knowing there was a nude component involved.

Part of me had secretly been wondering if the whole naked thing was just a marketing gimmick to accentuate the power of the workshop and the purification process we would go through. But two days into the workshop and the changes I had undergone were so profound that I had started to wonder if it was actually true.

Maybe these facilitators were going to call us out to get naked with each other, and that was the way they would help us make the fundamental shifts that would cement the work we'd been doing?

As I walked into the big and breezy workshop room on a sunny day in Los Angeles for the last time, the energy was different. There was a sense of calm and peace and nurturing love. That morning, there was not much chatting. We all moved softly and gently to sit down in a large circle.

Our facilitators, Preston and Alexi, waited for everyone to get settled in. Then Lexi stood up and slowly looked around the circle, meeting us all one by one in her gentle gaze.

"Well, you made it," she began. "Today is day three, the day of the Naked Truth. This is the day you get to be witnessed in all the beauty, purity, truth, and rawness of who you are. Without the shame, without the guilt, without the burden."

I could feel a lump start to form in my throat. And although I knew from my experience in Munich that the world wouldn't end at the sight of my naked body, a part of me started to worry about what people would think of me. Would I be judged?

But there was also a sense of an invitation to unburden myself of all the crap I'd been carrying my whole life around not feeling good enough.

Alexi continued to speak to us.

"Right now, you may be having all these thoughts and feelings coming through, but we've been preparing you for this for the last two days without you even realising it. All others will see when you're standing up there is your beauty. They'll be honouring you in your vulnerability and nakedness."

Preston got up and drew the blinds, blocking out the LA skyline from view. The room became dim and quiet.

"It's time."

The room started rustling with the sound of everyone taking their clothes off. Soon, we were all standing naked in a circle.

"Who will go first?" Preston asked.

One by one, my fellow workshop participants stepped into the centre of our circle and shared things they felt vulnerable about.

I was so surprised at what I heard. Many of the women shared vulnerabilities about their bodies. They felt fat, they hated themselves, they felt ashamed, they felt ugly. It blew me away how these absolutely gorgeous women, these goddesses standing in front of me, could feel that way about themselves.

When the men shared, I discovered that many of them had the same fears and hang-ups that I did. They hated their bodies; they felt their penises were small, or they'd experienced a woman saying they hadn't pleased them well enough...and it shaped their whole sexual identity.

We all have scars that we try to protect.

When it was my turn, I stepped into the middle of a circle with a hundred people surrounding me. I shared my vulnerability with them. I cried. I let myself be raw. And I felt completely seen, loved, and accepted.

But most of all, I felt the most incredible *freedom*.

These days, I have no issue with getting naked, either physically or emotionally. About a week before writing this chapter, my girlfriend and I stripped off our clothes and jumped into the ocean at a full moon party here in Bali. We didn't think twice about it. And it felt wonderful.

When I think about all the people and experiences I've attracted into my life since I began allowing myself to be vulnerable and showing up as my true self, I know that the ability to be vulnerable has been the greatest gift I have ever given myself.

Out of my vulnerability, I've created true freedom to live my life as completely *me*. Out of my vulnerability, I've created healthy boundaries of what nourishes and fulfils me. And I've also built in the permission and self-acceptance to ask for what I need from others.

In this chapter, I'll share with you how I did it.

. . .

THE CAGE OF SELF-PROTECTION

Just as the ego can block us from finding the path that's actually right for us, it can also stop us from truly connecting with others. The ego wants to protect us above all else. So, the concept of being vulnerable sends it into panicked overdrive.

The ego keeps us closed in our little protective cages. Never showing all of who we are. And we don't even realise what's happening. We certainly don't realise that our reluctance to be vulnerable is holding us back from experiencing the feelings of connection and belonging that we crave.

This craving for connection and belonging is fuelled by the millions of years of human evolution that have formed our core neurology, and yet, we deny it.

That's mind-blowing to me now. But I used to be blind to my cage of self-protection. I always thought I was an open guy. I had no problem saying what I thought or giving feedback. I didn't hide. Or so I thought…

Then, around three years ago, I remember my partner at the time asking me to share my truth. "I want your truth, Barry," she'd say. "Share with me what's really going on."

I didn't understand what the hell she meant. I was being truthful to her —what the hell did she want from me? "I've *told* you," I would say. "That's all there is." I'd stand there, hands open, eyes wide, feeling irritated that she was digging for something that wasn't there. I was an open book, couldn't she see?

Whenever she wanted me to share with her any of my vulnerabilities, I just had this automatic response, a complete rebuttal. A door somewhere inside me was shut tight, and she was trying to knock on it. But I wouldn't even acknowledge it was there.

"I *am* telling you! I *am* being vulnerable with you!"

But I wasn't really. I just didn't have any conscious awareness of, or access to, the deeper layers within me.

It was because of her persistence—that I viewed as simply nagging—and her challenging me on whether I was really being vulnerable that I started to realise that what I was sharing was just an automatic response. It was a mechanism to keep me safe.

I thought that I was sharing my truth, but in actual fact, I was sharing a mask that I'd designed to keep me safe. Because deep down, I didn't feel safe to be me. Deep down, I wasn't given the experience of life where it was safe to be me.

When I was a kid, I was regularly sent to my room when I got too emotional. "Go to your room and come out when you stop crying." I acted out and got sent to my room for that, too. "Go to your room and come out when you're ready to apologise."

By no fault of my parents at all—they were just doing what they had been taught—I learned that my authentic responses weren't welcome. And further, regardless of whether I thought I'd done the wrong thing or not, I was sent to my room with the condition that I wouldn't belong, wouldn't experience love, until I changed my actions.

Over years of this conditioning, I created a new "rule" in my ego: that expressing my authentic self led to a removal of love from my tribe.

Now, I'll talk more about authenticity and what it means in a later chapter. But before authenticity comes a willingness to be vulnerable. To show up as your true self and express how you really feel is really challenging at first because most of us grow up not doing it.

Not only that, from an evolutionary perspective, the deck is stacked against us. The reason I found it so hard to even access my deeper levels of vulnerability, let alone share them, wasn't just because of my twenty-something years of conditioning... it was also because of thousands of years of development every human being before me went through to create the particular brain neurology we have today.

Think about this—when confronted, all animals resist exposing their bellies. Because if a predator slashes at your belly, all your guts come out, and you die. You can take a slash on the leg, a slash on the arm, even a cut to the head. But that soft underbelly is where animals are most physically vulnerable. It's life or death stuff.

As humans, we operate on the same principle. Both physically *and* emotionally. What's the first thing we do when we get a fright? We hunch our shoulders, bend inwards, and bring our arms and legs in to protect our torso.

Emotionally, we have an automatic response that's just as—if not more— powerful than our physical reaction. Because our emotional reaction is not just an evolutionary response, it's been compounded by a lifetime of hurts, betrayals, and messages from society that being vulnerable is bad.

Men, in particular, are taught that being vulnerable and sharing what's really going on with us emotionally is not wanted or accepted by society. Crying is tolerated in a young boy, but for a man, it's practically taboo.

Thankfully, women are rightly breaking down the decades of oppression that society has placed on them. Think about how things have changed for women since the 1950s. That's a fantastic thing, and although there's a long way to go, the notion of what a woman should be, how they should act, and what they should do has changed a lot.

For men, a lot of the old 1950s oppressive stereotyping is still around today. There's a lot of unconscious assumption that men are the breadwinners, they are the backbone of the household, they are the protectors of their family.

Men that are perceived to be weak or underconfident get pummeled by society. So we learn to keep that stuff to ourselves, pushing it down and paving a layer of protection over it until we mostly forget our deepest pains and hurts. Mostly. But here's the thing…

VULNERABILITY IS STRENGTH

How many times have you been asked, "How are you?" and you just automatically reply "I'm fine," or, "Good, thanks"? No matter how you're really feeling inside? Even if you're actually feeling terrible?

Why do we hide ourselves from others?

Why do we wear so many masks?

Why don't we speak our truth?

Now, I'm not saying that we need to unload all our woes on the checkout chick at the supermarket who is just being polite. But how would it feel to start showing who you really are—including your vulnerabilities—a bit more with your tribes and networks?

If you haven't thought about this before, the thought of being vulnerable, even to those closest to you, scares the hell out of you. That's okay and totally normal. But allowing yourself to share your vulnerabilities with others doesn't make you weak. Not by a long shot. It is actually one of the strongest and most courageous things a person can do.

What might happen if you show vulnerability to others?

You might get laughed at. You might get ridiculed. Some people might distance themselves from you.

So what? Do you know what will also happen?

You'll become braver. Stronger. Happier. Freer.

You'll also start drawing people to yourself who are an energetic match. People who inspire you, who lift you up, who see you—all of you—and *love* you.

True strength lies in vulnerability. When you can show up wholeheartedly, completely as yourself, and share your absolute undenying truth, even in the face of rejection, even in the face of being ridiculed and laughed at and made fun of, that's strength.

When you practice being vulnerable, you become so deeply grounded in who you are and what you're about that nothing else matters. The true weakness is in feeling you've got to put on a mask and shy away from who you really fucking are just to belong!

It took years for me to start to slowly access more of my vulnerability and be okay with sharing it. Sure, initially, it was sometimes used against me. By partners who ridiculed me for my insecurities, by peers who weren't comfortable with my raw emotion. By staff who had a different idea of who I should be as the head of my business. You name it.

But those hurtful experiences gave me the most beautiful blessing: I survived them. Just like my first nude sauna experience in Munich all those years ago, I realised the worst had happened, and I coped just fine. So what was I so afraid of?

Think about the ancient part of our brains that is focused on keeping us alive. That critter neurology that is still trying to keep us safe from the sabre-toothed tiger. To the critter brain, the experiences we survive are marked as "safe." And those safe experiences become the experiences that our continued survival depends upon. Because we survived them, the brain wants us to repeat them. That way, it's doing its job.

As we've already explored, the problem comes when we want to have new experiences. Our critter neurology, our ego, all of our mind's power will try and stop us from doing something new. So we keep having the experiences we've already repeated...even if they actually sucked.

But here's how to hack that system.

When you share vulnerability, and someone throws it back in your face, although it creates an aspect of hurt which you want to avoid, the brain still marks the experience as survivable. At the critter level, which is where a lot of our brain-based decisions are driven, it's an experience you can go through again. And again. And the more you do it, the easier it becomes as you create more positive feedback loops for your ego to embed into your personality.

The most beautiful thing is that the more you practice sharing your vulnerability, the more you'll attract people and situations that accept and nourish that level of vulnerability.

All those past relationships I had where I was showing up and being vulnerable, and they couldn't handle it…they don't exist in my sphere of influence anymore. The staff? Gone. The friends, partners? Gone. I'm in a world now where the conversations I have are nourishing, and people get to meet me where I'm at.

If people don't want to meet me at my level, I simply and lovingly tell them that this is not where I'm playing the game. And we go our separate ways.

How do you think it would feel if all of your relationships, romantic or otherwise, allowed and encouraged you to show up as your whole self—no masks, no bullshit? And the people close to you loved you wholeheartedly for who you are, even the bits you feel shame around?

I've got to tell you: it feels fucking amazing.

You can live in this space, too. You deserve to.

VULNERABILITY AND TRUST

Whether you're aware of it or not, you're a part of a number of tribes or teams. It's how we band together for the survival of the group and always have since our cave-dwelling days. How well our teams operate to achieve their collective goals determines how well we succeed at what we want to achieve.

What does this have to do with vulnerability, you might ask?

The number one dysfunction in any team is a lack of trust. And I don't mean trust as in keeping someone's secret. I'm talking about trust in the relationship and the common outcome that we're committed to so strongly.

Sports teams, business teams, even you and your partner are a team. Even you and your family are a team. Your success depends on the trust in your commitment to your shared outcomes. Sure, there may be conflict. There may be points of difference. But we know we can remain in a connection of love because I can trust your truth, and you can trust mine.

Most of us were never taught that we can show up and speak our absolute truth, and love won't be taken away from us. In fact, many of us were taught the opposite.

But the thing is, if we're not showing up and following our heart and speaking our truth, we're not trusting ourselves. And therefore, we are not trustworthy to others. How can we maintain relationships based on integrity if we're not showing up as trustworthy by speaking our truth? If others can't trust us to tell the truth, how can they ever really trust *us*?

Back when I was first thinking and learning a lot about vulnerability, authenticity, and trust, I decided to try being vulnerable with my staff. This was pretty challenging for me because I was the leader in the business! Surely that meant that, like the stereotypical 1950s man, I was supposed to be strong, to always know what I was doing, and to never admit weakness.

What would happen when I "showed the cracks" to my team? Would they lose faith in my ability to run the business? Would they lose respect for me? Would they run away screaming?

One day, during our Monday meeting, I told them I wanted to try something new.

"I'm exploring the concept of vulnerability," I told them. "I believe that vulnerability is the key to success and living a connected life."

They all sat quietly, waiting for what would come next.

"So, I'd like us to share something today that we've never, ever shared with anyone else before in our life. Leaders go first, so I'll start."

I then went on to share with them that I'd proposed to my partner (who they knew because she used to work in the business), and she'd turned me down. I had never shared that with anyone because I felt so much shame and guilt around it.

And then something wonderful happened. My team started sharing their own vulnerability, too. But not surface stuff; they shared some very deep and significant traumas. Once I'd pulled off my own mask and shared something that was so close to my heart, others felt it. And that gave them permission to do the same thing.

I was blown away and completely honoured. I still am.

After that experience, every single one of us felt more connected, more liberated, more whole, and with a greater sense of belonging. We connected in a moment of fucking *truth*.

Now, if you're a boss, I'm not saying you should go to your team and ask them to share a deep dark secret with you tomorrow and expect them to be receptive to that! That was something that I intuitively felt I could do with my team because of the incredible culture we've built at The Game Changers.

Since that day, I've had so many experiences where I've shared my truth and vulnerability with a member of my team, and it's turned out to be exactly what was needed to open a door to somewhere better. It's helped the business to thrive beyond what I could have ever imagined. But if I had pretended to be some guy with all the answers and operated in my "Business Barry" ego space, I would still be stuck, facing the same challenges in my business.

It doesn't matter if we're talking about professional teams or personal teams; deeper connections and better relationships start with dropping a moment of truth, a moment of vulnerability into your connection with someone, and that allows them to be okay with their vulnerability, too. And so, a ripple effect begins.

Both individually and collectively, this is the essence of starting to shift our human consciousness.

EXPLORING YOUR VULNERABILITY

So, by now, you might be thinking, *Okay, Barry, I'll give it a try... but where do I start?* Maybe you're scanning your daily interactions at work and at home, looking for a place where you might get the opportunity to share a deeper piece of yourself.

Here's my advice—you need to create the opportunity for it to happen. Don't wait for a safe space to share your vulnerability—it doesn't happen that way. Your environment is your environment, and it's a direct reflection of you, whether good or bad.

If you feel that the environment you're in isn't fit for you to share your vulnerability, then that environment needs to shift. But it can't until you start sharing your vulnerability. You need to create the environment yourself. And besides, how can you know what a safe environment is until you start sharing?

It's not a chicken-or-egg scenario here. *You* create your environment. You're the leader of your life. Leaders go first.

Once you start sharing vulnerability, you'll start to notice a few things in the people around you. Who shows up but doesn't share? Who shows up and can hold the person who is sharing? Who can't handle it and turns to jokes or ridicule?

It's only through having an actual live feedback loop that you can consciously start shifting your world.

If you're looking for a place to begin, begin with your heart. Connecting to your heart is your deepest truth. It's not something that you do once, and you get there. Over time, the more you connect with your heart, the more you start to realise your absolute fundamental truths. I'm talking about the truths that are far beyond the conditioning and safety mechanisms that we've created to help us survive this physical existence.

Once you start your heart connection, you realise that a lot of what you believed to be true simply isn't. You simply have old biases, things you've told yourself so many times that you don't even question it. Once you start sharing those realisations with those that you love and care about most—and gain the feedback from their reactions—the more you start to shape a more honest, nurturing, and freeing environment.

But first, just recognise within yourself the feeling that something needs to shift. That knowing that you haven't been true to yourself. That you hide yourself from others.

So when you start doing your heart-based meditations and having new realisations, start sharing them in conversations with those around you, and notice what feedback you get.

Here are some questions to get you started:

- What's the one thing you carry the most guilt about?
- What's the one thing that you feel the most shameful about?
- What's the one thing that you secretly hope and pray that no one ever finds out about you?
- What's the one thing that you wish you could take back?

Think on these for a while. Ask them of yourself before you do your heart meditations, and record what comes up.

If your first reaction is, "I don't have anything like that," then that's a clear sign you need to dig deeper. Because we *all* have stuff like that. Stuff that hides deep within us. Gently thank your ego for trying to protect you and ask it to step aside.

When you've got your answers, I encourage you to find several people and share your answers with them. The liberation you'll feel, that sense of freedom when this thing no longer has power over you, is nothing short of incredible. The house of shame that you've built inside of yourself will start to topple over, bit by bit.

Notice who meets you at your level and who does not. Gravitate towards conversations that feel good to you, the ones that support you, the ones where people are curious and want to know more.

Trust that this is where you need to go. This is where you start to bring your real self to life. It's where who you truly are gets to peek out for the first time and feel the sun.

I'll be the first to say: "Hello. It's great to meet you."

CHAPTER 9

BOUNDARIES

"Stop asking why they keep doing it and start asking
yourself why you keep allowing it."

—*Charles J. Orlando*

"Ugh, not this dickhead again."

I was at my first Tantra workshop in Bali, where I was expecting to awaken a deeper sexual energy and learn how to access mental, emotional, physical, and spiritual bliss.

As I spotted Connor across the room, I couldn't believe it. What was he doing here? More importantly, how was I going to avoid him for seven days?

Connor was a guy I'd seen at the gym a few weeks before. He hung out with someone who had picked a fight with one of my friends in the past, so I immediately judged him harshly. As I watched him peacock around with annoying "yo, bro" bravado, I felt my lip curl in a barely hidden sneer. *Dickhead.*

Over the next seven days of the Tantra workshop, I did a pretty good job of avoiding him. We were in a large group, so there were plenty of other people to engage with during our periodic exercises.

But Connor was on my mind. Too much. Like an annoying song that gets stuck in your head, my thoughts kept drifting back to him. Why was my mind bugging me with this? I was supposed to be focusing on myself. Why was this guy bouncing around my brain?

On the last day of the workshop, our teacher told us to prepare for our last exercise. "Walk around the room and find someone you feel drawn to," they instructed.

I knew I had to find Connor. For whatever reason, I was drawn to him, despite not wanting to be. Maybe I needed to trust my intuition and find out why?

Five minutes later, awkward greetings were made, and Connor and I sat facing each other cross-legged on the floor.

As our teacher began speaking, I had no idea where this exercise was headed.

"Now I want you to tell each other everything that is a 'no' to you. Everything you don't like, everything that goes against how you want to be treated. One person goes at a time, and their partner is to hold the space for them to share."

Well, okay then. We could do this; it seemed pretty simple.

Connor went first. "I'm a 'no' to people lying to me," he began.

That's a good one, I thought. *That's one of my nos, too.*

"I'm a 'no' to being cheated on. I'm a 'no' to people being late to meet me," Connor continued, and as he did, I realised just how many of our nos were the same. As he kept sharing, I started feeling emotional as a realisation bubbled up inside me...*these were the same boundaries that I actually had for myself, but I'd never expressed them to others.*

In my mind, memories flashed of times where I'd said yes to things I didn't really want or simply said nothing at all. Times that I didn't express what I needed, and as a consequence, wasn't happy with what I got. I never realised how empty it made me feel until that moment.

After we both shared, we moved on to the second part of the exercise.

One after another, we were instructed to reach out and touch the other person in a semi-inappropriate way. Hand on inner leg, hand on face, that kind of thing. When we were touched this way, we had to grab their hand and remove it while saying no.

I was surprised at the shame I felt while removing Connor's hand forcefully and telling him no. Why had my whole body shivered with anxiety just then? Why did I feel like I was somehow being rude or doing the wrong thing when *he* was the one touching *me* without my consent?

In that moment, I remembered sitting at the dinner table when I was a kid. I could see the pale green linoleum and smell the steam of cooked vegetables on the stovetop. As I reached for food, I felt a smack on my hand that sent it crashing against my plate, causing a small eruption of clattering cutlery on the tablecloth. "No!" barked my dad. "Wait until we start dinner." I felt my cheeks blush with shame.

Snapping back to the smell of hardwood floor polish and humidity that afternoon in Bali, I realised that I had never asserted my own boundaries because, even as an adult, I was always afraid of that smack. Not a literal smack from my dad, but some kind of rebuke, rejection, or refusal from the person in front of me.

The truth was I had no idea how to express my own boundaries. Until I'd heard Connor articulate his own just minutes before, I'd had little idea they even existed.

After we'd done the exercise a few more times, our teacher raised his voice to the class once again.

"Now say no…but *with love.*"

I reached out and touched Connor. He grabbed my hand slowly and looked me in the eyes. "No," he said softly, gently.

And for the first time ever, I didn't feel shame upon being rebuked. Instantly, I realised, *Holy shit, I can say no, respecting my boundaries with love. And it's up to the other person whether they choose to receive that love or not. Their response is not my responsibility. It's their stuff to work through, and it's got nothing to do with me. It's not my story. And it's not my place to "fix it" for them.*

I burst into tears with the relief, the joy, and the *freedom* of this truth that I'd just unlocked.

I had received Connor's love because I was in my heart space, and I was experiencing love within me. I knew that if I'd felt guilt, shame, or anything else that we often carry around, I would have been defensive.

I'd played it out so many times in previous relationships, where something would happen, and one (or both) of us would snap straight to defensiveness or judgement. We'd grab our emotional weaponry, put on our armour, and begin the bad guy witch hunt: who is wrong and who is right.

But I was in a space of love. When Connor said no, I could feel his love. I could receive it. And so, in that moment, I was able to respect him *and* me at the same time. The emotion was stripped away, the "am I bad," "he is being mean," all that self-centred rubbish that our ego brings up when it feels threatened...it wasn't there.

Love was all there was.

Half an hour later, we ended the session forever changed.

"Barry, thank you so much," Connor said. "Thank you for holding the space for me to express myself and for not judging me."

I had to confess...

"You know what? I did judge you, Connor. When I first saw you at the gym, I thought you were a dickhead. I judged you for the company you kept and the situation your friend had caused before. But today, I just knew I wanted to put my judgements aside and actually get to know you. And I'm so glad I did."

We hugged. For what felt like ages. Eventually, we rejoined the group, teary-eyed and joyous.

We'd both just had the most amazing experience where we learned how to identify our boundaries, respect those boundaries, and say no with love...*without buying into the emotional drama that the ego tries to create.*

Knowing that I'm allowed to ask for what I want and that the other person is allowed to choose to accept that or not, without it being a reflection of me. It's a gift.

And I'd like to offer that gift to you.

So, follow me as we dive deeper into the realm of the head and the things within it that hold us back from following our heart's true message. Because not only does your ego and unwillingness to be vulnerable hold you back from living a fulfilled and heart-centred life, your perceived obligations to others can do so, too.

■ ■ ■

THE PROBLEM WITH BEING A PEOPLE PLEASER

Thinking about it now, I realise that in my past relationships, I didn't have any boundaries. I was a "yes man" who always believed that to make my partner happy, I needed to do what they wanted. At the same time, I had no awareness or respect for *their* boundaries. How could I, when I didn't have any of my own?

I didn't mind if someone walked in on me in the bathroom, so I assumed my partners didn't either (I was *wrong*!). I didn't mind if they were on the phone during dinner, so I assumed they didn't mind it if I took a few calls. And many, many other blind assumptions that meant that while trying to love each other, we were really grating against each other every single day.

There was never any alignment with what we both wanted and needed from the other. There was just blind assumption—I never imagined that the stuff I was okay with would not be okay with my partner. Because I had never established any boundaries for myself, I wasn't consciously aware of them, for me or for others.

The thing is, everybody is different. We are all having our own unique experience of the world. But I was only seeing the world through my own lens.

It wasn't until entering the relationship I'm currently in that boundaries started playing a stronger role. My current partner, Kate, is aware of her boundaries and willing to ask for what she needs. At first, that was challenging for me.

On nights that she wanted to stay at her place instead of mine, I felt a pang of hurt because what that meant in my mind was based on my fear of abandonment. Didn't she want to spend time with me? What was wrong with me?

Even though she had told me gently and with love that she simply needed some time to herself, I made it about me, which is what we usually do in relationships, instead of seeing our partner as a person with their own needs.

Here's a pattern I see a lot and have repeated myself many times:

One partner asserts a need that doesn't fit in with how we want to do things. For example, they may want to go out with their friends one Friday night instead of staying in with you. Instead of recognising that our partner is their own person with different needs than us, we make it about ourselves.

Our ego gets triggered. It flies into action, "Whoa, there! She doesn't want to spend time with you! She wants to go out and find another man! She doesn't value your company! You're in danger of being hurt! Defend yourself!" And so the fight begins.

By the time the dust has settled, you both feel like you've been wronged, and you are both 100 per cent pissed off. You both unconsciously (or maybe consciously) start to feel that you cannot get your needs met in the relationship, and it develops distance, a crack. Enough of these cracks, and it eventually breaks.

Can you think of a time when your ego flew into action to "protect" you when there was really no need? Can you think of a time when you made someone else's decision for themselves all about you?

Sure, you can, because we all have done it, many times!

But once you recognise it, you can start to change that pattern of behaviour. When you feel the burn of self-righteous anger starting to pump through your veins, you can start to tell your ego, "Thanks, but you're not needed here. This isn't about me; it's about them. And that's perfectly okay."

I honour Kate because she continued to ask for what was right for her, even if she could tell it was causing insecurities in me. She didn't start sacrificing her needs to meet what I perceived mine to be because she knew that would be detrimental to both of us.

And because she honoured her own needs by upholding her boundaries, a beautiful thing happened. I started to realise that I could ask for what I needed, too.

I'd never had that before. I'd never felt complete love and trust that if I asked for what I needed, that my partner would be completely fine with it instead of making it about them and letting their ego try to control the situation to keep them safe from whatever threat was perceived.

I started to notice that every time she went away and spent time by herself or did stuff with her friends, she would come back so much more loving and in a wonderful headspace to fully be with me. And I realised that the better she took care of herself, the better she was able to show up in our relationship.

And that goes both ways. It's not your job to make your partner happy. And it's not their job to make you happy either. It's your job to make *you* happy and express what's right for you. And vice versa. When you do that, you both turn up in the relationship as your best selves.

What this means is that if I look after myself and what I need for me, and she looks after herself and her needs also, we're both in a place where we can support and look after each other. It means none of the bullshit ego conflict comes up. And if it ever does, we will simply talk about it to learn each other's point of view, which dissolves the issue.

Instead of assuming what our partner needs, based on what *we* would want, have the trust that we will ask for what we need. In fact, asking for what we need is our responsibility to each other. Without that open and honest communication, there's a lot of guesswork required, which will never lead to a fulfilling relationship for either party.

We enter a relationship with all our past preconceptions. But if I turned up in my relationship with Kate and treated her the way my ex liked to be treated, the way I think she likes to be treated, or the way I would like to be treated…I'm not honouring *her*. I'm not understanding her.

Imagine if we all existed in an environment where we could express our desires and what we liked and didn't like…and have that met with curiosity, love, and appreciation rather than a projection of their trauma?

Imagine meeting someone who wanted to understand your past, not to punish you, but to understand how you want to be loved?

It's entirely possible, believe me.

But to start attracting these kinds of people in your life, first, you must make room for them to enter. And you cannot start doing that until you start telling the universe what you want. That often begins with telling it what you *don't* want.

NO IS NOT A DIRTY WORD

When was the last time you told someone no?

Did you feel a knot in the pit of your belly? Did you worry that you would piss someone off?

As kids, we're not taught to have healthy boundaries. Our world is simply: my parent tells me to do something, and I have to do it.

Even when we ask why we just get the answer: *because I say so*.

Their authority is absolute. And there are a number of good reasons for this. I mean, if a kid is about to run in front of traffic, the parent needs to know that when they yell "stop," the kid will instantly obey. Parents are our caretakers; their rules keep us safe as we're growing up.

But the flipside to this authoritarian structure is that as kids, we often don't get the experience of expressing what feels right for us and having the other person respecting our wishes.

Our mum and dad burst into our room without knocking. Or they make you hug a family friend even though you're uncomfortable. Our boundaries aren't a factor for them because we're just kids, right?

As a consequence, we aren't taught how to say no in a healthy, loving way. In fact, we are taught that no is an awful word, that it's rude and even selfish to tell someone no. But saying no is a crucial tool for a healthy existence as a human living on this planet with a gazillion other people!

Think about this:

A no to someone else is a yes to *you*.

The universe gives us what we ask for. If you're constantly saying yes to things that don't serve you, that's what you're going to get more of. The brain loves patterns, so it will keep seeking out the same path. The ego loves safety, so it will keep giving you more of what you have survived before.

If you keep saying yes to clients, they'll think, *Great! They want more work!*, and they will keep giving you more. If you keep saying yes to dirtbags who cheat on you, the universe will say, "Great! I'll keep sending them your way." If you keep getting walked over by your friends, they'll think, *They don't mind, I'll keep taking more and more.*

So why do we do it?

Why do we tie ourselves up in knots emotionally to avoid having a talk with a friend when their behaviour doesn't match how we want to show up in life? Why do we put our own needs on the backburner when someone else wants something from us?

Why is it so hard to say, "You know, that actually doesn't work for me. I'm saying no."?

I often think that what stops a lot of people from putting boundaries in place is fear or concern about disappointing or upsetting somebody else. We don't want to rock the boat.

But it's almost like we try to play God in those moments.

We think, *If I say no to them right now, they'll feel rejected, so I should just do it.* Or, *If I ask them to stop doing this thing that I don't like, they'll feel upset, so I'll just put up with it.*

We have a perception of what saying no would do for somebody else, but in that process, we're not allowing the other person to have their own experience. We're trying to wrap them in cotton wool. We're deciding what's right for them.

But here's the thing—who the hell are we to do that? We are not God. We don't really know what somebody else needs. We don't know all the nuances of how they were brought up or how they see the world.

The only thing we can really know is ourselves. And when we really start to get to know ourselves, like you're learning to do in this book, that's when we can create boundaries that support us to become the best version of ourselves.

These boundaries might be pretty simple things like not eating dessert that's been served up because we're already full. Or telling your friends you don't want to go out on Friday night because you need some chill alone time at home. Or asking your flatmate to not leave their dirty dishes in the sink because you value a neat and clean house.

You'll have bigger boundaries, too. Boundaries around fundamentals like trust, loyalty, love, honour. All the values and beliefs that make up who you are.

But when you go along with what you think others want simply because you don't want to let anybody down, that disallows you from managing your own experience of life.

And that's no way to live!

What do you put up with currently that you're actually uncomfortable or unhappy with?

When in your life do you tense your shoulders and tighten your jaw?

Where do you feel you aren't free to be you?

ASKING FOR WHAT YOU NEED

Creating boundaries is about loving yourself enough to ask for what you need and also respecting yourself enough to not take what you get.

When I was young, I was often told, "Take what you get and be grateful." While I understand the reasoning behind this, my parents not wanting to raise an entitled brat, that messaging becomes the unconscious voice that plays in your head for everything you want, not just material things.

But I didn't actually want some of the things I was given. Even so, if someone was offering me something, it was rude to turn it down. Because it would make the person offering it uncomfortable, and it certainly wasn't the place of a child to make an adult feel uncomfortable!

But this training often plays out detrimentally as adults because we end up taking what we get instead of asking for what we need. That sucks for us, and it stops the people that care about us from knowing how to show up in a way that supports and nourishes us, which isn't fair on them either.

For example, say a guy buys his girlfriend a rose, but she's actually allergic to roses. But she's been raised to be grateful for what she gets, so she thanks him and shows that she's happy to receive it.

So the guy thinks, *Great, the rose is a winner! I'm going to get them for her more often.* Soon she's getting roses every other week, and the itching eyes and watery nose they cause are driving her crazy. She thinks, *Ugh, roses again! Why does he keep buying these damn things for me? I hate them!*

Soon, she's unconsciously building all this resentment towards the guy because he keeps buying her something she doesn't want. But she's never educated him otherwise because she doesn't want to hurt him or let him down.

So she's not getting what she needs, and she's also denying her partner the opportunity to meet her needs.

Eventually, she might snap and shout, "Will you stop getting me fucking roses! Can't you see that I hate them?" And the partner will be shocked and hurt. Because he had no idea she really felt that way.

Can you imagine how different things would have been if she'd said from the beginning, "Hey, thank you so much for the roses; I really appreciate the time and thought you put into getting them for me. But I'm actually allergic to them. I really love sunflowers, though."

By asserting her needs with love, she honours the gift she's been given and educates her partner on her needs. When we don't take the time to understand our partner and what their boundaries are, it also doesn't allow them the space to understand themselves.

This comes up in sexual relationships as well. People don't express their desires and then have unsatisfying sex lives. Maybe they blame their partner. This can go on for years in some couples—what a tragedy that they spend so much time not fully experiencing pleasure with each other, just taking what they get instead of asking for what they need.

How different do you think the quality of their sexual intimacy would be if they started to communicate their needs in a loving way? "Hey, darling, I actually am not that into being touched that way. This is how I like to be touched. This is what feels good for me."

If you communicate your needs to your partner in a loving way, gently educating them on your needs, do you think they'll be upset? Of course not; they'll be thrilled that they are learning how to please you more.

"Thank you for sharing what you like and what you don't like. It allows me to love you more because it allows me to know you more."

It's funny how often we don't allow others to really know us or what we really want…and then get disappointed when they let us down by breaking an invisible rule they never knew existed in the first place. But if you don't let people know what feels good and what doesn't, how the hell are they supposed to know? It's hardly fair, is it?

Communicating your boundaries is actually an act of love. It allows others to really know you and love you. In a way, lacking boundaries is kind of like a self-defence tactic. Think about it—everything needs borders. Countries. Roads. Coastlines. Everything has a shape.

But when you don't communicate your own boundaries—the borders within which your true self exists—you never show others your true shape. And if people can't find where the real you begins, they can never get close to you.

BEING SELFLESSLY SELFISH

"But Barry, isn't it selfish to tell someone else no?"

I grew up believing that it was selfish to have asked for what I wanted, or to have turned something down, or to upset somebody, or to have made someone feel rejected or whatever their response was.

But after that session with Connor at the Tantra workshop, I started to realise that this wasn't my responsibility. I was playing God all those years. I thought I knew better. But that's actually being selfish. That is the paradox … the way I was showing up trying to determine what all the people around me wanted or needed of me and providing that, that perceived generosity or selflessness was actually me being selfish.

Because I wasn't allowing them to be responsible for their own experience, I wasn't allowing them to understand me or learn how I choose to show up and how I want to be treated. So I was actually doing them a disservice. I thought I was protecting them, but I was actually shutting them out from knowing me and loving me.

Understanding and expressing my needs—being "selfish"—is when I can actually be *selfless* … because by doing so, I also give permission to other people around me to do the same thing.

I give them permission to also express their deep desires, their essential needs. It can feel very exposing to ask for what you want because there's a whole bunch of stuff around self-worth that we can get caught up in, too. Do I deserve to receive this right now? Am I a worthy enough person to have my needs met?

There's also a whole bunch of guilt or shame wrapped up in expressing our boundaries, too. What will others think of me for wanting this? What will happen if they deny me? If they turn me down?

If others don't want to meet you at your level, you won't burst into flames. Instead, their denial is good feedback because it's helped you identify that that person is not a great match for you. It's nothing bad against you or them; it's just not a fit, simple as that.

TEACHING OTHERS HOW TO TREAT YOU

If you spend lots of time in your life feeling resentful, bitching about being disrespected or taken advantage of, playing the martyr, or living in low-vibe emotional states... I've got a harsh truth to tell you: it's kind of your own fault.

If your friend is always taking advantage of you, it's because you keep letting them. If your partner never satisfies you sexually, it's because you haven't told them how to please you. If you're always getting the short end of the stick, it's because you set yourself up for it.

If you don't define how you want to be treated, others will do it for you. And if you're constantly selling yourself a piece at a time... eventually, you'll end up empty. And besides, saying yes all the time is *exhausting*, isn't it?

Let me ask you real quick:

- Do you constantly do favours that are a stretch for you financially, physically, or emotionally?
- Do you take on so many responsibilities to please others that your wellbeing suffers?
- Do you constantly sacrifice what you want to please your partner?
- Do you secretly experience resentment, anger, or self-loathing, wondering how you can possibly escape the tangled web of commitments you've created around yourself?
- Do you find yourself regularly bitching about a friend, colleague, or situation?

By doing this, you're not actually helping anyone. Especially yourself. You're actually denying others from having the experiences they need.

Maybe your friend who constantly cries poor actually needs to be told no a few times, so they start being more financially responsible. Maybe your partner's self-esteem is taking a battering because he feels like he isn't pleasing you in bed and would love nothing more than for you to ask for what you want. Maybe members of your local community group actually feel robbed of the opportunity to contribute because you're always doing so much.

The thing is, when you set healthy boundaries that are in alignment with your integrity (we'll talk about integrity in the next chapter), you can actually be *more* generous to others because you have more of yourself to give.

The more your needs are met, the happier, more fulfilled, engaged, and present you are for the people around you. You can show up as your best self, not someone sapped of enthusiasm and totally disinterested. By establishing and upholding boundaries, the quality of your relationships improves, as does the quality of your output in everything you do in life.

It's like putting on your oxygen mask in a plane—secure your own mask first before helping others. If not, you all suffer.

BOUNDARIES AND VALUES

I've always set values in my businesses, and doing so has been a fundamental reason for our success. Values set the standards of behaviour and allowed me to make the right decisions for those businesses.

Whatever my question was, whether it was to keep a certain staff member, take on an opportunity, launch a new product I'd been thinking about, my line of questioning would be the same:

How does this fit with the company values? Is it in alignment? Does it meet them all, or just one or two?

The answer would always guide me.

But in the past year or so, I realised that I'd never really sat down and thought about my personal values, so how can I really define my boundaries? How can I know why some things feel right, and some don't? If I can't articulate it, how can I educate others on how I want to be treated?

So I sat down and worked out what feels good and what doesn't. From there, I realised what my personal values are:

- **Space**. I need the space in my life to grow and breathe. If I haven't got appointments backed up against one another, it allows me to feel freedom, which sparks my creativity and allows me to experience a sense of gratitude and appreciation. Because I've got time to stop and think, feel, create, and enjoy.
- **Wealth**. Wealth allows me to feel abundant and to contribute. Through wealth, I can create leverage, so I can do more things by investing my wealth in different places. I can help more people, I can create more value, and I can cause bigger ripples across the world.
- **Vulnerability**. This is a core value because it allows me to have connection, depth, and love. By allowing myself to be vulnerable and showing up as truly me, I'm creating a community of people around me that are playing the game of life at a similar level to mine. And those relationships are incredibly nourishing.
- **Trust**. If I don't feel I can trust someone and have an open, honest conversation in integrity, they can't be in my space. Because I only want to give my time and energy to those people I can trust in expressing all of myself without being judged.

Now that I have those values defined, it makes all of my personal and business decisions really clear. Your values work as a decision-making matrix, a kind of "magic 8-ball" that helps you determine what's right for you.

If I've got a big deadline looming on a project and someone asks me if I want to go hang gliding that day, I can weigh it up against my values.

Does it give me space? Well, I'm already under pressure with this project. Does it give me wealth? No, it's actually robbing me of wealth because I can't invoice for it. And going would mean that I'm not being vulnerable and trusting myself in expressing that this is not the right time for me right now.

But if I went anyway because all my friends were going and I felt social pressure to go, sure I would have fun at the time. But it would create pressure and tension around my big project that might bring up some resentment or friction, simply because I hadn't honoured my values and asserted my boundaries with love by saying, "Sorry, I would love to go, but it's not a good time for me right now. I can come with you next week instead."

On the other hand, if I was asked to go hang gliding on another day where I didn't have a looming project, the decision might be different. I would have the space to do it. It wouldn't be robbing me of wealth; in fact, I might make a good business connection with the person who asked me to go.

Do you see the difference?

My values work like my own personal North Star... along with my heart. My values help guide me where I need to go.

Your values might be similar to mine, or they might be something totally different. And that's fine. We are all having our own experience of life.

Have you ever sat down and given thought to what your personal values are? Most people don't. We are so busy leading our lives that we don't stop and think, *Do I really want this?*

Maybe it's time to start.

IDENTIFYING YOUR BOUNDARIES

As you're reading this book, and this chapter especially, a few things might be popping up for you in terms of how your needs are or aren't being met. Maybe you're realising that you feel resentment towards certain friends or your partner because they're not meeting your needs (that you haven't communicated to them!).

Take some time to sit down and ponder your values. Focus on your heart —what is it telling you?

If you're looking for a place to start, a good way is to first define what is an absolute "no" for you—in terms of money, friendship, marriage, sex, health, everything.

When Michelangelo created the statue of David out of a single block of marble, people marvelled at the feat. "How did you create it?" they asked. Michelangelo replied, "I simply removed everything that wasn't David."

So, let's start removing everything that's not you. Every decision you make to fit in with someone else to belong or to be liked. The obligations that you feel towards your friends, your partner, your colleagues. All the places you're staying in your life because of these unconscious agreements that you made a long time ago, that aren't serving who you are now.

But remember this: everything you get rid of makes space for something new to come along. And when you get clear on your yeses and nos and start communicating those boundaries, the universe listens. It gives you more of what you ask for. And new people and experiences start showing up that are more aligned with the space you're carving out for yourself.

In all my years of coaching, every time I worked with someone to envision their ideal partner, job, or business, they manifested it so quickly because the universe says yes.

And remember that just because you start getting what you asked for, that doesn't mean you have to accept it. If what you thought you wanted isn't quite hitting it, and you need to adjust, do it! Ask again. And again. Keep recalibrating until you find your sweet spot. It might take time, but you will get there.

So, let's begin. Get a piece of paper and draw a line down the middle. Mark your two sides of the page "yes" and "no." Then start brainstorming. Pick an area of your life and just begin. If you get stuck, think of what you don't want. That's often much easier. Then think of the opposite of that. Write it down.

You'll start to see patterns emerge that you can group together. You'll uncover themes. And then, you can start shaping what's important to you and define your boundaries for how you want to live.

Each boundary you create and uphold with love is another block of self-respect in the new internal structure you are building for yourself. Your house is getting strong! Keep going.

CHAPTER 10

INTEGRITY

"Whoever is careless with the truth in small matters cannot be trusted with important matters."

—*Albert Einstein*

"DID THAT SEEM OVERLY ENTHUSIASTIC TO YOU?"

I was sitting in a cafe in Canggu, enjoying an iced tea with my girl, Kate. We were having a lazy day, gazing out at the rice fields beyond the cafe as we enjoyed the warm yet breezy afternoon.

A friend of mine had just come in with his family and given me a massive hug.

"How are you, bro?" he exclaimed. "It's been so long. Let's catch up soon, eh?"

A flurry of hugs and kisses on cheeks and exclamations about how great we all looked followed. He came and went like a whirlwind of such incredible enthusiasm that it put a sour taste in my mouth. Because actually, we'd been playing the "let's hang out" game for months. But every time I contacted him to try and organise something, he didn't get back to me. Or we tentatively made plans, and he flaked hours before we were to meet up.

Even though he was super enthusiastic when he saw me that day, other times, I'd seen him around town, and he'd ignored me completely.

Something was starting to feel not right…and his over-the-top greeting on this day riled me.

"You know," replied Kate as he took a seat somewhere inside. "That seemed kinda forced. It felt fake."

I frowned, feeling annoyed. This was a great guy whose friendship I really enjoyed. But slowly, I began to realise I was bitching to Kate a lot about him never getting back to me. And I knew that if I complained about something more than once, it was a problem that needed addressing.

Now, this was a guy who had kids and a family and all the rest. I had no idea what was going on with him. He probably had very good reasons for being unavailable. Or cold. Or whatever. He obviously had other stuff going on. And that's fine. But the disconnection between what he was saying and what he was doing was really bugging me.

If he was super busy or just not interested, then why make such a big deal out of catching up when he saw me? I just didn't get it.

Soon, I realised that I needed to have a conversation about it with him. The whole thing was taking up a lot of my headspace that was far better used for more positive things! I was regularly thinking about it and puzzling over why he was not walking his talk. Why he was hot and cold. I wanted his friendship…but I was in a place in my life where I lived in integrity between what I said and what I did, and that was the type of energy I wanted to surround myself with.

In fact, the week before I saw him in the cafe, I'd spent a week in reflection to define my values. *What do I stand for? What do I believe? What is important to me?*

Among my values were integrity and vulnerability. And through those would come trust. I realised that what I wanted was not heaps of friends but, rather, a small number of friends—men in particular—that could hold space for who I am. That could hold all of me and how I was showing up in the world.

I wanted friends that I could go to in vulnerability when shit was happening in my life and be heard. Friends that would witness me and be there for me. Previously, I had thought that this guy was one of those friends... but for whatever reason, he wasn't able to hold that space and be there for me anymore.

Whatever the reason that things had changed between us, I needed to cut ties before it consumed all of my energy. I was using way too much of my emotional bandwidth on it, and I wanted to redirect my energy to where it was reciprocated.

I tried to make arrangements to see him and talk it out, but nothing came of it.

So, I wrote him a text.

"Look, I think you're a great guy. I really value your friendship. However, I'm super clear on who I want to have around me right now and who I'm calling into my sphere energetically. And I want to surround myself with people who are happy to meet me where I am at. I want friends who are willing and able to be there for me. And I've been noticing that for a long time now, you haven't shown up for me. I feel that I've put way too much energy into what's increasingly looking like a one-sided friendship."

It was basically a break-up message.

Before I sent the message, part of me wondered... was I just being a little sissy and complaining about nothing? I realised that no, this was my truth. And I had to operate in integrity with how I wanted to function in life.

I just needed to cut the cord with the situation emotionally, so I could focus on relationships that gave me strength instead of leaving me wondering about my value.

Now, this is a good guy I'm talking about. He wrote back saying he was sorry it had come across that way and apologised for not following through on his promises.

By that point, it was too late because I'd let go of the friendship. I wished him well and still really do.

The thing is, if he couldn't see what I was sharing with him because it's not something he recognised, then that's a clear indication that he just wasn't a fit for me values-wise. He wasn't in alignment with how I wanted the people around me to show up in my life and where I wanted to send my energy.

After I "broke up" with him, I immediately stopped having that sense of annoyance about the situation. All the negative emotions that had been building—they all disappeared. I could see him around town—Canggu is a small place—and feel well wishes towards him without needing to become matey or needing anything from him.

And the amazing thing was when I drew that line in the friendship, I almost instantly started attracting new friends that were more at my level of how I wanted to show up for others and be treated myself.

So now that we've come this far in Part 2 of this book (the head), you've learned how to take control back from your ego, to show up vulnerably and maintain healthy boundaries with others. But your work's not done yet. Because there's still a sneaky little habit that needs to be addressed before you can rest assured your foundations for fulfilled, heart-centred living are strong. And it involves your integrity.

■ ■ ■

WHAT IS INTEGRITY REALLY?

If you had asked me years ago whether I lived a life of integrity, I would have said yes. Absolutely yes. I'm an honest guy. I don't lie, cheat, or steal. I don't tell other people's secrets. That's all it takes, right?

It wasn't until I did my first workshop with the personal growth company, Landmark, that I realised I had it all wrong. I'd actually been living my life completely outside of my integrity…I just didn't know it because I didn't really understand the full depth of what integrity is.

The Cambridge Dictionary defines integrity as "the quality of being honest and having strong moral principles." But what does that actually mean? Is integrity something you have or something you do? Turns out it's both. To have integrity and to act with integrity are the same thing. You cannot do one without the other.

If what you're doing is against your personal values, you're acting outside of your integrity. For example, if one of my values is health, but I regularly buy my son a packet of sugary jelly snacks, I'm acting outside of my integrity. I'm not acting in accordance with how I truly want to show up in life.

Acting in accordance with your values means you *have* integrity. But having it is just one side of the coin. How do you *demonstrate* your integrity? How do you really live a life that is fully aligned energetically with what you want to put out into the world (and what you want to get back from it)?

It's this: you do what you say you're going to do when you say you're going to do it.

Seems simple enough, right?

But think about it…how often do you actually demonstrate integrity this way? How often do you actually follow through on the things you say?

I used to regularly make assurances to people and never follow through. I would promise things, and although I would usually get them done, it was never when I said I would.

"I'll pick up the kids at 5:30 in the evening," became, "Sorry, I'm running late," at 6:20.

"I'll have the info you need to you by the end of the week," became, "Sorry for the delay" the following Thursday.

"Let's do something special together this weekend," became, "We can maybe book a weekend away in June."

Make a quick mental list of the things you have justified not following through on in the past few weeks.

Oh, the traffic was terrible. I ran out of time to complete the document I promised a colleague. Whatever.

There's a reason for every time we fail to follow through on a commitment, and it's usually our own damn fault. We didn't account for traffic and leave early enough to leave a buffer in our travel time. We chatted with a colleague for twenty-five minutes about last night's reality TV show instead of working on that document we promised.

We can always justify why we don't complete or achieve a goal. But the reality is, most often, we don't actually allow ourselves the time and space to do it.

Showing up late was a shocker for me. I was always late. It wasn't even a conscious thing. I wasn't trying to disrespect anyone, but I guess I just would have preferred other people waiting for me than me waiting for other people. I was a busy man, right?

But what I didn't realise at the time was that I wasn't valuing other people's time. And how could I expect people to value my time if I wasn't first valuing *theirs* by showing up when we'd agreed to?

How could I expect them to trust me as a man of my word?

Because I wasn't. I thought I was a stand-up guy. And, in many ways, I was.

But I wasn't reliable. I wasn't *trustworthy*.

ARE YOU *REALLY* TRUSTWORTHY?

If you commit to doing things for others that you're not willing to actually follow through on, it's no surprise that the trust between you and others will erode. But have you thought about how you're damaging your relationship with *yourself*?

If you're not following through on the commitments you make to others, how can you ever expect to follow through on commitments to yourself? We're always more willing to let ourselves down first than we are to let others down, mostly because our drive to belong is so incredibly strong—we don't want to disappoint anyone. Even though we often do.

There have been many times in the past where I agreed to do something or made a commitment to do something without any intention of actually following through.

You can probably think of half a dozen off the top of your head right now, too...if you're honest with yourself, that is!

They're kind of little white lies that we tell to keep our social bonds nicely lubricated. So we don't have to upset anyone or let them down. So people like us.

"Let's catch up soon." No intention of actually doing it.

"I'll have a look at the document for you." Don't keep waiting because I'm not really going to.

"I'll meet you out the front of the venue." No, I won't. I'll be late, and you'll have to go in without me.

Every time we do that, we erode not just the relationship with the other person but with ourselves. We erode our integrity. And ultimately, we create a life that is not fulfilling us.

Back in Chapter 2, we spoke about making decisions. How we make hundreds—sometimes thousands—of micro-decisions every single day that form the path upon which our lives twist and turn.

In those moments where we're not following through on the commitments we make, those times where we're not living in a state of integrity ...that's a decision as well. And a decision to *not* do something is just as powerful as a decision to follow through.

Here's the kicker: our decisions create our reality. If we keep making the decision to not follow through on our commitment to go to the gym four times a week, as a consequence, we put on weight. As a consequence of that, we feel lethargic. As a consequence of that, we don't get out and enjoy many activities. Every decision has a knock-on effect, both short- and long-term.

"I haven't got enough money."

"My relationship is in the toilet."

"My friends don't ask me out anymore."

It's because the decisions you're making consciously and unconsciously are not honouring your boundaries and what's important to you. They're not in integrity with your real self. Every decision to skip the gym counts. Every decision to leave ten minutes later than you should to meet a friend counts.

When you let others down, sure, it sucks for them. But guess what? They can (and probably will) eventually get sick of it and walk away from you.

But the real tragedy is that when you let others down, you're actually letting yourself down. Those same excuses I told to other people were the same bullshit excuses I was using on myself.

"Oh, well, looks like you didn't hit that goal this month, Barry. Next month will be different."

What do you think happens to your own trust in yourself when you let yourself down over and over again? Here's what happens: it becomes okay to let yourself down. It becomes okay for you to bullshit yourself. It becomes okay to live in a fantasy world where you're not really responsible for your results, and you're okay with not achieving anything.

And that's no way to live!

You can waste years, *decades* of your life in this self-bullshit cycle. Many people have! Some live their entire lives this way. It's always someone or something else's fault. But you know what? By living this way, you're just abdicating responsibility for your own life. What a fucking waste!

How you do one thing is how you do everything. It's impossible to live a life where you're letting others down without first letting yourself down, and vice versa.

Think about it now: how many things have you flaked on lately?

And how did that make you feel about yourself? Pretty crappy, right? So why are you doing that to yourself?

The more you bullshit yourself and live outside your integrity, the more it will bite you in the ass one day when you realise that the reality you've created is far from the one you had intended.

If you're noticing some areas of your own life where you're out of alignment between what you say and what you do…

It's time to take some responsibility for yourself, don't you think?

TAKING PERSONAL RESPONSIBILITY

You can't call in the life you desire if you're not in alignment with your personal integrity. Living in integrity has to be a fundamental foundation of who we are. We all have a personal responsibility to call ourselves out on the areas where we feel we are not operating in a state of integrity with our values and how we want to show up in this world.

Think about the last time you complained about something. Maybe you were upset about a colleague at work. Maybe you were pissed at something your partner did. Or maybe you felt a friend let you down.

Did you have a conversation about it with them? Or did you bitch about it to everyone except them? In doing that, were you operating in a state of integrity? Probably not. So you're letting yourself down, and you're letting them down, too. Because they have no awareness of the impact they're having on you, so they're just going to keep doing what they're doing. All the while, you're building all this resentment and digging a deeper hole. All because you haven't held a space of valuing your boundaries and having a conversation to bring things back into integrity.

It's nobody else's responsibility to make us happy or make us experience anything in life. And yet, there are so many people stuck in relationships where they believe it's their role to make the other person happy. Or they're letting people walk all over them at work because they don't want to rock the boat and have a conversation around boundaries.

These conversations don't have to be abrasive or awful. As demonstrated in my Tantra workshop with Connor, you can say no with love. You can communicate your boundaries in a way that gives the other person every opportunity to step into a space of acceptance and love if they choose. Or they can feed their ego. It's up to them and totally out of your control.

I think so often we place responsibility on the government, society, our friends, our family, or our partners to make us feel fulfilled or happy. We lack that self-ownership because we're afraid of what others might think. But when you take personal responsibility for living your life in a state of integrity, you lead others to do the same.

There will always be a minority of people that pull you down. They will try to use what you share against you. Or they can choose to let what you're sharing bring you to a space where you're in better alignment with each other.

But you have a responsibility to do the work within you. You have a responsibility when something happens that isn't the outcome you wanted, to reflect on the part you played in getting that outcome.

Sure, it might be helpful to understand the part someone else played. But it's not your responsibility to make the other person act a certain way. You can educate them. You can use healing conversations to try to come to a place of mutual agreement or understanding. You can choose to be vulnerable and express how you're feeling. But you can't force someone else to react a certain way. You can only be responsible for your own actions and reactions.

But you cannot abdicate responsibility for your lack of integrity and lack of a fulfilling life. You *must* do something about it. Nobody else can do it for you. It's *your* life.

The good news is it's entirely possible to heal the distrust you've created with others and with yourself and start building stronger relationships both outside and in.

It starts with a healing conversation.

HOW TO CREATE CHANGE THAT STICKS

If this chapter is feeling like one big slap on the wrist, it's not.

We're human. We stuff-up. It happens.

What really matters is what we do *after* we realise we've done the wrong thing and let someone (and ourselves) down.

On the whole, the human race rarely does this part right.

Because when we stuff-up, our ego flies into action. Defend, defend, defend! The ego will also fight hard to justify our actions (or lack of them), throwing accusations and blame everywhere but on you. Even though deep down we know that we put ourselves in the situation to not deliver the goods in the first place.

And what did we learn back in Chapter 5? When the ego is in the driver's seat, we cannot go anywhere new. The ego will drive us around and around, repeating the same patterns in a desperate attempt to keep us safe from the low-vibe emotions we are feeling (blame, shame, guilt) because even though it's a shitty pattern, it's *survivable*.

As a consequence of this, our pattern of behaviour never changes. We never learn.

So what's the way out? How do we break free of this ego-fuelled road trip to nowhere?

The answer is in this four-step process: apologise, acknowledge, recognise, amend.

What that means is that if for some reason something happens where you can't fulfil your obligation, you need to restore your integrity—both with the other person and with yourself.

- Apologise: express that you're sorry for what's happened,
- Acknowledge: take ownership around what you did wrong,
- Recognise: show that you understand the effect your actions have had on others, and
- Amend: commit to acting differently next time, so it doesn't happen again.

Here's how to have a healing conversation when you're acting outside of your personal integrity:

"I'm sorry for not fulfilling my commitment to pick the kids up on time. I actually didn't leave enough time and space for the extra traffic at this time of day. The impact of this is that I've wasted your time, I've let you down, and I've let myself down. What I plan to do in the future is leave an additional ten minutes early so that even if the traffic is heavy, I'll still be there on time."

What would you rather hear—the above, or, "Sorry for being late again. The traffic sucks."

Having a healing conversation not only helps mend the crack in the relationship with the person you've just annoyed or hurt, it also creates a feedback loop for yourself.

Think about this—in business, you have systems. The results of each system are the logical conclusion of all the parts within it. But systems rarely ever run smoothly at first. There's always a stuff-up or a complaint, or a problem with getting the results you want.

So, we build feedback loops into our systems to refine them. We ask: did the system work? If not, what needs to be changed? Then we incorporate your conclusions into the system and run it again. And again. Until it runs just how we want it to.

Humans run on systems, too, even though we don't often realise it!

We run systems for nearly everything we regularly do. Making a cup of coffee. Doing the washing. Working out at the gym. We follow the same set of steps to reach our goal. And when the goal isn't what we wanted (a cup of sludge, powdery clothes, or abs that just won't pop), we tweak the steps within our system to try and get a better outcome.

The healing conversation is also a feedback loop for the system you're running. You got a result that was the logical conclusion of all the things you did beforehand. You didn't leave on time, and therefore you were late. That wasn't the result that you wanted, so you declare what you are going to do differently next time. You declare it both to the other person, and most importantly, to yourself.

Then you implement it. You create that change. That's how your future can be different from your past. It's important to note here that's how you can change *any* system that you're currently running where you're unhappy with the results.

Don't like something that's happening in your life?

Somewhere along the line, your patterns of behaviour, whether consciously or unconsciously, created the right environment for it to happen.

Remember how the brain loves to operate on patterns?

What would it be like if you started to only say yes to the things you actually plan on fulfilling and said no to the things that are not in alignment with you?

Saying yes only to things you will actually do is kind of like reverse-engineering your own success in keeping your promises, which then creates a new pattern of keeping your promises. And the new cycle keeps running, getting stronger and stronger until it happens automatically. You simply don't let yourself—or anyone else—down. Because you only say yes to what's in integrity with your real self.

Doing this is exactly how I changed my old pattern of flaking out to the one I'm in now, where I live in integrity and follow through on everything I commit to. But even more than that, once I started keeping my commitments to myself and reprogramming my being this way, I've actually become a powerhouse of goal achievement. This has helped me not just personally but in my business as well.

What would it feel like to say you're going to do something and know with every fibre of your being that you were going to achieve that goal? Whether it's picking the kids up on time or hitting my biggest sales target for the month, the intention behind it is the same. And the result is the same—I hit that damn goal no matter what. Things just align for me to do it.

That's what living in a state of integrity does for you. When I set a goal, there's no question I will achieve it. Because I have conditioned my brain, body, and spirit to know I follow through on what I say.

Change the pattern, change your life.

RESTORING YOUR INTEGRITY

A while ago, I noticed that I was in the pattern of complaining a lot. I was in victim mode, having the same conversations and feeling completely overwhelmed. I noticed that I was kind of spinning my wheels in life and not really moving forward.

So, I did this simple exercise that's similar to the one you did in the last chapter, where you worked out your boundaries. I got a piece of paper and drew a line straight down the middle. On one side, I marked "integrity," and on the other, "out of integrity."

Then I listed all the areas in my life where I thought I was living in a state of integrity with my values or out of integrity.

I covered exercise, finances, relationships, business, love, health— everything I could think of. I got into detail. My snacking on sugary treats. The time I was spending with my partner. My use of alcohol. What time I was going to bed.

Even when I felt I'd hit a brick wall and there was nothing more to write, I kept sitting with it because there was always more that I just wasn't willing to face yet.

Eventually, I ended up with a long list in front of me. I thought, *Wow, I'm doing some things really well. Pat myself on the back for those.*

But I also realised, *Fuck, there's a lot of things I'm doing that just don't align with my values. They don't reflect the way I want to show up in this world. And that's letting me down, and it's letting the people around me down, too, because if I'm not showing up as my best self for me, I'm not doing it for them either.*

Then I started to create an action plan to bring the things in my life that were out of alignment back into a state of integrity.

I want you to do the same.

Your action plan might look like changing some patterns of behaviour, building feedback loops, and having healing conversations. You might want to ring someone up and say, "Hey, I really want to acknowledge that I haven't been showing up for you lately. I've been cancelling appointments, which wastes your time and lets you down. This is what you can count on me for in the future."

Making the verbal declaration to someone else is important because, as I mentioned earlier, we are far more comfortable with letting ourselves down than others. Using a declaration makes you accountable to someone other than yourself.

Think about it. It's one thing to say, "I'm going to start eating better." There's no guts behind it. No skin in the game. No real force behind the decision. But by bringing the words into consciousness and bringing other people around your intention, you're committing to actually doing it.

Let's get metaphysical for a minute.

Our words create our reality. Our intentions create our reality. Our energy attracts other energy. So it's important to be careful what we put out there.

Everything in life is made up of atoms, photons, quarks, and other teeny tiny subatomic particles. Humans, plants, even waves in the sea are made up of many of the same building blocks. These tiny particles are electrically charged. They vibrate, squiggle, and wiggle. In doing this, they attract and repel other types of teeny particles. Like the plus and minus ends of a battery, all energy attracts (or repels) other energy.

That's the nature of life itself. Everything has to move. Everything has to attract and repel other things to do everything in life: create new skin, move our legs, grow our bones...everything comes down to how we use and transmit energy.

So, it stands to reason, then, that given this electrical force running within everything, those energies have relationships with each other, and the energy we project influences what we get back.

That's why we have to be careful of what we consciously put out there. If we moan and groan and complain...we attract more opportunities to do more of the same. Because you always get back what you put out. The universe says yes. It says, "Oh, this human is enjoying this story; look at how much attention they're giving it. Let's give them more of what they're focusing on."

But when we draw a line in the sand and say, "No, this isn't working for me," and we call out what we want, putting our intentional energy behind it, we attract what we're calling for.

"My boss is a pain in the arse," you might complain. The more you do it, the more the energy you're putting out tells the universe that's what you're focusing on. So the universe says yes. Let's give them more experiences like that because that's what they're calling in. That's where their vibrational frequency is sitting. That's the universal radio station they're tuned into— Bitch and Moan FM.

When we start asserting our boundaries, living by our values, and keeping in a state of integrity, things start to show up that are in alignment with that energetic track. Think of it as having tuned in to a new radio station. When you're living in congruence with your values, you're officially on YouFM. The signal is clear.

When you're not living in a state of integrity with who you are and what you value, the signal is scrambled, confused. And so are you.

Where our focus goes, our energy flows and our results show.

The words you speak, and your energetic intentions behind them, are important for helping you maintain your state of integrity (or get back into it if you've lost your way).

The more you say what you mean and mean what you say, the more you'll begin to manifest the types of opportunities, people, and experiences that are aligned with who you are and where you want to go.

I can think of so many examples of how I'm manifesting the things I ask for these days.

About a week before writing this chapter, I met up with the owner of an outsourcing business I used way back when I first started The Game

Changers. We hung out, and I gave him lots of advice for free because it's in alignment with my values to do so.

When I got home, I told my partner Kate how much of a great complementary fit his business would be with a particular business that I've recently built. His business had a lot of things set up that mine doesn't, and mine has things set up that his doesn't. It felt like we'd be a great fit and could really bring value to the other.

What do you think happened? I got a call from him soon after where he wanted to explore the idea of merging.

I wonder, did I even have the idea, or was I picking up his idea? All I know is that I put it out there, and bang! It manifested.

Do you remember back in Chapter 7 when I told you about how I wanted to get out of a company, and the next day the CEO rang me saying one of their sales reps wanted to buy my shares?

The amount of stuff I'm manifesting is getting kind of freaky, in the most wonderful way.

I honestly believe that the more we move into a space of integrity, the more we can manifest the things we ask for. Because our communication with the True Source, and the self, is totally clear.

So, it's time to begin communicating more clearly. Get clear on where you're operating within or outside of integrity. Where do you need to put some new boundaries? Where do you need to have some healing conversations? Which patterns do you commit to change?

This is where the rubber really hits the road. You're putting up the brickwork on the new internal house you're building within yourself. The House of You.

You deserve everything you get. One way or another...

So how will you get clear about what you're asking for?

CHAPTER 11

AUTHENTICITY

"Today you are You, that is truer than true.
There is no one alive who is Youer than You."

—*Dr. Seuss*

"I FEEL KINDA NERVOUS ABOUT SHARING THIS WITH YOU..."

My partner and I had just ridden my motorbike up to Ubud from our home in Canggu, Bali, for a craniosacral therapy session we had booked for the next day. (If we ever meet in person, ask me about it. It's incredible.)

After the long commute, we were winding down, lying in bed in our villa, a gorgeous little dwelling with an infinity pool that overlooked the luscious green jungle beyond. We were face-to-face within the cool, crisp white linen sheets, close and intimate.

A fan stirred up a faint breeze above our heads, moving the thin mosquito cloth that surrounded the bed. We gazed at each other, casually caressing each other's skin, exhausted but deliciously relaxed.

Something had been on my mind for a while, and I knew that Kate would give me the space I needed to speak my truth.

"I've noticed this fear inside of me around proposing to you," I said.

Her eyes widened slightly as I said this, but she didn't react. She waited for me to go on.

"It's not that I don't want to marry you, quite the opposite," I assured her. "I can't imagine finding a more ideal partner than you. But it's like I'm afraid of what could happen in the future. I'm afraid that you could leave me, or cheat on me, or you could, I don't know, *die*... I'm afraid of all these things that haven't happened."

I'd been thinking about proposing to Kate a lot. We'd discussed marriage, kids, everything that partners should get straight on before they make that sort of commitment. We knew where we stood—a great match, aligned on every level.

So, at first, I was reluctant to share my fear around proposing. It was such a deep, vulnerable fear, and I didn't want to appear as weak. And I didn't want to upset her, for her to take what I was sharing the wrong way. A movie reel of blow-ups from past relationships ran through my head...was I about to cause another one?

But in our relationship, we had been showing up for each other in the spirit of what you're learning about in this book: we shared our vulnerabilities. We communicated and protected our boundaries. We stayed within our personal integrity.

All that added up to us showing up as authentically ourselves. No hiding. No presenting a distorted version of our true nature. No bullshit.

Being my authentic self hadn't led me wrong so far, so I shared openly.

And Kate met me at my level.

Instead of reacting by letting her own fears and insecurities take over, she responded with a sense of curiosity and acceptance. She held space for me to explore my mess and discover where it was coming from and what it meant.

"Look," she began, "I can't promise you that we'll always be together. How can I possibly know that? How can *anyone* really know that?"

I've gotta admit, that was hard to hear at first. But as hard as it was, it was the truth. It was authentic. It wasn't the bullshit fairy floss promise that couples make when they're trying to make each other feel good. You know, the type of promises that end up with your ex smashing up your car with a baseball bat while screaming, "You told me you'd love me forever!"

Kate continued, "But what I *can* promise you is that I'm going to keep showing up for you. I'm going to keep being there for you and working with you for our relationship."

That's the *truth*. That's the absolute best promise any partner can make.

It's funny because after she said that, my fear disappeared. It had no power over me anymore. I had shown up authentically and told her my truth. She had done the same for me. And when the fear was brought to light, it was resolved, and not only that, the whole experience allowed me to love her even more!

I've spent so long coaching people around busting their beliefs and biases, and one of the most profound things I've learned is that when you actually just own your unresourceful traits, your fears, or undesirable behaviours, either they're resolved, or you find a more resourceful way to express them.

Living an authentic life is about allowing yourself to be fully expressed. But if you ignore the parts of yourself that you are afraid to show…they just get louder. The more you push them away, the more they try to knock your door down. But if you bring them to the light, they no longer have a hold on you.

It's like trying to ignore an infection. If you hurt yourself and ignore it, sooner or later, that infection is going to knock you onto your ass when it gets so bad you have to be hospitalised. It's the same thing with our emotions. They're there for a reason. They *need* to be processed.

Sure, they don't all need to be shared with everyone you know. Cheryl, the checkout chick, doesn't give a damn that you're feeling down today.

But emotions need to be expressed in some form, whether written down or shared with a friend, family member, or partner.

The more we can express ourselves truthfully, the more we can really move into ownership of our authenticity and the more we live our lives as *who we really are* instead of who we're pretending to be.

THE HONEY(MOON) TRAP

People talk about the "honeymoon phase" in relationships. They say it lasts about three to six months. "Oh, you're in your honeymoon phase," they'll say. "Enjoy it while it lasts!"

The reason that there is a honeymoon phase at all (and especially why it ends) is that people show up as an inauthentic version of themselves from day one.

Have you ever tried to present an inauthentically polished version of yourself just to be accepted? From a partner, an HR manager, friends, whoever? Just for their approval?

Maybe you've even gone to the extent of pretending to like things you don't actually like, just to try and bond with the other person.

What's the fucking point?

Nobody can keep up a false facade forever. And besides, who would even want to? Sooner or later, you'll get comfortable. Or tired. Or both. Then your real traits start to slip in. The outdoorsy adventure-guy image you projected in the beginning ends up as a set of brand-new runners gathering dust by the door and a Netflix "previously watched" list a mile long.

Your partner starts thinking, *What the hell? He said he loved to hike every weekend. Now I can't peel him off the couch.* Then their needs are not being met anymore, and the cracks begin to get wider and wider until you both carry so much resentment towards each other for not being who you thought they were…and the kicker is that you set the relationship up to fail by setting those unrealistic expectations in the first place.

But if you show up as your authentic self from the get-go, you're going to quickly find out who is a good match for you and who is not. And I'd rather get to the right person quickly rather than waste time and energy trying to create a false facade with someone who isn't actually right for me. I don't want to wait five years before realising that my partner cannot actually handle who I am.

In the past, I didn't show up authentically because I was hiding…and within three to six months, the wheels started falling off, and the honeymoon period started to wane!

Maybe you've had a similar experience?

It's the same in business, friendships, and basically every human interaction. We present the version of ourselves that we think others want to see in job interviews. But who would want to work in a job they're not going to enjoy because it's not a good match?

Or we pretend we're just like other people in our friendship circle because we need to be liked and accepted. But we feel lonely as hell because the people we're surrounding ourselves with aren't actually on our level.

Our need to belong is a strong driving force…but we don't belong just everywhere and anywhere. Nor do we need to.

Think about this: the more space you give in your life for the things that aren't the right fit for you, the less space you have for the things that will actually nourish and fulfil you.

The more I show up as authentically me, which includes sharing my insecurities, weaknesses, fears and frustrations, the better my life becomes. My business runs better. People show up in my life who are better suited to the level I want to play at. I attract opportunities aligned with my goals.

When I live in a state of expression of who I truly am, the universe puts the experiences and people in front of me that I need.

Try it, and you'll see.

AUTHENTICITY AND INTEGRITY

Authenticity and integrity are not quite the same things. Yes, they are close. Entwined even. But there's a slight difference.

Authenticity is when we're showing up as our truest self. If I'm being authentic, I'm showing up as all of me. There's no part of me consciously trying to be anybody other than who I am. I'm expressing my desires, my boundaries, what makes me tick…it's all there.

I'm an open book. No mirrors, facades, or masks. Authenticity is a state of *being*.

Integrity, however, is a space of *doing*. It's when we say we're going to do something, and we follow through on it. Integrity is a mechanism for trust, for both the big things (*can I trust that you will keep your marriage vows?*) to the little things (*can I trust that you'll pick up what I asked you to from the store?*) and all the things in between.

Can I trust that you're going to do what you say?

So, integrity is about standards and the choice to uphold them, while authenticity is about one's distinct nature and the full embodiment of it.

And the more you show up in a space of personal integrity, the more you live an authentic life.

WHO DO YOU THINK YOU ARE?

If you're going to start living authentically, first, you need to understand who you really are. And in my ten years of coaching people from all walks of life, I can tell you that not many people have actually taken the time to sit and figure that out.

Instead, they let the ego take the reins and drive their direction through life, collecting experiences, people, and material things that make them feel good. But eventually, it comes crashing down when they reach forty or fifty and realise that no matter how much stuff they fill themselves up with, they still feel hollow.

That's why it's so important to make sure that you stay aligned with your heart and do some internal work to figure out what's really true about you and what's a construction that you've unconsciously created to keep you safe.

A lot of this is done in your heart-based meditations. The more you connect to your heart, the more truths about yourself will bubble up to the surface.

There are tools that can help you do that, too, like DiSC profiling.

I remember going to a workshop years ago and learning about it. DiSC is a personal assessment tool that measures different aspects of your personality. The DiSC assessment examines how a person ranks in the four areas of behaviour: Dominance, Influence, Steadiness, and Conscientiousness (Wiley 2013).

- Dominance: direct, results-oriented, decisive, competitive, problem solver
- Influence: charming, enthusiastic, optimistic, persuasive, inspiring
- Steadiness: understanding, team player, patient, stable, sincere
- Conscientious: analytical, diplomatic, precise, compliant, objective

We all have these traits within us, but everyone's makeup is different. Understanding your profile and your partner's profile can help you figure out how to work together better.

For example, you may score highly in Dominance and Influence while your partner ranks in Steadiness. So, you might get frustrated that they need more time to consider decisions than you do. But when you understand that it's part of their personality profile, you're more likely to give them the time they need (and avoid a lot of conflict!).

We use DiSC profiles for candidates at another one of my companies, Alchemy Outsourcing, too, so we can match the right virtual assistant with the right type of job. There's no point matching a person who has high Influence energy in a data entry job because they'll go crazy without interaction with people. But a high C would thrive in that kind of role.

Anyway, it's a terrific learning tool on both a personal or professional level, and I recommend that you take one for yourself.

When you do your DiSC profile, you'll learn that you have both a natural and adaptive profile. When I first did mine, I remember my natural profile was a high D S, where my adaptive profile was S C. Why were they so different? Why was the way I would adapt my natural behaviour so different to my true nature?

I had a realisation—it was because of my upbringing. My father was a strong D. Very outcome-focused, always at work, trying his hardest to provide for the family when I was growing up. But my filter, or my perception of him, was that he wasn't there for me as a father when I was little.

My dad grew up with an absent father himself, and his own parents had struggled with money during his childhood. So, he was working hard to provide an income and security and safety for us because he wanted to give us a different experience than he had during his own upbringing.

But I wanted a dad who would pick me up and take me to sports practice. I wanted someone who would be there when I got home from school to hang out with me. That was my perception of a father-son relationship.

So, his authentic representation of who he was was different from my perception of who he was. And I remember going through this DiSC process and realising, *Fuck, this is why I've been so worn out my whole life. Because I've spent so much of my energy trying to be somebody else.*

I was avoiding being authentically my true nature because I didn't want to be like my dad. As a consequence, I tried to avoid showing up in my own life, with my own family, in the same way he had shown up for me.

So, I went into business thinking, "I'm going to work my ass off now, so when I eventually have a family and kids, I can be there for them, unlike my father was for me." I shaped my whole life around trying to be unlike my father because my perception was that what he did wasn't nourishing. It didn't serve me. It didn't give me what I wanted.

The irony is that I ended up just like him, working all of the time building my first multimillion-dollar business to the point that it eventually all fell apart, and I went bankrupt.

Once I had this realisation after discovering my DiSC profile, it led me down the path of a six- or seven-year journey of slowly learning to own my traits. Of owning my characteristics, owning who I was.

I didn't have to be like my father; I still had a choice. I could *own* being the type of personality that was outcome-focused, direct, a fast mover... and still be there for my kids, partner, and loved ones.

His blueprint didn't have to be my blueprint. But I had categorised everything I was under the one umbrella. And I was working like hell to avoid it—and trying to avoid being who I really was energetically sucked the life out of me.

If you feel the same way, you're not alone.

SHINING A LIGHT ON YOUR TRUE NATURE

Most people have a perception of who they wish to be. We try to create values not by eliciting things that are the most valuable to us but around what we aspire to be. And we work like hell to try and be that aspect of ourselves, that version that is approved.

But that's not authentic. It's not the whole thing. It's not who we really are. So we try to suppress the rage and the anger that comes up, the hurt of the sadness. So often, I see people in relationships, men especially, suppressing what they really feel because they're worried that their partner cannot hold the space for them or that their partner will leave them.

And what happens is they suppress these feelings for so long until their partner just asks them to take out the trash, and they blow up and absolutely rip into them.

It's not actually about the trash. It's about the fact that they've suppressed all these things for weeks, a month, or even years. They have not expressed their true, authentic nature, and it eventually has to come out. The dam breaks. What we suppress gets expressed.

It's happening all the time in nature. Think about a volcano. Think about the way the earth works. Pressure builds, and we have to release that pressure.

In previous relationships, I used to get angry pretty much every week. Because I was not in an environment where I felt safe to express my true, authentic self. I was not nurtured to show up as authentically me.

So pressure built and built and would regularly result in a blow-up, often over something simple or small. Because I was trying to hide who I really was. I was afraid of who I really was. I was afraid that if I expressed my true self, I wouldn't be loved.

But the funny thing is that the more I tried to avoid all those parts of myself, the more they kept rising to the surface and the more they had control over me. The moment I started to give those parts a voice and movement, they no longer had control over me. I now control them.

Think about someone at school that had a secret over you. Maybe in primary school, you set the class turtle free. Maybe you put sand down Johnny's underwear. I don't know what you got up to back then. Or maybe you had a secret in high school that someone had over you. Hidden crushes, petty crime (been there, teenagers can certainly get up to some mischief!).

If you'd just owned it and expressed it, all that pressure would have diffused. Your secret would no longer have had any power over you. Sure, you may have had some explaining to do... but surely that's better than the sickening feeling of all that pressure? All that *hiding*?

Are you getting an idea of the true cost of not living authentically? Of spending your life in the shadows? A life spent in a hole deep within yourself, not getting any nourishment or sunlight?

What happens to a plant if you hide it in a cupboard? It withers and dies. Well, we're all going to die; that can't be changed. But we *can* choose to give ourselves the nourishment we need to thrive in life... or spend our precious time on this planet simply letting ourselves slowly rot.

Which do you choose?

. . .

At this point in my life, living authentically as *me*, I feel completely free and liberated. There's nothing anyone can say or do that can hold power over me. Because no matter what comes up inside of me, I know that I'm surrounded by people who hold the space for me to express it.

Before, I was constantly living in fear that something I said or did would be taken the wrong way and create conflict. I hid myself and lived life in the shadows. And I was constantly creating all these stories and situations to keep me safe (that would blow up in my face because I was operating outside of my integrity).

Nowadays, I'm learning to love all aspects of me and learning that all my fears, all my insecurities... they're all just part of the little boy deep inside that's trying to keep me safe.

I can recognise that the little boy is not the same as the thirty-five-year-old man sitting here typing these words. But by not giving myself permission to be expressed, that little boy stays trapped inside of me, stuck in fear.

If you're waiting for permission to be you, this is it. I'm giving you permission right now.

Bring your authentic self into the light.

You deserve to live as who you truly are. To feel full. To feel free. To feel liberated. To feel love inside and around you.

We all do.

DEALING WITH YOUR UGLY BITS

Many years ago, when I was in a relationship with the mother of my children, I used to end up in a rage within ten minutes of coming home. As soon as I walked into the environment, I'd feel pressured and pissed off, and the rage grew. I wondered at the time what the fuck was wrong with me. Why did I behave in such a way?

It wasn't until many years later that I read *Keys to the Kingdom* by Alison Armstrong that it clicked into place for me. In the book, Armstrong writes about the stages of development in men and explores the ways men are different from women.

One of the things shared was that while women, in their feminine energy, can flow from one activity to the next seamlessly, men need a bit of transition time. It talks about how if a woman does not give men that transition time to when they come home, it creates tension in him and distance between the two of them. But if they allow him some space straight after they get home, he will transition to where he's fully open to receive you and to be there and support you as a woman.

This was a little Eureka moment for me. So that's why I always felt pressured and angry when I got home from work—I had no transition time to just chill and adjust! It was something I thought was wrong with me. Something I tried to run away from, something to hide.

But it always bubbled up to the surface.

I remember one day coming home, hopping out of my ute and into the scorching Perth heat. I noticed that the grass was turning yellow on either side of the light pink pavers that led me to the front door of the house I shared with my partner and kids.

Great, I thought. *The sprinkler system is busted.* It was another thing to add to the list of one hundred things I needed to do around the house. And that was on top of the five hundred things I needed to do in my business.

As I opened the wire door, I noticed that one of the hinges had come loose. Another thing. Then I entered the house, and the kids came barrelling at me, yelling and pushing and generally just being young kids.

My partner, Trin, yelled at me from up the hallway, "They're yours now! It's your turn."

Suddenly, it all became too much, and I just blew up.

I felt like nobody had any idea of all the pressures I was under and the weight of the responsibility of running my business on top of everything I needed to do in the household, as well as trying to be a good father to these beautiful kids that had an unrelenting need for my attention.

A part of me knew that Trin was having a similar experience, having just been with the kids all day and probably wanting to do some things for herself, just like I was.

Looking back now, if I'd just accepted that I needed some time before being hit with all the energies and demands of my partner and kids, I probably could have communicated it to my partner then.

I could have said, "Hey, Trin, I'm not sure why, but I've got this pattern of getting overwhelmed and angry when I get home. I realise it's detrimental to all of us, and I want to change it. Could you please give me fifteen minutes of space when I get home? I know you've got things to tell me and things you need me to do, and I am committed to being there for you, but I just need this time."

Expressing your needs that way is a lot better than snapping, "Will you just leave me the fuck alone for a minute?" And it's going to get a much more productive response!

My point is that even the things you're ashamed of, scared of, and not wanting to accept…there is a reason it's all there. Good or bad, wrong or right doesn't matter. Those labels are just the ego trying to keep you in its control.

What would happen if you accepted the things about yourself that you find ugly?

If instead of trying to hide or repress, you decided to approach these things with curiosity instead? To ask yourself what are the driving forces behind your behaviour, and how can you create some healthy boundaries and express your needs to others?

STEPPING UP AND STEPPING OUT

By now in the book, we've talked about being vulnerable. About making better decisions and expressing healthy boundaries. About values and staying in integrity. When you start putting all this learning into action, you will be able to show up authentically.

It's time for the rubber to hit the road.

It's time to start living in the space of authenticity.

All this talk of living authentically may seem kind of woo-woo or "soft," but living authentically is actually the gutsiest, bravest, most badass thing you can do. Most people are shit scared of showing who they really are.

I promise you, people won't run screaming when they see your true self (and if they do, they weren't the right person for you anyway).

Sure, sometimes it will create conflict when the people around you might not understand or accept the way you're showing up in life now. They'll say you've changed (when you've actually just become more of yourself), and they might fight to maintain the old status quo (because it was comfortable for them).

But that's easy to navigate when you know how. And you'll learn how to have healthy conflict in the next chapter.

And sure, it might turn out that your job, your partner, your friends...they all might not be ultimately right for you. You've got to be ready to accept that once you start showing up authentically, some might stay, and some might go.

About the ones that go: you might be afraid to be without them right now. But would you rather live your life hiding yourself and staying small or have the most amazing experiences with partners, friends, and pursuits that light you up?

So often, we attract people in our lives based on the inauthentic vibration we're expressing to the world. The energy we project is given back to us, remember?

With that in mind, how can we ever attract our tribe if we're not first showing up as all of who we are? Given what we attract in is what we put out there, if what we're putting out there is an inauthentic version of us because we're afraid or fearful of being rejected or whatever, we're not fully owning who we are. Then we're going to attract others that are in the same space.

Like attracts like.

But if we're being authentic, we're going to attract authentic relationships. We're going to attract people who can hold the space for us to be all of who we are. We're going to attract people who fuel us to thrive and live our very best lives.

I know this because I've done it. And you can, too.

If you're recognising that you're on the wrong track with your career or business, your loved ones, your friends, it's time to break the cycle. All of the things you've learned so far in this book all add upon each other to help you move towards your authentic life as the Real You.

Being vulnerable. Creating boundaries. Saying no and expressing your needs. Embracing all of who you are.

I guess the question is...are you ready to accept and love yourself for who you are? And to have the faith in yourself that whatever happens, it's what you need to grow to where you need to be?

If you're not quite there yet, that's okay. Take one step at a time to move closer to that space.

And for what it's worth, I accept you. For all your "ugly" bits, too. All your broken bits. All the bits you're trying to hide. I'm sending love your way.

CHAPTER 12

HEALTHY CONFLICT

**"What we've got here is failure
to communicate."**

—The Captain, Cool Hand Luke

"I HATE YOU, DAD. *I HATE YOU*!"

Tears streamed down my son's face as he raged at me.

I stood there, aching to take his trembling little body in my arms and hold him tight. But I didn't dare. His anger was all-consuming. And it was totally justified.

Two minutes earlier, we had been happily playing in the pool at my villa in Bali. The sun was shining, Banyan tree branches were swaying in a gentle breeze, and life was full of big smiles and the cackling laughter of my two sons as they splashed around.

Then I made a thoroughly unwise decision.

I picked up my son, Leo, outside of the pool in a big bear hug and went to throw him in. But Leo struggled at the last minute, and I fudged it. He flipped into the pool, coming frighteningly close to hitting his head on the edge of the pool as he went. Thank goodness he didn't get hurt at all. But what an awful shock.

Obviously, I instantly regretted what I'd done and was thankful that my momentary brain fade didn't cost us more dearly.

Leo was understandably shocked and upset. As soon as his head popped up in the water, he started screaming at me. He knew how close he'd come to serious injury, and he was furious. My other son stopped splashing around and stood still in the pool, watching the scenario play out with deep concern for his brother.

The tears ran down Leo's face as his emotions peaked. He climbed out of the pool and began to storm off while cursing at me, his feet making wet thumping noises on the hard concrete as he marched away.

"You could've killed me! I hate you!" he yelled.

Naturally, I stood there and copped it. All of his anger. Because I deserved it! I'd made a split-second, stupid decision, and it impacted both of us. It was on me. And Leo had every right to express his feelings about it.

But in that moment, I also chose to demonstrate a very important lesson.

You see, Leo is highly emotional, just like I was when I was a kid. I've noticed that the moment he feels he's done the wrong thing, he jumps into either justification of why he's done it or into aggression, anger, and denial. Or he jumps into blame, pointing the finger at somebody else. His ego basically uses all the tricks in its toolbox to save him from the pain of feeling like he's done something wrong.

From knowing how he's grown up and what he's been through so far in his short life, I know that he feels that if he does the wrong thing, then love will be taken away. Or his mum or I will love him less. Deep down, he fears he won't belong. That he won't be accepted in our family tribe.

So, he tries to avoid being the one that's in the wrong. When I first saw this in him, I remembered the same thing in myself looking back throughout my *own* history.

When I was younger, I was so quick to jump into rage and aggression when I thought I'd done the wrong thing. Denial, blame, justification, anger. All of it. Because I couldn't stand the guilt and shame of being the one at fault.

I saw the incident in the pool as a great opportunity to teach my son how to take responsibility at times where we do the wrong thing. How to not get stuck in the trap of finger-pointing and deflecting blame.

Essentially, how to deal with fucking up in a healthier way.

"You're right," I called after Leo. "I was careless. It was stupid of me. It didn't turn out how I intended, and I could've seriously hurt you."

Leo stopped and looked back at me with tears still streaming down his face.

"I'm sorry," I said earnestly. "I take full responsibility. And it won't happen again."

Leo started yelling at me again in reply. His body was still trembling from the shock of it all. I stood there and let him yell, holding the space for him to express all the fear that came up in him as a result of my actions. I allowed him to express all of his emotions without shutting him down.

Because I created those emotions in him! I had created this turmoil in my child. Who the hell was I to tell him to shut it down?

When he was done, when he was all yelled out and had begun to process the shock of the near-miss and my response to it, it was time to complete his lesson.

"One thing I want to share with you, Leo. Did you notice how I took responsibility for that?" I asked as we shared a healing cuddle. "That was my fault. I owned it. Did you notice that I didn't blame you? That I didn't justify my actions? I just owned it."

I could see that Leo was getting it. I didn't take responsibility simply to teach him a lesson—I took responsibility because it was my fucking fault! But that didn't make me a bad person unworthy of love. It just meant that I was a person who had done a stupid thing and made amends for it in a space of honesty and love.

Behaving this way in all my relationships has a huge impact and power in my life. And it will for my boys, too, as they grow up knowing and using the tools I give them for healthy conflict resolution and healing, both with others and within themselves.

How often do you take responsibility when you fuck up?

How often do you hide?

. . .

REVISING OUTDATED PROGRAMS

Every day, I see so many people living in a realm of denial, blame, or justification …for what?

The blame, the aggression, the deflection, they're all automatic responses. They're the ego jumping into action to protect us from feeling bad about ourselves. It happens so fast that it's not even a conscious thought. It's a reflex.

The question I want to ask is: where did you learn that?

At what point in your life did you learn that that was the way to conduct yourself so deeply that it's now become a safety mechanism? A mechanism to keep you *safe*.

When did you feel that if you fucked up, love would be taken away from you?

At some time in your past, love or belongingness was taken away from you when you did something wrong.

Maybe when you were a kid, you dropped the milk, and your parents were pissed, and you felt terrible and wanted to avoid feeling their disappointment in you ever again. You wanted to avoid feeling that way so much that you created this knee-jerk reaction to look anywhere for another reason for your fuckups than where your focus really belonged: at yourself.

So, you developed a mechanism that you thought would get you out of it. And maybe it worked. Maybe lying to get yourself out of trouble has worked for you in the past. Maybe blaming someone else, maybe even anger has made someone else submit.

So, you unconsciously play out the same survival mechanism, over and over. To stay safe.

But what has it given you?

Has it allowed you to be a powerful manifestor that's created the life you wish to live? Or has it broken up relationships? Lost friends? Created a whole bunch of pain for you to be here right now, reading this book, looking for answers?

I know for me, it certainly didn't give me any of the amazing things in my life that I have now. It created distance. It created a loss of love. It created many friendships where they didn't have my back because they couldn't trust me to own my shit.

The undeniable, immoveable fact is that we all fuck up.

All of us. There's not one person on the planet who has lived their entire life not putting one foot wrong. If there is, I'd bet my house on them being the most inwardly repressed, frustrated, miserable person in the world because they've spent their entire lives in fear of pissing anyone off, sacrificing their own needs to belong.

We fuck up.

It doesn't mean that we're bad people. We're just people who sometimes do bad things. Or stupid things. Or dumb things.

But too often, we make the dumb thing we did part of our identity. Remember: it's not who we are; it's something that we've done. It does not define us. We internally carry around so many "facts" that we decided about ourselves long ago into adulthood.

We let a friend down and decide we're a bad friend and not worthy of friendships. We hurt someone and decide that we're a brute and perpetuate that cycle from then on. We said something stupid and decided we should hide our opinions from the world for fear of ridicule.

We tarnish ourselves with this brush of identity. But we are not our actions.

We. Fuck. Up.

We're not perfect—we're an eternal work in progress. So stop living in the perpetual loop that your ego has you stuck in—a loop of self-blame, self-anger, self-justification, self-resentment. It starts within, and then we project it out.

Time to change the reel, don't you think?

Because there's a big difference between "I am bad" and "I did something bad." And besides, what is "bad" anyway? Bad according to who?

When we label things "good," "bad," "right," "wrong," it creates a separation. And it stops you from seeing the path to where you really want to be.

Up until the last few years, I spent my life avoiding conflict because I thought it was bad.

But conflict is actually not bad. Quite the opposite.

Don't get me wrong here—unresourceful or unhealthy conflict such as yelling, physically fighting, intimidation, and so on … they only make things worse. Unhealthy conflict doesn't help anyone and is a highly dysfunctional way of operating.

Unhealthy conflict is justification. It's blame. It's victimising. It's excuses. It's denial. It doesn't lead to any positive outcomes.

But conflict is a powerful tool when dealt with in the right way. It's necessary for driving great change and progress. No one necessarily has to do something wrong. Both parties might simply have a difference of opinion or different way of doing things. That's just fine. If we all agreed on everything, nothing new would ever get invented. We'd still be getting around using horse and cart because everyone agreed that a mechanised vehicle was a ridiculous idea.

Conflict is not bad, and neither are you.

So instead of saying, "I did this bad thing," how different would it be if you said instead, "My action just then didn't get the result I wanted," or "It wasn't a fit for me"?

Instead of labelling yourself as good, bad, whatever, strip away the emotion and ask, "Are my actions and behaviours and words getting me what I want?" Since you're reading this book, something tells me they're not…

Start giving yourself the space to go away and reflect. Listen to your heart, your intuition, and you'll find your truth. You'll find your path to progress. And drop the ego. Leave it at the door. It will only lead you astray.

It takes a bit of work at first, because...

YOUR EGO WANTS TO RAGE

By this point in the book, you're probably starting to give your ego a little side-eye. You're realising it can be like the interfering aunty who is "just trying to help" (while always making things worse).

Conflict is a space where the ego really thrives. It loves that space because there's always so many low-vibe emotions jumping around. It's easy for the ego to turn the dial up to eleven and turn you into a raving crazy person.

But the thing is, conflict is a part of life.

Conflict is going to arise. And when it does, you have two choices.

You can express it in an unresourceful way. You can yell, get pissed off, and put the other person on the defensive. You can get up in your ivory tower and start hurling objects at anyone who dares to approach.

Doing this, you're going to be met with *more* conflict, nine times out of ten, unless you're with someone who is super understanding and can talk you down off the ledge, which is rare. And besides, it's not someone else's job to help you handle your own damn ego.

By handling conflict in an unresourceful way, we don't get what we want, and we attract other situations to get pissed off about. The universe gives us more of what we focus on, remember?

The good news is that there's another option.

We can learn to express ourselves vulnerably, wholeheartedly, from an authentic place in integrity with what we want and expressing it.

Whether you like it or not, there's always going to be conflict. People have different opinions, different priorities, different ways of seeing the world. We all have our own reality, remember?

Of course, there's going to be friction in life, which is why it's so incredibly important to learn how to resolve conflict in a healthy way that creates productive and positive outcomes. This applies to every relationship in your life—business relationships, friendships, intimate partnerships…everyone.

The quality of your conflict resolution reflects the quality of your outcomes in life.

The thing is, to have healthy conflict, you've got to have trust that you're both not fighting for yourselves; you're fighting for a mutually agreed-upon goal.

Whether that goal is a relationship succeeding, a business project getting done, or whatever else, when everybody's fighting for the same goal that exists outside of themselves, it's so much easier to take the ego-driven identity and emotional noise out of the conversation.

You're fighting for the greater good. When your sights are set high, ground-level personal ego shit doesn't matter.

WHAT ARE *YOU* FIGHTING FOR?

Conflict usually starts the same way. Something will happen that causes one party to get triggered somehow.

The unresourceful way of handling it is to hand the reins over to the ego and let it jump into action to try and protect you. It will send you straight into denial or blame, justification, anger or aggression, pushback, all that sort of stuff.

Thinking about my own relationships, I've noticed a significant difference in how I handle conflict with my current relationship and my past ones. I used to repeat an unresourceful conflict cycle with past partners. One of us would get triggered. The other would react. Then it was battle stations for both of us.

We'd both draw a circle of protection around ourselves and load up on emotional weaponry to protect our position at all costs. Looking back at it now, I get the image of two giant stone towers spaced about fifty metres apart from each other, with each person standing at the top shouting and throwing spears and arrows. Both are so focused on protecting each other's position on top of the tower that they can't even hear what the other is saying.

Not really a good way of resolving conflict, don't you think?

If that description sounds familiar about how you and your partner deal with conflict, think about this. What would it look like, instead, if you got down from your tower and met in the middle, on neutral ground where you didn't have to protect your tower?

What if, instead, you approached the conflict with curiosity about its source?

All conflict can essentially be boiled down to a lack of communication. When you don't see each other's perspective, you cannot understand it. As a result, they seem like a crazy person with ridiculous demands. And they probably feel the same about you.

Then you start to drift apart.

But when you care enough about something, you don't *want* to drift apart. You both want to work together to achieve your shared goal. It could be a business vision or a relationship outcome. When you care about the thing you're both trying to achieve and put it first, that's when you can climb down from your tower and meet each other in a neutral space.

The only way to resolve conflict in a healthy, productive, and positive way is through understanding each other's perspective. And the only way to do that is through communication.

When I have conflict with my partner, Kate, I put any knee-jerk ego reactions aside and consciously move into a space of curiosity to understand her perspective. Because I can trust that we both want the same thing, which is for our relationship to flourish.

So instead of fighting to defend our own standpoint, we fight for our shared goal: our relationship.

In business, the principle is the same. Say you have two business directors. They both want the business to succeed. They both want it to be successful. That's the shared outcome. So when they have differences of opinion about how to execute various things within the business to achieve that goal, they need to step out of their own ego space, stop defending their own position, and step into a neutral space in the middle, where they can actually listen to each other and come to a mutual understanding.

The moment I dropped the me-versus-you viewpoint and integrated the idea of both parties simply having different views, I stopped reacting emotionally to conflict.

As a result, I was immediately able to have better conversations with others when seeking to resolve conflicts. They started reflecting my own healthy approach to conflict resolution. Instead of approaching the situation fuelled by emotion, they instead brought curiosity and a desire to achieve mutual understanding to the conversation.

Whereas before, I would attract a lot of relationships that were just endless battles. Everything was always a fight.

Most couples fight over the same thing. They just have a different perspective on that thing. The problem is that instead of both stepping into a space of curiosity about it, they draw a line in the sand, build their tower, grab their pitchfork, and start protecting their own ego instead of focusing on their shared goal.

The reason the mother of my kids left me was that she felt that she wasn't heard, understood, or supported. She felt that she was doing it all on her own. But the funny thing is, I felt the exact same way. I was slaving my guts out in my business, trying to be successful, not for me, but for them. I was always working my butt off to do what I thought was required, which was to provide for my family.

She was doing the same thing, but because we weren't able to communicate, because there wasn't the *trust* that we were working for a mutually agreed outcome, there wasn't healthy conflict.

Because there was no curiosity-based communication between us, there was no understanding of each other's perspective. She didn't understand what I was doing or why I was doing it. And vice versa. All I could see was that she wasn't appreciating what I was doing and supporting me. And vice versa.

Although we were both doing our best and working for the same goal (providing a good life for our family), our approaches were different. And we didn't know how to handle the conflicts that arose because of these different approaches in a healthy, healing way.

Instead of communicating from a neutral position, we just hurled barbs at each other from way up the top of our towers, surrounded by our emotional weaponry as we tried to protect ourselves from hurt.

And we grew apart.

USING NON-VIOLENT COMMUNICATION

A book that really opened my eyes to the huge role that communication has in healthy conflict was *Nonviolent Communication* by Marshall Rosenberg, PhD.

I read it at a time when I was in a relationship that was really up and down. My partner was regularly triggered, but instead of opening a dialogue, she would poke at me until I snapped. The ensuing fight would release some of the tension she was feeling but cause a lot of destruction to our relationship.

A lot of people use conflict this way.

I used to do it to my mother when I was young. I'd poke and prod until I got a reaction. And I never knew why I did it. I just didn't have a conscious understanding of it back then. What I've realised in recent years is that I did it for connection. I always lacked connection. But I didn't know how to ask for what I wanted. I didn't know how to express my needs in a healthy fashion.

So, I would poke and poke until she reacted.

Maybe there's someone in your life who does this to you?

They aren't able to communicate their feelings and needs for whatever reason. Maybe they don't know how. Maybe they aren't self-aware enough to understand what's really driving them. Maybe they don't feel they can share safely. Maybe they were "trained" from a young age not to share their deeper feelings. Or maybe they are practising an avoidance strategy—the emotions are there, but they don't want to deal with the cause because it's too painful.

Either way, as you know by now, emotions need to be expressed. And they *will* be, whether in a resourceful or unresourceful way.

Any negative emotion is a communication problem. Any single time that we're experiencing some form of anger, frustration, or other negative emotion, it's a communication issue, whether it's that we haven't communicated our needs or desires to somebody around us, or whether we haven't honoured these *within ourselves*.

I read *Nonviolent Communication* during my search for a better way to communicate with my partner when she was triggered. It's a book I recommend you read for yourself because effective communication is the foundation of *everything*. Without being able to effectively communicate our thoughts, feelings, and ideas with each other, the human race would never have made it out of the cave!

The book presents a different way of speaking that is less you-centric, and therefore, lessens the risk of the triggered person feeling like they're being criticised.

For example, you might say, "I feel sad when you don't tell me you love me because my need for connection is not being met."

You're essentially taking ownership of your emotion when the thing that triggers you happens. It's very different to saying, "I hate it when you don't say you love me." That kind of sentence is focused on what you did, while the non-violent way is focused on how I feel.

Or, "I feel a lot of shame when I ask for what I want sexually because I feel my need for safety is not being met." You own it. You share with them what it is that they're doing that creates this emotion coming up inside of you. And you share with them what needs are not being met.

Because at the end of the day, we're only getting triggered because of past wounds. It's never about the person in front of you. It's never about what they did to you or what you did to them. It's about what your actions brought up inside of them and reminded them about.

This way of communicating also means that you take the time to stop and really sit and process what's happened and get to the core of it. It requires you to ask yourself, "What's really happening here? What old wounds are being opened up inside of me to make me react this way?"

Then the next step is to have a conversation with the other person, so they can know all your past wounds, hurts, and adversities, *not to use them against you, but to love you better.*

Because if you knew that doing certain things is triggering old wounds in your partner, and you have a common goal of peace, harmony, love, and connection in your relationship, why the fuck would you keep doing it?

Your partner cannot know what's triggering you if you don't tell them. Likewise, you cannot know what's triggering them if they don't tell you. And if you don't know what your trigger points are, you're both just going to keep hitting them again and again until you drive each other away.

That being said, it's not your job to help them bring it out and deal with it. And it's not their job to help you do the same either. It's your shit. Your responsibility.

If you want to show up in your relationships—whether personal, business, or whatever else—in congruence with your shared desired outcomes, it's your responsibility to work on your shit and help them understand and resolve it with you. It's your job to show up in the most supportive way that you can.

By having the conversation this way, it gives the other person the opportunity to own it and to step forward into a space where you can both work to resolve the issue. Instead of saying, "You make me feel this way," and shoving blame down their throat, it invites them to step forward into a mutually healing space.

DE-ESCALATION DURING A BATTLE ROYALE

The wide-ranging natures, histories, and coping mechanisms of people, in general, mean that sometimes you'll have a great deal of trouble getting to a space of healthy conflict with someone, no matter how hard you try.

What if someone's coming at you, and they seem determined to fight no matter what?

Obviously, they're in a space of heightened emotion. Their ego is yahooing and getting out their shiny knife set, ready for a Tarantino-esque bloody showdown.

This is where your boundaries come in.

It's where you say something like this:

"Look, I can see that you're really frustrated right now, and something I've done has upset you or triggered you. I'd love to talk this through with you. However, the way that you're showing up right now is not appropriate, and I'm not willing to have this conversation. Let's circle back in half an hour. Take some space, go for a walk, and let's chat in half an hour."

If this is an ongoing pattern in your relationship, a way to approach it is to have a conversation when they're *not* triggered and experiencing heightened emotion. You could say something like:

"Barry, I've noticed that when either of us is triggered, we try to have it out, and it ends up in more conflict and things being said that we don't mean. So, I'm going to propose now, while we're in a space of love and peace, that in the future, whoever is the calmest at the time calls a time-out. We'll take half an hour, go and sit somewhere else, be still and reflect, and then come back."

It's all you can do. Then it's up to them to accept your intention or not.

And sometimes, people just won't want to play at your level.

Let's face it, when you start expressing your changing desires or needs vulnerably and in integrity with authenticity and having healthy conflict, everything's not necessarily going to come up roses with every person you interact with.

Life doesn't always snap neatly into place!

You may still come across people that you just can't stand. You might meet some older versions of you and want to avoid them like the plague. You might be met with people who, for all your efforts to communicate rationally, might just want to kick off and chuck stuff at you.

That's where you've got to understand where your boundaries are and be willing to enforce them. You've got to ask yourself, "How much of this carry-on am I willing to tolerate?"

Remember the story I shared about my son at the beginning of this chapter? At this point in his development, he deals with conflict in an unresourceful way. And although I do have a boundary in place there, I am willing to tolerate a lot of his behaviour because, in many ways, I have created it. I've created this in him because he's modelled me for so many years. He watched how I dealt with conflict and is doing the same thing.

He's modelling the dad that overreacted. That blamed. That justified. That didn't take responsibility. He's modelling *an older version of me.*

Therefore, I'm more tolerant of him than people like my colleagues or friends. I have a standard of how I allow others to interact with me. And if you're not able to show up in integrity and authentically, owning your shit and allowing me to do the same, then there's no place for us to have a relationship. I'm simply not interested in playing at any level lower than where I'm at.

I have a different approach with my son. And that doesn't mean that I'm not operating in a space of integrity with him because I've got a different boundary with him than I have with others. You can have different boundaries for different situations. That's okay. It's not a one size fits all kind of thing.

Even so, with my son, there's still a boundary there where I reach the point that I need to put a pin in it. "Okay, mate, I've sat here, and I've listened to you. We've had this conversation, and I'm not going to tolerate this any longer."

Your own boundaries will be different for each person in your life, too. And sometimes, they will be pretty damn short!

HOLDING THE SPACE

There will be many times in your life where you will unconsciously react to something. An emotion will come up. Annoyance, fear, hatred, shame, something negative. Now, there's no point in denying that the emotion is there. As you know by this point in the book that ignoring it or pushing it down doesn't work.

Healthy conflict is about not projecting that emotion onto someone else. It's yours. They didn't "make" you feel anything. Something they did (whether knowingly or unknowingly) triggered an old wound in you, and it brought up this emotion.

Healthy conflict is about allowing the emotion to have space and having the curiosity to understand more about its deeper cause. It's not about telling people how they should express their emotion but holding the space for them to communicate what's going on.

It's important for you to not tell them how they should be.

"Oh, can you stop swearing?" "Can you stop waving your hands?" "Can you lower your voice?"

No. Just let them express themselves. Within your boundaries, obviously —if they are behaving inappropriately, you need to let them know. But remember, it's not personal. It's not about you. Even if they are saying, "You did this, you are that, you, you, you…" Nine times out of ten, it's really not about them.

And if you hold the space for them to share all they need to share, then you get to the core of what's really there. You allow them to express in their wholeness whatever's going on, but it's not done in a violent way or an aggressive way. And it's not a projection upon the other person.

When you get to the core issue of what's going on—the trigger—then you can make a commitment to not do the thing that triggers them again. If you feel you cannot avoid doing the thing that triggers them, then you need to work on that problem and come to an agreement on how you're both going to lessen the impact of the trigger while still both having your needs met, at least partially.

For more complex behaviour-reaction patterns, more communication to reach an understanding and establishing mutual agreements might be needed.

All of this requires you both to be committed to the shared outcomes you want for the relationship. If the other person doesn't give a damn about your feelings or isn't willing to participate in the discussion, then they are not the right people for you, and it's time to exit them from your life.

GETTING TO THE CORE ISSUE

In the last few chapters, there's been an underlying theme. You've probably picked up on it: *truth*.

Integrity, authenticity, vulnerability, boundaries, decision-making, connecting with your heart... they all require you to operate in a space of truth. Truth with yourself. Truth in how you act. Truth in showing the world who you are. Truth in what you want and need. Truth in how you choose to show up in the world.

None of it works unless it comes from the truth. *Your* truth.

Operating in integrity and being authentic, expressing it, communicating, being vulnerable at what's going on with you and expressing what's really there... it all allows you to have healthy conflict. Which is *good*.

If you don't have healthy conflict in your life, there's one or two things happening. Either you don't give a shit about anything, and you have completely resigned from life (and I sincerely hope you haven't!), or you're just a pushover. You're not expressing what you want.

And this is why secretly (or even publicly), you're bitching about everything. Because you're not actually taking a stand for what you fucking want! You're suppressing all of that because you just want to get along.

This is what I was doing for *years*. I was suppressing myself so much that the resentment, frustration, and anger built up inside of me so much that my partner would ask me to do a really simple task and I'd just fucking blow up. She would not understand why, and neither could I!

My rage wasn't about what she'd asked me to do; it was about all the hundreds of other times I was not allowing myself to express my truth. All the micro-sacrifices that I made and became resentful for. All the needs I had that I didn't know how to ask to have met.

It all builds up. And that's where conflict explodes into something very, very ugly and totally destructive.

In my life right now, I seldom get angry. Because of the way that I operate, the emotion just doesn't come up for me anymore. It doesn't get a chance to. I ask for what I need. I express and protect healthy boundaries. I show up authentically. I approach conflict with curiosity and a desire to understand the other person's perspective.

When you operate that way, there's no friction. There's no hiding. There's no opportunity for little niggling issues to be hidden away and fester until they build pressure and cause massive explosions. It just doesn't happen.

Am I saying I'm some kind of Buddha-esque picture of tranquillity and peace? Of course not—I'm still human! Sometimes I feel shitty. Sometimes I get a bee in my bonnet and feel a bit feisty.

But here's the thing—100 per cent of the times that I feel that way, I can relate it back to the fact that I haven't spoken my truth. Somewhere along the line, I let something slide that I should have stayed in a space of integrity on.

And therefore, it's my own damn fault. Nobody else's. Because how the fuck are they supposed to know what I need if I don't tell them? How are they supposed to know who I am if I don't show them? It's all on me.

And you know what?

That's just fine.

PART 3

THE HAND

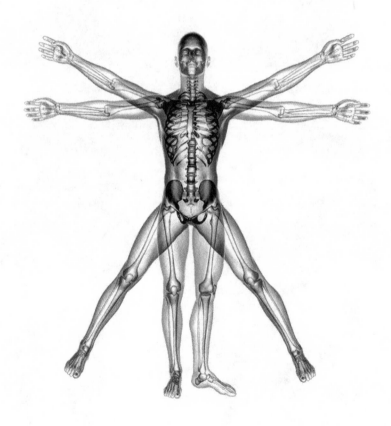

CHAPTER 13

EMBODYING THE HEART AND MIND

"There is freedom waiting for you,
On the breezes of the sky,
And you ask, 'What if I fall?'
Oh but my darling,
What if you fly?"

—*Erin Hanson*

OH SHIT... I JUST LOST $106,000.

My heart sank as I looked at the computer screen. My dream of easy riches was gone.

Years ago, my ex-girlfriend and I started a cryptocurrency portfolio. It was during one of Bitcoin's big booms, and we decided to give it a try. We put $10,000 into it, bought some diversified coins and waited to see what happened.

Eventually, the portfolio grew to $116,000. My ex said, "I feel like it's time to pull our dividends out now." It was her intuition.

I didn't agree. I didn't check in with my own intuition, and I didn't listen to hers. I got greedy. I really wanted to ride that wave.

"Nup," I said to her. "We're going to make a million bucks with this. Let's stay in."

A month later, the portfolio was worth $5k.

Needless to say, she wasn't impressed…and I had learned a big lesson.

The crypto portfolio eventually rose to $10k again. But by that time, our relationship was a bust. When we separated, we split the money, and she got out.

But I kept sitting on my $5k patiently.

Three years later, something happened with one particular coin that I had bought with no real reason why. My intuition had just called me to it. *This is going to go really well*, I had thought.

So, I bought 26,000 of them. It cost me $2k at the time.

A month or so ago, I started noticing it go up. And up, and up, and up …until my $2,000 investment gained me over $100k.

I asked my brother, who is an avid crypto trader, to chart the coin so I could see what it was doing and get an indication of when to sell out.

A couple of days later, he came back with his findings.

"Yeah, you should sell out now," he instructed me. "It's gonna pop."

But something didn't feel right about it. I decided to hold.

But I questioned myself…was I being greedy again like I had been years ago when my ex advised me to sell?

After meditating on it for a while, I was certain that if the coin tanked and I lost all of my gains, I would be totally okay. After all, I was really losing my original investment of $2k. The rest didn't really exist yet.

So, I held on.

A few days later, I spoke with my brother again. He had charted the coin and gave me a call. "Hold onto it, Barry; this coin's still got legs," he said.

So, once again, I held. And held. And held…

Until the other night, I had just come back from dinner with my girl. We were in bed about to make love, and all of a sudden, I reached over for my phone and started tapping away on the screen.

"What on Earth are you doing?" Kate asked, obviously (and rightly) perplexed!

"Sorry, babe," I said to her. "I've just got the strongest intuition. I have to sell that coin right now."

"Okay…" she said, amused.

So, I sold it at $500 a coin.

The next morning when I woke up, I checked in on coin stats. The coin I had sold the previous night had taken a dive, and it was heading down in value by the minute.

But you know what the funny thing was? The highest value it had reached was $502. I'd sold out about as close to the top as possible.

That's intuition. That's what using your intuition can do for you.

■ ■ ■

Now, I'm not saying that when you tap into the higher power or Source, that you will suddenly be able to predict lotto numbers and never lose a bet. The story I just told you isn't about the money. I just used that example to show you the kind of crazy shit that starts happening once you start developing your heart connection and tapping into your intuition.

The reality is that when you build a relationship with your heart and learn when it's sharing something with you, *you will hear the truth.*

It's not a yell. It's not something loud. It's more like a whisper. Which is, I guess, why people ignore that voice so much and for so long…

Let me tell you now—this type of stuff happens to me all the time now. I'll feel I should get on a plane now, and the borders will close the next day. I'll feel I need to look into an opportunity, and days later, it will fall in my lap.

The more you practice what you're learning in this book, the more you lead with your heart, the more amazing stuff like this will happen to you, too. When your energy aligns in flow with your heart and your truth, doors that were previously hidden to you begin to unlock.

And life gets pretty spectacular.

. . .

THE BEST JOURNEYS
DON'T FOLLOW A STRAIGHT LINE

As you're reading this book, you might feel a bit like I'm bragging, gloating, or otherwise showboating at how wonderful my life is and how easy things happen for me.

That Barry, you might be thinking, *what a fucking show-off. It's easy for him, not for me.*

The thing is, it's taken me a bloody long time to get to this point. And my path has not been straightforward, nor has it been easy. It has wobbled around plenty.

The way my journey unfolded over the past fifteen years began first with a spiritual awakening (which I talked about earlier in this book). That led me down a years-long path of heavy spiritual development. I'm talking about reading and listening to books, going to workshops, learning from spiritual mentors and teachers, and a *lot* of self-reflection, heart meditations, and internal work.

And when I say workshops, I mean *workshops*. Before I found Irmanysah Effendi's heart-based works, I tried everything. Chakra cleansing. Colour therapy. Breathwork. Buddhist principles. The list goes on.

And they all worked and gave me results. But there was still something missing for me. Something not quite complete. Something unanswered.

It wasn't until I walked into that first Reiki workshop many years ago, heartbroken and lost, feeling that I was fucking my life up but not knowing any other way, that I had a sense of coming home.

I remember it clearly. The people around me, my instructor, right down to the fake Persian rug that was wearing out in the middle on which we all sat at the beginning of the course. I remember the musty smell of old dust and incense.

And I remember the feeling that came over me as we progressed on that first day.

This is it, I thought. My body tingled with excitement, and something in my heart clicked into place. I knew that this was what I'd been looking for for years… without even realising that I had been searching.

From that first Reiki course, it was an ongoing practice every single day. I dove heavily into it, and the more I discovered, the more I felt shifts within my mind and my heart.

I was changing. And I just knew I was *finally* on the right track.

Then the bankruptcy happened.

As I shared earlier, I built up a multimillion-dollar business that depended entirely on me. I was the lynchpin that everything rested on. The single point of failure. When eventually I couldn't keep up anymore, it all fell over, and I went bankrupt.

As you could imagine, when I went bankrupt, I hit near rock-bottom pretty hard.

And yes, there was a bit of low-vibe emotions going on. Blame, denial, anger… I went through all of it for a little while.

How did my life fuck up so bad? I'd ask myself. *I'm a good person. I've been taking meditation classes. I've been trusting God. How could I have attracted this kind of trauma?*

All the while, I was metaphorically shaking my fists at the sky, even in the deepest throes of angst about what was happening to me… in my heart of hearts, something felt right about it.

I was free. I had a chance to start again and do it differently. Do it better. I had a chance to reset and learn from my mistakes. I wasn't on the right path before, working eighty-hour weeks and never being there for my partner (who, in fact, left me because of just that).

Somewhere along the way, my trajectory through life had veered off course. It happened slowly at first, and then, before I knew it, I was shooting off to somewhere very different as I worked like a dog trying to keep my broken, unsustainable business afloat.

I was so focused on the wrong things. I wanted to win. I wanted to make lots of money and be successful and provide for my family and all of the things that most business owners want. But I was going about it entirely the wrong way... because I knew no other way to do it.

I'd been brought up in an environment where hard work = success. Most people have. We feel that the harder we slog our guts out, the greater the reward. That's a lie. A big one.

And it's keeping millions of people all over the world stuck in a perpetual cycle of trading time for money (whether in your own business or not).

Somewhere along the way, my well-meaning but ultimately misaligned intentions had led me into a space where I was not living my best life as my best self. But I was too focused on keeping my break-neck momentum going to really notice.

So, the universe made me stop. With a screech, a thud, and a hell of a shock. But still, I was forced to stop. And when I did finally stop racing towards oblivion... there was the space and quietness inside me that I needed to hear what my heart had been gently saying the whole time.

What the hell had happened?

Well, here's the thing.

When you first start to listen to your intuition and trust your heart, you need to realise that there have been many years that you have spent *not* listening to it.

There have been many years following your will, your desires, and whatever else, and that has created infrastructure around you that needs to be pulled down.

You're kind of like a shanty townhouse—over the years, you've added a wall here, a roof there, an extra room over there…and for the most part, you're protected from the elements.

But you can't *move*. You can't see out of the windows. You can't sleep straight. All those little building problems are compounding. And compounding.

It's getting pretty uncomfortable living in the house you've built around yourself, right? It was for me. But you stay there because, where else will you go? What will happen if you start knocking walls down and letting the light in?

But unless you start rebuilding your structure, it's just going to get tighter, darker, and more uncomfortable to live in.

Sure, to rebuild, you've gotta knock some stuff down. It's a bit scary. It can sometimes be hard. And sometimes, you'll feel you're going backwards or just creating a big mess. But that's necessary.

In The Game Changers, we actually guide our members through a period where they take various structures and processes down in their business so we can see where things break.

Through this kind of stress test, we can see which pieces are working, which are not, and which aren't even necessary. During this time, the business owner will feel like they're going backwards, and they might even experience a dip in certain numbers.

But after we tear away the stuff that's not needed, get to the core, and rebuild their business structure correctly, they experience a resurgence that shoots past their biggest goals quickly, easily, and scalably.

But not if they don't have faith in letting go of the things they don't need.

This is what I think stops a lot of people from going down their own spiritual path in the beginning. They have an awakening and all of a sudden are like, *Oh, I need to trust my heart. I need to listen to my heart.* And they expect everything to become perfect.

But what they're not realising is that they have years of infrastructure that's been built around them, keeping them "safe." But it's been keeping everything else out. Mostly love. The ego keeps love out. It keeps us from truly connecting and experiencing unfiltered love from one another.

There's a lot to get rid of.

And then there's facing all the years we went against our heart, against divine guidance, and created trauma and negative karma and things like that.

Depending on how much you followed your ego, your will and desire will dictate how much that infrastructure will need to be knocked down.

So be prepared for things to appear to fall apart. To shift around a bit. Some people will go, but others will be attracted in. Some opportunities will fizzle, but others will appear.

TRUSTING YOUR HEART

When you start trusting your heart, you won't necessarily get what you want immediately. Holy curtains do not open wide, sun shining, angels coming forth singing. No, it's nothing like that. There is no God-switch that flips, and the universe instantly reorganises itself into your own private bliss pattern.

So, while at first, you won't get what you want…you actually will get what you need. Even if it hurts. Even if it looks like your house is falling down around you. Even if it doesn't look like you think it should look, it's what you need to *grow*. To learn the lessons the universe has been trying to teach you. To recalibrate your direction and go where your heart is trying to lead you.

If you allow that to stop you from trusting, your heart will never reach the place where your life is in consistent flow and constant nurture and support of *you*. You have to be prepared to go through the process and trust that it's going to be okay.

Even if you feel you've taken a few steps backward, it's all clearing the clutter and paving the way for you to rebuild better, stronger, happier, and more fulfilled than ever before.

Look back on any negative situation in your life. Most of the time you'll find a lesson there. You can look back and realise that situation was actually needed for your greater development.

Did it still suck? Hell yes. Speaking for myself, my bankruptcy was an incredibly painful experience. But do you know what? It happened because I wasn't listening to my heart. If I had, I would have started dismantling the business six months prior. But I didn't, and it wasn't until my life was crashing down around me that I finally listened.

Maybe you can think of a situation like that right now. An abusive relationship. A bad business decision. A toxic working environment. At some time, you knew you had to get out, didn't you?

And when you finally did, for all the pain and suffering you went through, you learned from the experience, didn't you? Often the most painful lessons are the most life-changing.

For me, the bankruptcy was so traumatic, but in my heart, I was consciously aware that there was something that felt okay about it. At the time, I couldn't logically make sense of that. Everything that made me feel like a successful man suddenly fell away from underneath my feet, as though I'd been building with sand the whole time. In my heart, I heard a voice saying, "Something good is going to come from this."

And obviously, where I am right now in life, living in Paradise, running multiple successful businesses, in an amazing relationship, growing my wealth every day, and happier than I've ever been ... it only came after I was willing to knock down so much of what I had built.

In fact, when I think of where I would be right now if the bankruptcy hadn't happened, my guts churn. I would probably still be working eighty-plus-hour weeks, my health failing, my relationships hanging on by a thread, feeling lonely, lost, and utterly overwhelmed every single day. What fucking misery!

That crash and burn is what led me to think, *Well, okay, how did I fuck this all up so badly?* And that's what led me to find Neuro-Linguistic Programming (NLP)—a behavioral technology geared towards achieving one's goals—and begin to understand my own mind, and how our beliefs and our thoughts create an aspect of our reality...and that we can *change* our reality (James 2021).

So let me ask you:

What things don't *you* need any more? What are you afraid to let go of?

What are you holding on to so tight because you think it's keeping you safe...but in actuality, it's keeping you from flying?

A NEW HOLY TRINITY

This book reflects my own journey of awakening. In the same order. I found spirituality, dove deep into that, then went into NLP. But at the same time, meditation was the foundation. That's why I shared the heart meditations with you earlier on in this book.

A lot of people will get into all kinds of personal development avenues just like I did. They'll become a Tony Robbins fan, listen to Deepak Chopra podcasts on repeat, and whatever else.

But they're missing this foundational piece. Just like I was. They're so caught up in their positive affirmations and quotes, but those things can't really call through what they want and need from the universe because their heart, mind, and body aren't aligned openly.

And so, the things they're desperately trying to manifest...just don't happen.

Because they're missing the final piece of the puzzle: *embodiment*. This is all about how we bring our heart and mind into the world through our actions and interactions with others.

Everything we've covered so far in this book on the heart and the mind exists within us. But we cannot neglect how we embody all of this and bring it to life in the physical world.

To get to this point in my life, I had to be willing to show up fully in heart and mind but also in body, too. Our heart, mind, and body are intrinsically linked, after all. Neglect one part of this trinity, and the others will not operate at their full potential.

If we're not expressing our truth to others, how can we ever expect to get what we want and need? If we're neglecting our own physical health, how can we expect to have the energy to live a vibrant life? If we're not demonstrating our values in the way we show up for others, how can we expect to attract our ideal tribe?

Thinking and feeling are important. But they're nothing without *action*. Without movement. Without some kind of physical representation.

It took me a long time to understand the importance of embodying our beliefs.

I remember having an experience, years ago, after beginning to practice NLP on my own thoughts, habits, and beliefs, when I found the missing piece.

I thought, *Oh, this is it. I've gone to develop myself spiritually. Inside, energetically, I'm connected to the Source. I listen to my intuition. I'm all set.*

And I realised that I could actually start coaching people from a place of intuition and help facilitate what I call "holographic change" in them. That's why I was able to get very fast results, far beyond what other NLP practitioners could. Because I sat in that place of intuition, I trusted that when having a conversation with my client, whatever I was feeling were their feelings. There was a representation within me.

So, when I coached in that place of what I was feeling and what was showing up intuitively, it allowed my clients to have that breakthrough far faster than doing the whole NLP process, which took forty-five minutes to access the negative belief. Whereas, I could access it in five minutes.

Even so, I blindly went through this period for another six or seven years, thinking I'd cracked the code. *It's like yin and yang,* I thought. *You've got the heart and the mind. That's it, right?*

But then, about two years ago, I did a workshop with Preston Smiles, a personal freedom and leadership coach based out of Austin, Texas. In the workshop, Preston incorporated a lot of embodiment practices. We did breathwork, we did movement, and some somatic work (which is essentially a range of specialised movement therapies).

What that means is moving and shaking the body, all with the purpose of releasing trapped trauma, pain, and negativity that we are still holding physically.

And that's when I had this third awakening…I'd found the Holy Trinity of self-development. We have the mind, *the body*, and the heart.

Think about this for a second:

Do you have tense shoulders? Stomach problems? A sore neck or headaches?

In a nutshell, where does your body hold tension?

We all do it. From the time we're young. I believe it's where a lot of our physical problems come from. Energy and tension that haven't been released and have just built up for years and years.

When we experience trauma, we hold it in our body. But we never get taught how to release that trauma. We go to therapy and do whatever else we need to do to ease our mind…but the body? Nope. We don't even think of it. But it's there.

Think about cats and dogs. The first thing they'll do when they wake up from sleeping is stretch. After birds have a fight, they'll perch somewhere and beat their wings a few times to release any residual tension. But we don't do those things as human beings (at least, not many of us).

Here in Bali, there are a lot of street dogs. Sometimes they attack each other. And the first thing they do when they get to a place of safety is they shake. Shake it off. Many animal species will regularly give their bodies a good shake. What they're doing is releasing trauma from their body.

But we don't, so the trauma gets stuck. This is why we develop these patterns; we get limited mobility and different symptoms in our physical body …because we store all this energy and emotion.

If you've ever had a breathwork session, you understand how the power of simply breathing can release pockets of trauma and negativity, so it gets shifted. When I did Primal Scream therapy and experienced that intense emotional release during my scream, I burst into tears right afterwards. After a lifetime of being taught to keep my voice down and be quiet, the experience of emotionally directed screaming was absolutely life-changing.

In more commonly accepted modalities, it happens, too. Physiotherapists, chiropractors…they will all tell you many stories of clients who cry when the source of tension in their body is released. Some will shake. Some will experience euphoria.

This is where the mind-body connection demonstrates itself so profoundly.

As I've said many times in this book—and will continue to say—emotions need to be expressed. When you push them down, they don't go away; they just fester and turn into black awfulness inside of us.

Think about the last time you experienced a traumatic event. Doesn't need to be major. It could be something as small as getting a fright. Dropping a glass on the floor.

What's the first thing you did? You stopped breathing. You might have even gasped. This affects your breathing pattern moving forward.

You probably also tightened up your body. Even when you relax your shoulders and your stomach, there is still some tension left behind, some part of us that is still holding it because we haven't shaken our body to set it free and reset.

Personally, I've had all this tension in my body my whole life. Sore knees, sore shoulders, sore hips. It's always been there, but I never fully realised it until I started to release it. That's when I noticed just how limited my movement was in my hips or back.

If you've ever had a chiropractic session, you walk in thinking things are pretty much okay, but after you get adjusted, you realise that previously you could only turn your head fifteen degrees, now you can turn it forty-five degrees.

Where do you feel the tension in your body right now? Focus on your shoulders. Your neck. Your back. Your stomach. Your hips. Then focus on relaxing them. Chances are you're carrying a lot of tension you weren't even aware of. You're the frog.

That's why as we progress into the last part of this book (actions), physical embodiment becomes so important.

This is where you need to start exploring ways you can move your body and find a flow that allows you to connect with the heart and mind.

For me, I exercise, I go to the gym, I go surfing. I do things where I'm physically moving my body to allow the energy from my heart to move through it. You might choose to dance. To skate. To run.

We'll get more into the daily practice of the "holy trinity." But for now, I want you to realise that self-development, spirituality—whatever you want to call your quest to become the best version of yourself and live your best life—requires you to work on all three. Mind, body, and spirit.

It's why I've structured this book this way. In three parts:

1. Heart (Being) Feelings
2. Head (Doing) Thoughts
3. Hand (Having) Actions

ENTERING THE NEW WAY OF BEING

Even in the act of reading this book, you're going through a similar journey as I did. Of course, your own journey will take time to unfold, but you now have a guide to refer to along the way.

You now know the work. You know it's time to listen to those whispers, to practice heart-based meditations, to show up in authenticity and integrity. No, there will not be some magical green light from the sky that clicks your entire life into place. But the more you do this work, the more you will find things fall into place and a greater sense of flow. You might first have to take a few steps backward—and break the old structures down before you can rebuild—but it will all be worth it in the end.

For me, life has become easier. There's a lot less noise. I'm a lot less distracted by the hustle and bustle of life, and I feel really focused on where I'm going.

Two or three years ago, I would spend the majority of my time making sure I got back to everyone that day. I just couldn't stand seeing that little red dot on my phone bleeping its notification at me. I would go insane and feel glued to my phone...and kind of resentful of it.

But now, sometimes, I don't get back to certain people for days. And I'm not stressed about it. Because I no longer have that feeling that the world is going to end if Heather doesn't get a reply today. My whole business is not going to burn down. No one is going to think any less of me.

And the only thing that's changed is *me*.

I've become more grounded and more in the flow of life. Because I'm in tune with my heart and my intuition, and because I'm showing up authentically and in integrity, I'm led in the right direction. Even if something happens that seems shitty at the time, a few days later, I'll see why it was actually a blessing.

I listen.

I know when I need to spend some time healing. When I need to take action on something. When I need to check in with someone.

I'm in tune with where I need to be and how I need to show up.

And I trust my truth.

The more I operate in this space, the more opportunities just seem to fall in my lap, without me having to do much to find them or get them.

It's true: life can be easier. And not just that, it can be fucking wonderful. You can have more of what you want and need.

If you feel something inside of you that is calling you forward, trust the process. You might not feel things changing right away. It might take a week. It might take a month. It might even take a year. But the important thing is that you keep going.

Start embodying the internal changes you're making. Start demonstrating them. Not only will taking action help cement those changes within you, but it will also start to influence and change your experience of the world around you.

At first, it takes effort, just like starting any form of new motion. Starting a car. A bird taking off. Turning a wheel. The beginning requires the most energy. But when that momentum starts building, it's easier to stay in motion. To glide. To fly.

So, keep taking one step forward every single day.

I know you can do it.

CHAPTER 14

PROGRESS OVER PERFECTION

"A journey of a thousand miles begins
with a single step."

—*Lao Tzu*

IN JANUARY 2015, FREE CLIMBERS TOMMY CALDWELL AND KEVIN Jorgeson successfully climbed a new route up the Dawn Wall on the Southeast face of Yosemite's monolithic rock formation El Capitan.

The Dawn Wall is essentially a 3,000-foot vertical sheet of mostly sheer granite that was previously thought of as impossible to traverse. It took them six years to plan the new route and nineteen days to climb it.

Throughout their ascent, Tommy and Kevin lived on the wall, pitching tiny hanging cots into the sheer rock face where they slept, washed, and cooked with thousands of feet of empty air below them (Bisharat 2015).

Each day, they would make achingly slow progress up the rock. They fell thousands of times as they attempted millimetre-wide footholds and handholds again and again. Everything hurt. The skin on their fingers shredded after continuous eighteen-hour days spent endlessly grabbing tiny razor-like granite edges.

Then came Pitch 15. Tommy had divided the long climb into thirty-two sections, each requiring a rope attached to a belay and anchor to hold their weight for the many times they would fall. Pitch 15 was an incredibly technical section that required grabbing two of the most difficult holds on the entire rock face.

The crux holds of Pitch 15 are some of the smallest and sharpest holds I have ever attempted to hold onto, Tommy later wrote on his Facebook page.

For six days, Kevin could not get past Pitch 15. The brutally difficult sideways traverse gave him almost nothing to hold. The world watched Kevin try and fail, again and again, and wondered... Kevin was holding his climbing partner back from progressing further. What was he going to do? He was stuck.

At times, Kevin thought of giving up. But instead, he focused on all he could do to move forward, which was to break down the movements required to make the leap to their smallest degree and keep practising getting them right until he was finally across.

Every day, he made minuscule changes in his approach to try and find the exact series of movements that would lead to success.

He eventually made it across and joined Tommy to ascend the summit together. Their epic achievement is still considered one of the hardest rock climbs in history.

When later asked about his choice to keep going even when it seemed impossible he'd make it across Pitch 15, Kevin said, "I don't want to be the guy who *almost* climbed the Dawn Wall" (Bisharat).

■ ■ ■

THE MYTH OF ACHIEVEMENT

As I was growing up, I occasionally heard the phrase, "It's about the journey, not the outcome." I remember having a deep sense of remembrance or knowing around this concept. It's like something deep inside of me rang true, even though I hadn't really had enough experience in this lifetime to have that knowing yet.

Even so, I still couldn't totally take it seriously. The rebellious, impatient teenager that lived inside of me called bullshit. *How can it be about the journey when I am fucking miserable? My journey fucking sucks.*

I was very much stuck in the state of, "I'll be happy when…"

I'll be happy when I get the girl. I'll be happy when I get the job. I'll be happy when I get the house.

And on, and on, and on…

In hindsight, being where I am in life now, what I can realise is that I wasn't able to enjoy the journey because I was always focused on the outcome.

All I was looking for was to belong. To be loved.

Without realising it, I actually thought, *Once I get the job, my dad will be proud of me. My mum will be proud of me. I'll have a place in this world because I'll belong.*

Looking back now, I've achieved many things. But with each achievement, I was only more driven to reach another outcome.

I'm sure you can relate to this.

Most people spend all this time and energy chasing an outcome, only to achieve it and realise that it didn't feel like they thought it would. And then they find something else to chase.

Like a rat in a maze constantly chasing that next piece of cheese, they just go around and around, always hungry. Never satisfied.

Or there's the other end of the spectrum—people that have been chasing an outcome their whole life, and they finally get to the point where they realise that something's just not right. That nothing is making them happy, and they're feeling more lost than ever before.

Cue mid-life crisis!

Looking back at my own pattern of goal achievement and dissatisfaction at the fleeting dopamine buzz, I thought I wanted the thing. The girl. The job. The flashy material stuff. Or the achievement. The six-figure payday. The big, successful event.

But really, all I actually wanted was to feel that sense of self-love, belonging, and worthiness within me. I wanted "proof" that I was not all of the shitty things I feared I was deep down.

The moment I started to experience that self-love, belonging, and worthiness, everything changed. I started enjoying my journey so much more. And the journey actually became more fulfilling than any outcome I had achieved before. Because when I had those internal things, I was in a constant state of emotional bliss.

And guess what? I actually started to achieve my outcomes a lot quicker.

I'll show you how you can start to do it, too, but first, let's clear up some common roadblocks.

COMPARISON AND IMPATIENCE

The major reason we give up on things is impatience.

We want it now, and if it doesn't happen, we get tired of trying and move to another shiny object. Or we look at what other people have, compare ourselves to them, and feel frustrated and inadequate.

We see our school friends on a yacht on Instagram and suddenly feel like our lives have come to nothing. We hear about the success of one of our colleagues and feel like we're not good enough.

But the thing is, you cannot compare your Chapter 5 to someone else's Chapter 13. Everyone is on their own journey and at different places on their path.

The more you spend time looking at the greener grass on the other side and comparing yourself to others, the less energy you have to progress on— and enjoy—your own journey.

I remember how on many of my spiritual teacher Irmansyah Effendi's retreats, there would always be people having difficulty with the concept of patience, of being okay with playing the long game.

"Oh, but I still have all these negative thoughts about where I am in life," they'd say. Or, "But I still get angry at my partner for not supporting my work schedule," or any number of different "but I" statements. Lots of objections and reasons why a longer approach wouldn't work for them.

And Irmansyah would always say the same thing. It took me years to truly understand his words.

He'd ask, "If you start walking towards that door over there, and I take one step, am I there yet?"

"No, you're not," everyone would reply.

"What about if I took two steps or three steps?"

"Not yet," everyone would answer.

"But what if I just keep taking steps forward every day? I would eventually reach the door, right?"

Of course, everyone would agree.

So why, then, did we feel that no matter how hard we worked and how much we tried, we never felt like we were getting anywhere?

It took me years, but I eventually realised I was creating so much story and negativity and emotion around the fact that I worked my butt off, but I didn't get to my goals.

I thought I was walking to the door but never reaching it.

But the problem was that I kept moving the goalposts every time I made it. Every time I did achieve something, I'd barely acknowledge it. Because by the time I got there, I was already focused on the next phase, so reaching a goal never felt like I thought it would.

I figured I wasn't aiming big enough. Not high enough. Not grand enough. Surely if the goal was bigger, I would feel amazing when I achieved it, right? I'd get that blissful dopamine rush I was craving.

So, I kept chasing more and more.

But the truth was, I wouldn't have been happy reaching *any* goal. Because I didn't have the love and acceptance inside of me to truly appreciate and recognise my achievements along my journey.

And fuck, working my guts out all the time but never getting there? It was so emotionally and physically draining!

Surely, there's a better way, right? (Hint: there is, and I'll show you.)

DEALING WITH FAILURE

Look, sometimes in life, you're going to fail. It's going to happen, so you may as well get used to it now.

But failure isn't actually a bad thing at all. Failure can be helpful because it gives you feedback on what *not* to do. This brings us closer to finding the way that works!

The problem with failure is that we tie so much emotion into it. We make it mean something big and ugly in our minds. And in doing so, we grind our own progress to a halt.

If you find yourself giving up often, it's time to improve your relationship with failure.

Just say I make a coffee for you, and you hand it back and tell me, "Yuck, Barry, that tastes like crap!"

Is that a reason to go and sob in the corner, vowing to never step near a coffee machine again? Of course not. It's just feedback. It's an opportunity to ask, "Okay, can you tell me what I got wrong with it? Did you want more sugar? Do you like frothy milk? Can you show me how you like it done?"

Whether your goal is making a cup of coffee, learning a new language, building a business, or climbing El Capitan, the process is exactly the same. The only thing that makes El Cap seem much more unattainable than making a coffee is the emotion we attach to the goal.

The bigger the goal, the more the emotion.

Stuffing up a cup of coffee is easy to get over. Because it's a small thing, right?

But failing in business, missing our equivalent Dawn Wall ascent...we make these things mean so many horrible things in our heads. That we're not good enough. That we're not smart enough. That we're not brave enough. Or whatever else.

But when you remove the emotion, you've simply discovered a way that didn't work. This means you've got a whole lot of data to help you find a way that *does* work.

The only way you'll truly fail is if you stop trying.

I could have given up after failing in my kitchen joinery business. I could have said, "Oh, well, I tried this business thing, and I just lost everything, took all these people's money, and I'm a bad person. So, I should just crawl into a hole and die."

But if I had done that, I wouldn't be where I am now. I'm afraid to think of where I'd be. Probably working for somebody else, feeling super miserable and unhappy, possibly still living back in Tasmania.

Sure, sometimes I still react to things emotionally. Some days, something will frustrate me, and I'll get that fleeting feeling of impatience, irritation, and the desire to just chuck in the towel on whatever it was I was trying to do.

But it doesn't last for long.

And man, I used to live in a world of constant reaction. Everything was so fucking annoying. Because I was always looking at where I wanted to be and feeling frustrated that I wasn't there already. I was always looking at the top of the mountain instead of the gorgeous valley full of flowers that were around me.

And because I couldn't enjoy the journey, I had a difficult time ever reaching those goals I set. Can you relate? How many things have you given up on just before you might have had a breakthrough?

Tommy and Kevin failed literally thousands of times before they climbed the Dawn Wall.

What's *your* Dawn Wall?

And what are you going to do differently from now on to manage your climb?

KEEPING YOUR COMPASS TRUE

You might be wondering how to know when to keep going…and when we're focusing on the wrong goal. Maybe in other circumstances, Kevin would have never made it up the Dawn Wall and died an old man still clinging to that rock.

Nobody wants to spend years trying to achieve something that ultimately doesn't give them anything they want.

As with many of the questions you might ask yourself when thinking about the concepts in this book, the answer lies in your heart.

Our heart is our internal compass that truly allows us to start to know, feel, and understand how we should be showing up in life right now.

Listening to the heart is how we progress the fastest. That means saying no to things that don't serve us, that aren't aligned with our boundaries or values, and saying yes to things that are.

But we often muck our progress up by listening to our brain instead of our heart.

Our brain is fueled by the scaredy-cat ego, remember? It's trying to keep you at the base of the mountain where it's safe.

It's why we get so set in our ways. It's why we get stuck into thinking that there's only one way to reach a goal. But working in front of the computer for fourteen hours a day is not the only (or best) way to build a business. Going on a gazillion dates is not necessarily the best way to find a partner who is a true match.

It's not always best to copy everyone else. And you don't have to stay stuck in the ways you've always done something, simply because that's all you've done to this point.

Everybody grows up modelling the people around them. We model our parents, to begin with, then other people at school, in sporting or social clubs, and then as we move through teenagerhood, we model people in our friendship group or outside influencers that we aspire to become. But their way is not necessarily the right way or the best way.

So many people have solutions within them, but they don't follow their inner voice because the solution feels too different. They discredit it, believing it's too easy or that there must be a catch.

As I said earlier in this chapter, we see that in business owners that want to work with The Game Changers all the time. The easiest, most straight-line solution can be right in front of them, but they'll think there's no way that such a simple solution would actually work. They won't step forward and take it because of their own hidden biases from how things were taught to them growing up.

Think of some of the beliefs that you have around your goals.

Do you believe you need to work hard to make money? Do you believe that someone like you won't find an ideal partner? Do you believe that you can't lose weight?

The truth is you can do anything you choose to. The only reason we don't reach our goals is that we go about them the wrong way, don't use the feedback we're getting to improve our approach, and then let our ego psych us out and stop us from moving forward altogether.

There are plenty of ways to leverage the resources you have around you to reach your goals easier, faster, or with less heartache than others have reached theirs... but if you don't listen to your heart's intuition, you won't see the way forward.

People create a whole lot of bullshit for themselves because they're not listening to their heart. Sometimes, your heart will tell you that you need a day off. Maybe you've been working ridiculous hours, or there are other things going on, and you need some time for self-care. Then that's absolutely what you should do.

Just the other day, I took a day off to go surfing and have lunch with a new connection here in Bali. Thanks to my heart's guidance, I intuitively felt like taking a break was what I needed to do. Turns out that the person I went to lunch with came back to me the next day and offered to buy me out of a business I wanted to exit.

That kind of stuff happens to me all the time because I'm showing up in a state of alignment with my values and integrity. I listen to what my heart tells me, and I trust that it will guide me true.

And it does. It isn't easy at first. But it's really that simple.

So, remember to check in with your heart, okay? It will show you the path forward. Even if that path doesn't always go in a straight line!

SETTING YOUR INTENTIONS

The other day, my partner, Kate, and I were packing to go to a breathwork session in Ubud, which is commonly regarded as the most spiritual area of Bali. We had our clothes, water bottles, and toiletry bags laid out on the big wooden table in our dining area.

Our little ginger cat, Nacho, was skittering up and down the length of the table, knocking things over and generally attempting to trash our attempts at neat packing.

Kate asked me, "What's your intention for this workshop?" I thought about it for a minute, then shrugged. "I didn't really have one," I told her. "I'm just happy to go along and enjoy it."

Then she made a comment to me that really made me stop and think for a minute. She said, "Barry, you never seem to have any wishes or intentions. It's almost like you don't want anything."

She was right, in a way. I don't have goals or intentions the way I used to. Sure, I still have goals I'd like to reach. Recently, the thought of growing my first business to $10 million a year popped up. And I thought, *Yeah, I'd really love to do that. If we grow that big, we will be able to help so many more people.*

When those kinds of thoughts come up, I'll put a plan around the goal and take action to move forward towards it. And I know I'll get there because I've built trust with myself and stay in integrity. I've spent so long following through on what I say that, nowadays, I do what I say I'm going to do without even thinking about it. It just happens. The pieces fall into place.

On the other hand, I do approach my life as a whole much differently. I used to have these long lists of goals, strategies, and plans. And I was so caught up in the busyness of it all. I was so consumed by these plans and all the pieces within them that I was not living in the moment and enjoying the small things.

These days, I enjoy having a cuddle with Kate in bed every morning and going surfing. I enjoy a nice cup of coffee or a beautiful meal. In previous years, I could have been looking at the most beautiful sunset that has ever been, and I wouldn't have really seen it because, in my head, I would be thinking of a million other things.

Maybe you can relate to this?

I'm not saying that being more present and enjoying the moment will remove all responsibility. I still have a really full life. I have businesses to run. Kids to raise. A partner to be there for. There is still plenty of "stuff" on my plate.

The only thing that has changed is *me* and my perception of reality.

Take everything away from me, and I will still find joy in the little things. I don't need money to go surfing. I don't need money to enjoy a cuddle in the morning. I don't need money to enjoy a nice sunset.

The more successful I become, the more I hear people say to me, "Oh, it's easy for you because you have money."

But I had to go through the journey of acquiring all this stuff to realise that it wasn't actually what made me happy.

There have been a lot of studies tracking what people say at the end of their lives. I've never come across an interview where someone says, "I wish I'd worked more hours." Or, "I wish I'd made more money."

What people wish for at the end of their lives is more time with family. They wish they'd stopped to smell the roses more and enjoy the special times in their lives.

Or they wish they hadn't held onto their anger or resentment towards someone for so long. They wish they'd stressed less. That they'd enjoyed the day-to-day moments more. In hindsight, what really matters in life becomes really clear.

What really matters to you?

And how can you honour it more in your everyday life?

BUILDING YOUR MUSCLE MEMORY

The first time you go anywhere, it's slower and harder than the next time and the next. Because that first time you're not 100 per cent certain of how to get there. You grab a map and plot out your path. You might try a few shortcuts that don't work out. You walk slowly as you look for street numbers to find the building you're after.

But once you've found your way there once, it's so much easier to go there again. You don't need to keep checking a map. You know which route is the best. You walk confidently and quickly.

It's the same with doing anything in life or business. It takes a while the first time. But once you know how, you can do it again and again, quicker and quicker each time. There was once a time when tying your shoelace took you five minutes and was a total pain in the arse. But now you do it in seconds without even thinking about it.

Once you build a business to a million bucks, it's very easy to do it again. Once you have built a business that can work without you, it's very easy to do it again. Once you've created wealth, it's very easy to do it again. Because you know the way. Just think about all the millionaires that have been bankrupt and made their fortune back again. There are more than you probably think!

I spent years building my first business to a million bucks in annual turnover. I made all the mistakes and spent loads of time figuratively wandering around in the dark, looking for a light switch.

But by the time I got there, the journey there had given me all the information I needed to know. So the second time, it happened much quicker and easier. Now I have a number of businesses that are growing astronomically faster than my first one.

However, without that journey towards my first seven-figure business, I wouldn't have all the other multiple seven-figure businesses that I do today. You cannot skip ahead. Sure, you can get coaching and training from others who have achieved your outcome before to get there faster (which is what we do at The Game Changers).

But at the end of the day, the journey still has to happen within you.

Because there are a lot of beliefs that have to change. And there are certain ways that we connect with our sense of self and sense of identity that have to change, too. Once that change has been created, it's easy to replicate the result because we're no longer out of alignment with who we need to be to reach that goal.

It's all muscle memory. The first time you start going to the gym, it's hard. You are sore for days. Your muscles ache and groan. It takes a lot to get to the certain size you want or weight you want to lift.

But if you have six months off, when you go back to the gym, you'll reach the level you were before quicker than the first time. Because you've already created these pathways within yourself to the result. And your body knows what to do.

So with everything in life, there is a certain amount of knowledge and insight that having "been there and done that" can give you. But half the problem is that the early version of you probably isn't open to listening to it.

If someone had told me exactly how to get to my goals many years ago, I probably wouldn't have listened. I chose instead to complain and feel shitty about my lack of progress.

I wasn't yet the person I needed to be to reach my goals. Not to mention, my goals were likely misaligned anyway.

We see it at The Game Changers all the time. Business owners will tell us about the courses or coaching they'd signed up for before, but "it didn't work." When we dug deeper into why it didn't work, it wasn't necessarily the training that was the problem. It was that the business owner simply didn't want to take the path that had been laid out for them.

Because they second-guessed it. They thought, *Oh, no, that doesn't apply to me, I'm different.* Or they didn't want to do the "hard stuff" that the path required. Sometimes, they thought the path was too simple to be true. Or any of the many other reasons they discounted the information they were being given as false.

The truth is that life's often not nearly as hard as we make it. Everything that we want to achieve takes a certain amount of actions done in a certain order. That's it.

But we second guess ourselves. We get tired of trying. We let defeat, impatience, or doubt creep in. Often when our goal is just around the corner.

You actually get a hell of a long way in life simply by showing up.

I've known some incredibly smart people who have never gotten a single business off the ground because they kept giving up. And I've known many people of average intelligence who become multimillionaires simply because they kept showing up—every day—and taking steps forward.

It's not intelligence, or luck, or being born into wealth, or anything outside ourselves that dictates what we can achieve in life.

It's showing up every day and putting in the steps required to reach the goal. Whether you want to learn to meditate, find an ideal partner, build a successful business, or become a better person, everything requires you to make the journey from who you were to who you need to be.

Some journeys are longer; some are shorter. But if you keep moving forward and keep analysing the results you get and refining your approach with every next step, you'll certainly get to where you want to go. But if you stand still and do nothing, you absolutely won't get anywhere.

LETTING GO OF PERFECTION

I started living by the mantra "progress over perfection" a few years ago. Because I realised that I had been putting so much pressure on myself to be perfect. And I noticed that our clients at The Game Changers put so much pressure on themselves to be perfect, too.

They waited for the perfect time to launch their new product to the market. They waited to turn their Facebook ads on until their funnel was perfect. They waited to hire their new staff member until they had all their systems in place and everything was perfect.

And this perfectionism was costing them a huge amount of time, energy, and money. And more importantly, it was costing them a lot of happiness, too.

But perfection doesn't exist.

If you look in nature, nothing lines up. Nothing's completely perfect. There's always a bit of variation here and there. Things are cracked and broken and torn, and still, there is incredible wonderment and beauty in that.

Yet, we have this obsession with perfectionism. But who are we trying to be perfect for? Whose approval are we trying to get? Whose love are we looking for?

And on the flip side, what would happen if something wasn't perfect? Would the world end? Would we lose everything?

There's a lot of biases and beliefs that are keeping people stuck around things like:

I don't want to be judged. I don't want to get it wrong. I don't want to show that I don't have the answers. I don't want to be found out.

But you could spend your entire life trying to get something perfect, and it still might not be right in the eyes of somebody else.

Whose life are you trying to live? Who are you trying to get the approval of? Are you living your life for yourself or for someone else whose opinion could change at any moment?

Living in truth, living a fulfilling and nourishing life is when you can be fully self-expressed, liberated, and own all of who you are.

"Progress over perfection" is a phrase that I began to use to relinquish some of the enormous, crushing pressure that I put on myself. Because every single day, I tried to work harder than anybody else. I tried to get things better than anybody else.

And do you know what?

People still judged me. Stuff still didn't work in my business sometimes. I still got things wrong in the eyes of others.

It didn't matter how hard I tried to make everything perfect.

So really…what was the fucking point?

I wondered, what if I started focusing on making progress instead? What would life be like if I stopped torturing myself and just focused on doing the things that needed to be done, one at a time, and trusting in the process?

When I started approaching my goals in life this way, I first set my goals according to what I thought would fulfil me. Things I thought would give me the sense of achievement that we all crave.

But these days, my goals are very different. Now, I often go after things for the growth I'll experience in the process. I am curious as to how far I can push myself to discover what I am actually capable of achieving. And every time I achieve something that I haven't done before, who I am as a person expands.

This was a big shift from thinking, *I need to make $10k a month* or placing all my focus on buying a house or car or whatever other materialistic thing I was chasing.

My new goal of growing The Game Changers to $10 million isn't about the money. It's about doing something I wasn't capable of doing before. It's about helping more people build businesses that give them the lifestyle they want and the ripple effects the growth will have across the world.

I know that to reach that goal, I will have to become a far greater version of who I am today. Because if I was already capable of doing it today, I'd have already done it.

So, I'm going to have to upgrade my mindset. My problem-solving abilities. My leadership abilities. My risk-aversion profile. Everything. And along the journey, I will become a greater version of myself.

It's about the challenge and the growth within me. I am not in a highly emotional state about it. It might take ten years, or it might take two. The time is irrelevant because the game is with myself.

And I'm focusing on progress over perfection. I'm focusing on the fact that if every single day I choose to take a step towards my goal, I will get there. Some days, I might not feel like working and go surfing instead. I will keep checking in with my heart and do what intuitively feels right for me.

But every single day, I still work on taking at least one step towards that door.

Sometimes, things will pop up that show me I'm not on the right track. Sometimes, I will not manage to take that one step forward one day. But you know what? That's not a reason to validate all of the things your ego is screaming in your head as it tries to keep you in the same comfort zone as before.

If you miss a day or two, it doesn't mean that you're not good enough, that nobody loves you, that your upbringing didn't set you up to succeed, or whatever rubbish your ego is telling you. It's just feedback. It's data that you can use to assess why you didn't achieve that step forward today and create a better plan for successfully taking a step forward tomorrow.

Even when you feel like you're not making progress...you are. Look at where you are right now and where you were five years ago.

Compare the two.

You've done a lot since then, haven't you? A lot of growing, a lot of learning, a lot of trying new things, of building your life, growing relationships, and so much more. Even if you've had a lot of painful experiences, you're wiser now than you were then, yes?

Did you even notice your progress? Or have you been so focused on the next mountain that you've forgotten to have gratitude for this one?

Life is beautiful. Not all of us get to enjoy it for long. It's about time you started loving your journey a bit more, don't you think?

Before you continue to the next chapter...

Go and enjoy that cup of coffee. Look out the window at the sky. Take stock of how far you've come in the last five, ten, or twenty years of your life. Feel the accomplishment of making it this far.

And then come back, fresh and ready to progress to what's next.

CHAPTER 15

DAILY RITUALS

"We are what we repeatedly do."

—Will Durant

"WHY IS THIS HAPPENING TO ME? I HATE THIS DAY ALREADY!"

It was a sunny Thursday morning, and I was lying in my bed in Palm Beach, Western Australia.

The morning started like any other. I woke up, and before both eyes were even open, I rolled over in my king size bed to grab my phone. Squinting at the sunlight that was streaming through the window from the oceanfront outside, I turned my phone off aeroplane mode and tried to focus as I watched the notifications stream down my screen.

I scrolled and scrolled, checking various apps and emails as I went through the stream of updates, questions, and things to do. Eventually, I landed on Slack, the messaging board we use for internal communications at The Game Changers.

My heart sank as I read the message from our client care captain, Salve.

"Greg M is leaving," it said. "Team FYI, please cease payments immediately and commence the client offboarding process."

A wave of anger and frustration hit me. *How could this have happened?* As I got out of bed, I was in a foul mood before my feet even hit the floor.

Immediately, I sprung into damage-control mode. I started messaging my team and trying to get more information about what had gone wrong with Greg. I flew into the shower, skipped breakfast, and didn't do my morning meditations. My mind was 100 per cent occupied with feeling like shit that this client had left us.

And do you know what?

That morning dictated how I spent the whole entire day. I spent the whole day pissed off. And even more than that, everything went wrong that day.

I mean *everything*. Random shit that you wouldn't believe.

It was like I was walking around with a rain cloud over my head. A cosmic neon flashing sign with a big arrow pointed at my head saying, *Fuck with this guy! He's full of negative energy; he must want some more!*

I fell over and tore my knee. Every meeting I had with my team was shit. People cut in front of me in traffic. Someone stuffed up my lunch order. My car had a flat tyre.

Now, it was all just situational stuff that shouldn't have had such a massive impact on me. On any other day, none of it would have even bothered me in the slightest.

But by the end of *this* day, I felt like absolute shit. I felt like life had grabbed me, boxed me around the ears a bit, and then dropped me into a rubbish bin.

As I sat at home trying to stop my head from spinning at the absolute shitshow my day had been, I realised something very important.

Fuck, I created this.

Sure, a client had left, and that sucked. But I chose to read that message from Salve before I'd even fully woken up. I chose to start my day reacting to other things. And I chose to let that experience set the tone for the rest of my day.

I almost laughed at how stupidly simple, yet utterly profound, that was. I made a promise to myself then and there: that day would be the very last time I set myself up like that.

The funny thing is, I'd been telling myself for weeks that I shouldn't check my phone first thing in the morning—that I should control how I set up my day. I'd been hearing it from other people, too. My heart had been whispering to me...but I hadn't listened.

So I set myself up for success. I downloaded my morning meditation, so I could do it without needing internet access on my phone. The next morning, as I woke up and grabbed my phone to turn off my alarm, I resisted the urge to turn on the internet and check my notifications.

To this day, I remember really clearly how hard that was. My dopamine addiction was so strong. Even though checking in every two minutes ultimately made me feel like shit...I still craved knowing what was going on. Fear of missing out sure does have a barb in its tail to bite you on the ass!

But I stayed true to my intention. Instead of going for the dopamine hit, I hit play on my meditation video and spent twenty minutes in deep calm and positive energy. By the end of the meditation, I felt amazing. My positive outlook was bullet-proof. *We can attract five more clients*, I decided. I wandered downstairs and began a series of five morning rituals to take care of my body, mind, and spirit.

Then it was time to begin my working day.

At the time, I was still in the primary sales role within the business. That day turned out to be one of my highest sales days ever. I think I signed five or six more clients. Every interaction I had with my team was great. Even though a highly valued staff member resigned that day, instead of feeling shitty, I felt okay and trusted that I would be given what I need from the universe.

I was a different man.

That night as I sat down to dinner, it hit me how much we create our own experience. I had two days side by side that were as different as they could be. On the first day, everything that could have gone wrong did. The next day could've easily gone like that, too, especially when my team member quit. But because of how I chose to get up and start my day, the whole entire day was different.

I finished that day feeling on top of the world. It was such a strong confirmation that we create our own experience of life.

From that point on, I decided to never again blame anyone or anything else for the experiences I have in life. Good or bad, it's all on me.

And that's really helped me recognise those moments when I was sabotaging myself, when I was blaming others for my lack of results, and when I was jumping into all those unresourceful behaviours. It has helped me to recognise those patterns, and instead of blaming, ranting, or raving, now I ask myself one question:

How have I created this experience?

I take responsibility for my own shit instead of palming the blame onto someone or something else. Because when you do that, you disempower yourself. By telling yourself that someone else is responsible for your results, you're giving *them* the power over your life. You're bowing out.

Fuck that. I am in control. I teach the world how to show up for me. By taking responsibility for myself, I can create my own experience of life that is much better than bouncing around like a pinball reacting to everything outside of me on an endless loop.

Which would you prefer?

. . .

OWN YOUR DAY (OR BECOME ITS BITCH)

Most of us live in a highly reactionary state. We are not in control of our days and spend our time pinballing from one problem or task to another.

Sadly, it's because we have handed over control to others.

It starts small at first...we don't uphold boundaries here or there; we answer an email or two after hours, we skip breakfast in favour of getting the kids to school or getting to work early, but then it builds and builds.

And before you know it, your entire day is completely controlled by the people around you. Clients, staff, kids, partners, friends. All you do is jump from one "have to do this" to the next.

But we set ourselves up for it.

For many years, I'd wake up, reach over and grab my phone, and start checking apps before my eyes were even focused. I'd check WhatsApp, Messenger, texts, and then emails. If I was feeling particularly sadistic, I'd have a quick scroll through Facebook or Instagram.

And before I even got out of bed, my day was controlling me. I remember that I used to experience my days feeling anxious, out of control, and overwhelmed. Every day was a whirlwind.

Nowadays, I set my phone to aeroplane mode, so I get absolutely no notifications until I choose to turn them back on. And I only look at my phone after I've had my morning cuddles with my girl, meditated, and whatever other self-care activities—my daily rituals—I choose to do.

The reason that daily rituals are so important, more than anything, is because they mean that you are owning your day before your day owns you.

If you're waking up to incoming messages from other people, demands from your children, and other outside noise that you blindly obey, you're setting a negative framework for the whole day before the day has even really started. You set the scene for being out of control. And what's worse, without even knowingly doing it, you start to create unconscious beliefs that you can't do anything else. That there's no other way to live...that this is "just how it is."

Those beliefs are the voice that's saying, *But I have kids that need to be fed breakfast,* or *But I have people at work that rely on me.* Well, that might be true, but you can control when and how you meet those needs.

You teach other people how to treat you. *You* create the boundaries in your own life.

Don't you?

If you answer a phone call from your boss or your client on a Saturday, you unconsciously tell them that it's okay to call you on the weekend. If you don't respect your time, they won't either. Why should they?

If you answer the demands of your children at six o'clock in the morning, you're unconsciously training them that you're available for whatever they want at that time.

Where in actual fact, they're not going to starve if they wait an hour for breakfast. They're not going to die if they don't get your attention at the crack of dawn. Your business is not going to collapse if you don't answer that phone call on a Sunday.

And if you reason that by taking care of it now, you're saving yourself time later, you're kidding yourself. Because there will always be more of whatever you're letting in.

Over the years, you have taught the world how to interact with you. If you've got a million things to do and multiple entities making demands of you and your time, the sad truth is that it's your fault. At some point, you've let these patterns begin, and now they're self-perpetuating.

The good news is that you trained the world this way once, so you can retrain it whenever you choose to!

It starts with filling your own cup.

FILLING YOUR CUP

Society teaches us that taking care of ourselves first is selfish and a bad thing. I think that's a bunch of BS.

On an aeroplane, we're instructed to put on our own oxygen masks first before helping a child do the same. If you think that's a crazy idea, how much help do you think you'll be to everyone if you've passed out due to lack of oxygen because you tried to help them first!

Apply this to your everyday life.

Taking care of yourself equals keeping your cup full. Filling your cup replenishes your stores of mental, emotional, and physical energy. Every day, we all need something that's nurturing us spiritually, mentally, and physically. That's how we fill our cup, which allows us to show up at our best.

If you're not filling your own cup, how can you fill the cups of others? If you're not taking care of your own physical, mental, emotional, and spiritual health . . . you're not only going to be operating at about 30 per cent of your own capacity, but you're not going to have much left to give others. You're going to be cranky, stressed, tired, and generally feeling far from your best.

Empty cups lead to burnout and breakdown. They lead to feeling like you're just going through the motions of life, too tired and uninspired to appreciate the amazing gift of your time on this planet.

That's no way to live.

So why do we put others before ourselves?

Once again, the answer is our need for belonging. We want to feel connected to a tribe.

We reach for our phone every morning because we're craving connection. We're looking for some form of a dopamine hit, but ultimately, what we're really looking for is belonging.

The crazy thing about it is that social media networks were created for us to experience more connection, but they've actually achieved the opposite. We are more removed from each other than ever. We feel more alone than ever.

I said to my son the other day, "Why don't you get off your Xbox and hang out with some friends?" Do you know what he said? "But Dad, we don't do that in our generation anymore. We meet online, and we play games together online."

Is that how fucked up the world is right now that people can't even meet up face to face anymore? Even before COVID hit, this is how things were. Calling friends on the phone is a rarity these days—instead, we look at their Facebook feed and feel like we're connected because we're seeing what they are up to. We like a picture or send a quick comment. But it's not really connecting on a deep human level.

And we crave that connection. Which is why we keep reaching for that phone. There was a study done a while ago that found the average user touches their phone over 2,000 times a day (Naftulin 2016). I know that, for me, when I first installed my iPhone monitoring app, it found that I used to spend eight hours a day on my phone, which is astronomical.

We crave connection. And we look for it in virtual spaces that offer escapism instead of actually living the human experience. We post on social media and keep refreshing to see who likes our update because that will make us feel worthy and as though we belong. We scroll Instagram and get depressed because everyone's painting a picture of their amazing life, and ours doesn't match up. And so, our need grows. The cycle continues.

Yet, fundamentally, what we're missing is that connection and belonging to self. We're missing the essential connection with who we really are. And that's where waking up and having a daily ritual can create that connection in a profound way.

It fills your cup.

YOUR NEW FIVE SERVES A DAY

Health and wellness associations worldwide recommend eating five serves of vegetables a day to maintain great health. Your daily rituals are a new kind of five serves, but instead of just nourishing your body, they nourish every part of your being.

Here's how it works.

Every day, aim to do five things:

1. One thing that gives you fun, such as hobbies.
2. One thing that nurtures your spiritual self.
3. One thing that gives you health.

4. One to make you money or build wealth.

5. And one to build knowledge or evolve your mindset.

This can look however you want it to. As long as you're doing something that sits in each of these "essential five."

When I started doing my daily rituals, at first, I looked around me and saw what people I admired or aspired to be like did, and I did that, too. And it kind of worked, but ultimately, what made the most difference was checking in with myself.

I took the time to think about what made *me* feel good.

Everyone is different, but what I found was best for me is to wake up, sit up, and meditate. A lot of people get up and exercise first and then meditate. But I found that once I had exercised, I was way too energised and thinking about all the stuff I had to do that day.

Now the first thing I do is have cuddles with my partner, which is very nourishing from a spiritual aspect. There's a lot of loving and connection in that space. Then I'll get up and have water first thing, which is great for the body. Then I'll meditate, which is something for my heart. Then I'll get the kids off to school. Then I'll do some yoga or stretching, or more vigorous exercise like walking or running. I'll listen to a podcast while exercising to incorporate something for my mind at the same time.

Then I will go for a surf, come back and have a healthy breakfast, and set my intentions for the day. I might spend some time learning the guitar or something that nurtures my creativity. I do whatever I'm feeling that day, as long as it's in tune with what my heart tells me I need.

For you, it might look different.

You might do yoga. You might drink green smoothies. You might go for a walk in the morning and listen to your favourite podcast. You might meditate or pray. You might journal and set your daily intentions. You might go for a run. Or a bike ride. You might go to the beach and just sit and watch the waves. There are so many different things you can do.

Everybody has a different recipe for their ultimate cup filling, and you need to find what resonates with you. As long as you're feeding your mind, body, and spirit, you're on the right track.

My daily rituals take me anywhere from fifteen minutes to three hours, depending on how much I decide to do that day. But I always check something off for my heart, mind, and body, no matter how small.

And I always start with the heart. I start in spirituality and in grounding myself. If I do that, my days run better, smoother, and more productively than if I just jump straight into action. And by doing that, I'm also building that connection with myself.

For you, your daily rituals don't need to be a three-hour journey. It could just be fifteen minutes. I don't care how much you've got going on in your life, everybody can create fifteen minutes of time in their day if they truly prioritise it.

If you think *I've got kids, I can't do it*; you can. You can get up earlier. If you didn't sleep very well, that's exactly why you should get up earlier because you'll need a lot less sleep if you meditate more, if you exercise more, and if you nourish your body more.

If you've got a busy workday, there are things you can do to create that fifteen minutes of "you time," too. Schedule a meeting with yourself in your calendar. Start maintaining your boundaries with staff or colleagues who previously had the rights to your attention at a moment's notice. Do what you need to do.

If you're thinking, *That's easy for you, Barry, you've got this lifestyle now where you don't have to work* ... that's bullshit. I have my kids living with me. I have multiple businesses. I have household staff to organise. I have stuff on my plate, too.

But I get up earlier to make sure I do my daily rituals every single day. And the more I take care of my mental, physical, and spiritual health, the better I feel and operate.

So, take the time to think about what fills your cup.

What feeds your body, mind, and spirit?

And where are you going to create the time for your daily self-care?

DECIDING ON YOUR RITUALS

If you're feeling the urge to start brainstorming what your daily rituals will be, you're already setting yourself up for failure.

As I have mentioned before, this book is divided into three parts, which represent three actions—being, doing, having—for a good reason. You can't jump straight to the having until you sort out the being and doing parts first. And you shouldn't jump into doing without first deciding on the rest, either.

If you have already whipped out your phone and are looking up a meditation app right now, you're jumping the gun. You're jumping straight into the doing phase without first deciding who you need to be and what you want to have.

If you simply pick a ritual at random, or because it's "cool," or because your friend does it and she looks really happy... you're going about it the wrong way. And your daily rituals will not make you feel any better.

To truly get great results in anything, the doing needs to be supported by first understanding the outcome you're looking for. What is the thing you actually want to achieve by having a daily ritual?

And you also need to understand the being part of your goal. Who do you need to be to successfully achieve that result?

When we jump into the action of doing, without understanding who or why, we will always fail. Because we don't understand who we need to be to get there and what we want to have in the first place.

Without this understanding, we're floating around in the middle somewhere, wondering why we're not getting results. It's because we're focusing on the wrong things and not setting ourselves up for success.

So, the first thing to think about is what you want to have. Decide on why having a daily ritual is important to you.

A good place to start when figuring this out is to look at the ways in which you're not in control of your day right now.

Do you allow the demands of your partner, your kids, or your business to dictate how you spend your day?

Where do you find yourself complaining or feeling the most resentful? They're the signposts of where you're not setting yourself up to be in control of your day. Where you feel the shittiest is where you're the most reactionary.

Where in your day do you feel most like a ball battered around a pinball machine?

And how can you change your approach to your day so that you're not feeling this way?

Start there.

DEBUGGING THE TIME MYTH

I've coached a lot of people around their own identity of self.

People think, *I'm a mother. I'm a husband. I'm a business owner.* And whatever else. Those identities shape our behaviours. Not always in a conscious way, but they do.

And we let those identities define what we prioritise and how we spend our time. We think that we don't have time to exercise because our kids get up early in the morning. We think we don't have the time to meditate every day because work keeps us too busy.

But do you know what?

We all have the same amount of time every day.

We can take the time to exercise, meditate, or do anything else we want to prioritise. We can get up an hour early. We can skip watching Netflix for an hour at night. Does that mean it's easy? Perhaps not at first. Especially if you're not a morning person!

People resist getting up an hour early because they feel like they're missing out on sleep. But the reality is that if you got up earlier to nourish yourself and take care of yourself, you'd actually start to require less sleep at night.

We tell ourselves that the reason we're tired is that we're not sleeping enough, when really, better nutrition, yoga, and meditation gives us much more energy than that extra hour of tossing in bed.

This is where there is that conundrum in our minds, and it's based on the identity we've created for ourselves.

I have clients that wake up at four o'clock every morning, so they've got time to do their daily rituals before the kids wake up and their business day starts.

It's a matter of priorities.

People will say, "Oh, I don't have the money to get a haircut," and then spend $40 on a pack of cigarettes. They'll say, "I don't have the time to go to the gym," and spend hours watching TV at night.

But if it's enough of a priority, then you do whatever is needed to get it done.

There are plenty of ways to leverage more time or money out of your day by being smarter with the resources you have available.

Organise carpools with the other parents in your kid's sports team to give you a few nights off driving. Start making coffee yourself at home instead of paying $6 at a cafe every day. Order a few ready-made meals a few times a week to save cooking and cleaning time. Or batch your cooking and do the month's dinners on the first Sunday of each month. Cut back on pay-per-view subscriptions and spend the money on an exercise app instead.

Either we'll find a way, or we'll find an excuse.

The next time you say, "I don't have time," say to yourself, "It's not a priority for me," and see how that feels.

You have the same amount of time as anybody else in the world. But how you choose to spend that time is up to you. How much time do you spend watching Netflix, sleeping in, playing on your phone, checking social media, and other activities that aren't moving you towards who you want to be?

Is that time you're spending worth it? Is it producing a return on your investment, if not financially, then emotionally, physically, spiritually? Are you getting healthier, stronger, or fitter? Are you becoming calmer, less stressed, more present? Are you learning and expanding your skillset?

If not, perhaps it's time to switch some of your time to things that do produce a positive return on investment (ROI).

Everything that you do in life costs you something and gives you something.

What do you do, and what does it cost you?

Is the payoff you're getting back worth it?

AN EASY WAY TO FORM NEW HABITS

Don't get me wrong; I'm not expecting a superhuman effort from you.

I know that it can be hard to start a new ritual at first. After all, you're already running your day according to another set of rituals that are much more firmly established. Now you want to change things?

Uh-uh, says the ego, *that sounds hard. It sounds like possible pain* (short term at least). *Let's bypass it*, says the ego. *It's cold, stay in bed. You're tired. The kids are too loud today. You've gotta do all these things, and you don't have time.*

What the ego is really doing is keeping you on the track that you're currently on. Your comfort zone. The ego loves comfort.

But your growth lies beyond your comfort zone. You want to go there, but it can be so difficult at first! So, what to do? Well, here's a really handy tool that can trick even the most stubborn ego-centric mindset into developing new patterns of behaviour. I use it all the time myself to get new habits started.

To embed your new habit, create the connection in your heart and mind around why you want to create the habit. What is it you're wanting to get out of it?

For example, just say you want to create the habit of having a big glass of water when you wake up. What it might be giving you is that when you start the day hydrated, your body and brain don't feel so lethargic. You feel more alert and ready to start the day. That's your outcome, not so much the process of drinking. When you connect to the outcome strongly enough, the process will take care of itself.

Another thing to keep in mind is a concept Tony Robbins coined called NET time, meaning No Extra Time. What this term entails is linking aspects of your daily rituals with things you're already doing (Team Tony).

As an example, one of my goals is to learn Bahasa Indonesian. So, I incorporate eating breakfast and lunch with learning and practising this new language. By combining something new with something I'm already doing, it makes forming the new habit much easier.

And it's also a way of leveraging more value out of my time. Nourishment for the body and brain at once!

What can you combine in your daily life with a new ritual?

BUILDING CONSISTENCY

For a long time, I was really inconsistent with my goals, rituals, and life in general! I would have lists everywhere, post-it notes on my wall, reminders everywhere about the things I wanted to achieve.

- Do yoga
- Meditate
- Learn the guitar
- Learn to surf
- Go to the gym
- Hit my dietary macros

I would have dates across the top. Every day, I would try and tick off as many of those things as I could in the morning. Depending on how my day worked out in terms of meetings and so on, some days, I would get more done than others. But because I was so committed to completing what I started every single day, I'd get through the list.

Even if they weren't complete in the morning, before I went to bed, I'd assess my list. I haven't meditated today. I haven't done yoga. Or whatever else.

Then I'd do it before bed.

The more I built that commitment muscle, the more those tasks started to become second nature. And because I'm a very visual person, having the checklist on my wall where I saw it every day helped enormously.

Habit-forming is nothing more than being consistent at doing something. It's that simple. Yet not always easy.

I'm not saying I'm superhuman. I get that sometimes it's tough to keep consistent. Over the last week, there have been multiple mornings where I just didn't want to go surfing. Don't get me wrong; I love doing it. But some days, it's been raining. Other days, the bed is so comfortable, and I don't want to get up.

But each time, I forced myself to go, and do you know what? The best sessions I've had have been the times I was most resistant to going.

It would have been very easy to listen to that voice in my head that says, *Barry, just press the snooze button again* ... But the issue is, once you open that door to becoming someone who doesn't keep your word, especially to yourself, that starts an avalanche that grows from flaking on small commitments to bigger ones.

Small hinges swing big doors.

What you do doesn't matter that much. The *doing* is what's important. If you've been going to the gym every day and you wake up and really don't feel like it, then go for a fifteen-minute walk instead. But still, do something that's aligned with your physical movement.

By doing that, not only do you keep forming the habit, but most importantly, you continue to embed that you're somebody that consistently follows through on their commitments and intentions.

According to Phillippa Lally, a health psychology researcher at University College in London, a new habit usually takes a little more than two months—sixty-six days to be exact—and as much as 254 days until it's fully formed (Lally et al. 2009). But everybody is a bit different. Some habits will come easier than others. The more your new habit is at odds with your self-identity, the harder it will be to form. But you will get there.

Consistency is key, so focus on that. Don't feel you have to take massive action every day. Taking massive action is great, but it requires a lot of sudden energy and change. And if you're not used to doing it, what happens the next day? You're spent. You don't follow through, so you don't achieve shit. What a waste.

I'd rather do something small every day and improve incrementally than force myself into this big burst of energy for one day and then give up because it's too hard maintaining that level of gruntwork.

For me, what's created my own success is consistently showing up. Even when I haven't wanted to. Just like my spiritual guru Irmansyah Effendi teaches, every single day, I got up and walked towards that door. Some days, I've taken many steps; some days, I've only taken one or two. But every day, I'm doing something to get to that door.

The day I get up and decide that something is more important than my ritual, that's the day I abandon that practice.

Now, if we abandon a daily ritual because it's not working for us, and we've made a conscious decision around it, that's great. But if we abandon our practices because we can't be bothered, or we tell ourselves that we don't have time, then we're dismantling the way of being that we've taken so long to nurture and create.

And that's a bloody shame.

So don't feel you have to move mountains in a single day—you don't. Start small.

Even if you start off spending just five minutes a day doing your habits, do it. And then build up from there. Keep doing it consistently until it becomes a habit. Believe me when I say that every minute you spend doing your daily rituals will have a compounding effect.

If you get off track, get back on. Maintain your commitment to yourself. Sure, we all have outside forces that push and pull us. Shit happens.

But at the end of the day, the only one responsible for your life is *you*.

And if you don't take control of how you choose to live it, others will do it for you.

How do *you* choose to live?

Decide on your rituals, then make them happen. It's that simple.

FINDING MORE TIME

You'd be surprised at how much time you actually waste each day.

A few minutes on Instagram here, a quick email check there... it all adds up. Without even knowing you, I'm absolutely sure that you could gain the time for a couple of daily self-care rituals simply by cutting out the time detritus from your current day.

But let's do this the easy way. As with everything you want to do or achieve in life, it's easy when you have one thing: data. With data, you can determine where you are now and plot the path through reverse engineering to where you want to be.

So do me a favour, okay?

Install Rescuetime on your computer.

Get a time tracker app for your Smartphone.

They'll give you a report of how you spend your time each week on those two devices. I'm sure you'll be surprised at the results.

And for everything else, there's a really handy tool that we use at The Game Changers called The Task Audit™.

Essentially, you get a piece of paper and create four columns: time, activity, category, priority.

Then you record every task you do and how long it takes you, for two weeks. At the end of those two weeks, you'll have a clear view of what types of things eat up your time. When you see those patterns, you can think of how to utilise that time better.

For our business clients at The Game Changers, we advise them to only spend time on the things that fall into the top priority category: high-level activities that only they can do. For the others, they have three choices: delegate to somebody else on their team, outsource it to an external provider or delete it altogether.

You can apply the same strategy in your own daily life.

For example, just say you spend five hours a week doing laundry. You might decide to outsource your laundry by hiring a laundry service to take care of it each week. There's five hours you can spend filling your cup.

If you spend too many hours on your phone, you might decide to reduce time-suck activities by putting an app on your phone that limits your social media time or alerts you when you've spent more than two hours on your phone a day.

As I said earlier in this chapter, there are plenty of ways to leverage your time differently. You just need to get over your limiting thinking (*I can't because...*). The truth is that your own identity is limiting what you think you "have to" do. Especially if part of your identity is that you give to others before yourself (which ironically means that over time you have less and less to give).

If you think you can't, the truth is that you just don't want to.

Either you'll find a way, or you'll find an excuse.

It's entirely up to you.

■ ■ ■

START TODAY

Don't underestimate the power of setting up each day intentionally.

Doing daily rituals marks a fundamental shift in the way you show up in life and the way that others show up to meet you in life. They shift the way that your entire world interacts with you.

So, make the decision now to start incorporating daily rituals into your morning. Try to start with three and see how you go. But make the commitment right now.

It doesn't matter at this point which rituals you choose, whether drinking a glass of water, meditating, doing yoga, or whatever else.

Sure, those things are important, but the most important thing is for you to build the framework of waking up in control of the way your environment interacts with you.

That's what daily rituals are fundamentally about.

You might need to put some boundaries around how your kids interact with you in the morning. Or you might need to put boundaries around your phone or your employees. That might take a small period of adjustment, but that's ok.

Because what's the alternative? Think about how worn out you feel right now. How much do you really have left to give?

If you're running yourself down each day, feeling more trampled on and exhausted as the years go by, for fuck's sake, it's about time you took control!

Daily rituals for the mind, body, and spirit are vitally important for a well-rounded, happy, and productive life. You're not being selfish or wasting your time by moving your body, stimulating your mind, and feeding your soul. By helping yourself, you're able to help others at a much higher level than giving them the last 20 per cent of your energy each day.

So, start filling your bloody cup, okay?

CHAPTER 16

SELF-LOVE

"You've been criticizing yourself for years, and it hasn't worked.
Try approving of yourself and see what happens."

—*Louise Hay*

"I DON'T WANT TO SPEND CHRISTMAS WITH YOUR FAMILY. I THINK
I should leave."

I sat on the bed in a spare bedroom of my childhood home in Tasmania,
fiddling anxiously with a frayed stitch on the quilt cover, wanting to go back
and join the warmth and laughter with my family in the living room. My
eyes widened as I tried to comprehend what my partner was saying.

We'd arrived just hours before, excited at the prospect of a few days spent
with my whole family over Christmas. It was a time I cherished, especially
because I only got to do it every two years as we swapped family Christmas
celebrations each year—one year hers, one year mine.

I was still giddy from hugs with my mum and dad, from wrestling with
my kids and seeing their beaming faces, from sharing a beer with my brothers,

from stacking our gifts under the tree, from the smell of Mum's roast cooking in the oven.

And now she wanted to leave? Before we'd even made it through Christmas Eve? What was going on?

I stared at her, flabbergasted and hurt, but also not surprised deep down. Our relationship had been full of love, and we'd shared many wonderful experiences together. But at the same time, we'd always experienced massive amounts of conflict.

You know those relationships that are always breaking up or making up, always up or down...the rollercoaster ones? The ones where friends roll their eyes when they hear about your latest blow-up and ask you why you stay? That was us.

Don't get me wrong; there was a lot of love. But for various reasons, we just couldn't seem to stay on the same page for long. Whether it was emotional baggage, unhelpful conflict resolution patterns, not showing up authentically, and whatever else...there was always something blocking us from becoming a truly aligned and fulfilled partnership.

Desperate to please her, I had been trying to change myself to fit what I thought she wanted me to be, something I know now was never going to work. But back then, I would try anything. Psychologists, workshops, relationship coaches...I did it all.

And along the way, I deepened my relationship with myself and my own heart connection. I started to value and love myself. To realise that my needs and boundaries were important, too. To understand that regularly bending to meet someone else's expectations is not a healthy way to live.

And so, on that Christmas Eve, as we were sitting in the small, cream-walled spare bedroom of the home I grew up in, and she was telling me she wanted to go and see her family instead, something came out of my mouth that I didn't anticipate.

"No, this is not okay." What had I said? On the many other times where we'd had some kind of conflict like this, I'd told her to do what she needed to do. I'd put her first and myself second.

But this time, I felt different.

"Look," I continued, "We spent Christmas with your family last year. This year was supposed to be with my family."

I could hear a sudden roar of laughter and clacking of plates coming from the living room as my family set the dinner table, intermingled with the faint tingle of Christmas carols on the TV. I wanted so much for us to go into the warmth and comfort of their company and enjoy Christmas with them.

"All my family are here. All my brothers have flown in. My kids are here. You made the commitment to see my family this year. I understand that you miss your family, but I want you to keep that commitment."

"I need some time for me," she said.

"I understand that, and I know it's a full and noisy house, but it means a lot for you to be here. This is the only time I get my family all together, and you're a part of that. I don't want to have to wait another two years for this opportunity again. It would really mean a lot to me if you could stay. What if you took an afternoon to yourself instead of leaving completely?"

She blinked a couple of times, perhaps surprised that I had stood my ground on the issue. Perhaps she felt I was being selfish. She got angry.

She told me that I didn't love her. That I was trying to get rid of her. And a bunch of other things that came from a place of rage.

This unhealthy pattern had played out in our conflicts often. Usually, I would lose my certainty and courage in who I was and go into pleasing mode to try and resolve the situation.

But as much as I wanted us to be happy again, this time, I wasn't going to participate. I wasn't going to sacrifice what I needed to "prove" to her that I loved her. It wasn't helping either of us.

All of the conflict and problems we'd gone through in the relationship rushed in all at once, overwhelming me. I was getting lost in the mess we were creating, losing sight of who I was and what I wanted.

I knew I needed to love myself enough to do what was right for me. I was done with twisting myself into knots to try and fit someone else's expectation of me.

"I do love you," I told her. "I love you more than anything in the world. It's because I love you that I'm taking a stand on this. This is what's important for me and for us right now. And if me standing here telling you that spending Christmas with you as part of my family makes you feel that I don't love you, then there's absolutely nothing else I can do. If you want to leave, then pack your bags and go."

As I finished speaking, my stomach dropped, and my adrenaline surged. I started shaking. With anger? With fear? I don't know. Part of me wanted to take it all back, to relent and give in to whatever she wanted just so she would be happy and love me again.

"Fine," she said and bent down to pick up her suitcase. As she threw it on the bed and started packing clothes inside, I brushed past her and went outside to gather my thoughts. The squeaky front wire door slammed behind me, and I stood for a minute blinking back tears in the cool nighttime air, staring at the chipped white paint on the front porch railing and trying to come to terms with what had just happened.

Fifteen minutes later, she was gone... and I tried to face Christmas with my family amongst the awkwardness of the fact that she had just left me, and everybody knew it.

Being without her hurt like hell. I felt like I had sunk into a dark pit and didn't have the strength to get out. It was hard to interact with my family —even my boys—because I felt so alone and somehow ashamed that the woman I loved was not by my side.

When I got back to our apartment in Melbourne after Christmas, all of her stuff was gone. All that was left were my things and a crushing sense of enormous emptiness. This was really it. She was really gone.

This is a woman that I loved deeply for many years and still have great respect and admiration for today. A beautiful, wonderful person. I'll be forever grateful for the lessons she taught me.

Looking back, packing up her stuff and leaving was the best thing she could have done. Because we both knew it wasn't working, but we loved each other so much that we kept smashing ourselves together, trying to force the pieces into place. And perhaps for many years more, we would have continued to do just that instead of finding our happiness apart.

Now I know that all the times I loved her more than I loved myself, all the times I didn't honour my boundaries, all the times that I played into unhelpful patterns... it didn't help either of us. It wasn't honouring her, just as it wasn't honouring me.

Hindsight has shown me that we were always going to end. But I prolonged our struggle for so long, sacrificing my own self-love for that of somebody else. It was never going to work because how could she have truly been happy with me when I was an empty cup?

My existence had been wrapped around her, but my own lack of self-love and self-worth meant that I could never be fulfilled. Nor could I really share with her from a place of abundance and strength... it was always from a place of emptiness and lack.

The reality is that during our relationship, every time I felt she didn't put me first, she was actually just reflecting my own lack of self-worth back at me. After all, the people in our lives are simply a reflection of ourselves. She so beautifully showed me all the areas of my life that I wasn't connected to.

She showed me where I needed to grow, develop, and love.

What lessons are the people in your life teaching you right now?

YOU ARE ENOUGH

Looking back on my life, I was always so super hard on myself. I was always my biggest critic. Nothing I ever did was good enough. I was never good-looking enough. I was never smart enough. I could never articulate my words clear enough.

It was my default setting to look for whatever was wrong in whatever I was doing. And what was wrong was always linked back to one thing: me.

I don't even know where I learned to do that. Where do we learn to be so negative about ourselves? It feels like the majority of the whole world is playing in that space, whether they show it publicly or not.

Sometimes, we all feel like we're not good enough.

So, we feel the need to prove to the world that we *are* good enough. And we do that by playing with a hundred selfie filters on Instagram, buying hot cars, rubbing shoulders with celebrities, or whatever else.

The reality is that we are all whole, perfect, and complete...yet not finished.

We all have the opportunity that whatever situation we find ourselves in at any point, no matter how bad we have fucked up our lives, we have the power to rebuild it in a positive way.

But we don't always see that power. Instead, we keep ourselves disempowered by beating ourselves up.

And to what end? Who is it really serving?

As I said in the last chapter, you need to take care of yourself before you can take care of anybody else. You need to put your oxygen mask on first, right? But the truth is that a lot of people spend their whole lives giving to others wholeheartedly, yet not giving themselves the same level of care.

We constantly show up, loving everyone else before we love ourselves.

If you do this, why?

We are all worthy of love. Especially from ourselves. No matter how flawed and fucked up we feel. No matter how many mistakes we have made. No matter how many regrets we have. We all deserve love. And it starts from within.

If you don't feel like you are worthy of love, consider this:

If you line up a bunch of six-year-olds in a row and walk down the line looking in all of their faces...which one of them is not worthy of love?

None of them, right? They are all worthy.

What's the difference between them and you? A few decades of living.

Some mistakes, perhaps. Some regrets. But part of us is still that six-year-old child. We are still worthy of love.

You are still worthy of love.

EMBRACING YOUR UGLY BITS

Self-love is about loving yourself and all the gifts that you've been given, even the ones that you don't particularly like. Even the ones that you are afraid of or ashamed of. The anger, the rage, the shame, the guilt, the judgement. The funny nose, the big ears.

Back when I was at school, I'd get teased every day. About a lot of things, including my ears. I had big ears, and I got called things like wingnut dumbo, big ears, and other names. Kids can be pretty cruel! I'd go home every day crying about it.

My parents would tell me we could always get them pinned back if I wanted. But Mum would also say, "Look, Barry, this is what you've been given. This is your gift. If you were meant to be given ears that sat back, then you'd have ears that sat back."

I never got them pinned back, and even though I was tormented by them at school, I've never had an issue with them since leaving. My ears haven't changed. What has changed is *me*.

Looking back on it now, I'm so grateful for having the experience of the bullying and teasing I went through at school. Because without it, I wouldn't have the resilience I have today. I wouldn't have the determination. I wouldn't have the fire in my belly.

Did I want it at the time? Fuck no! But I also know that a lot of the kids from my old school aren't doing so well now. They're stuck in medio-cre jobs they probably hate because they never developed the resilience to push further.

In my life and business, challenges come—oh, and there have been many! But they don't even present themselves as challenges anymore. Instead, they are opportunities for me to find out who I am by fixing them and moving through them.

The fact is that we don't live in a fairy floss world full of rainbows where everything is great all the time. Sometimes, life will knock you down. But you develop the sense of resilience and self-love to be okay with whatever happens.

Because the harmonious, peaceful utopia people are looking for is not outside of themselves. It's within us.

The utopia is learning to be who you need to be to face whatever comes to you. The only way to do that is to find a way to love all of us.

It can be hard at first, especially when you commit to showing up authentically and vulnerably.

At the beginning of my current relationship, I didn't want to keep repeating patterns of the past. So, I chose to show up fully as all of me. It was incredibly challenging, especially at the very beginning. Stuff would come up that I was so ashamed to share. But I would still share it.

And this weird thing happened. My partner, Kate, would just love me through it. She didn't laugh in my face or use it as a weapon against me or any of the things I was afraid might follow. She just met me where I am and held the space for me to be me. Amazing what can happen when you trust your heart, right?

In fact, my willingness to show up as all of me—even the bits I'd rather hide—has ended up being one of the qualities that she loves the most about me.

It's easy to present yourself in the best light and be the version of yourself that you love the most. But that's inauthentic and ultimately another mask that stops us from truly receiving love. Because how can anyone really love you if they don't really know who you are?

Sharing all of yourself is hard, and not everyone is ready for this level of vulnerability. I've had partners in the past who used my weaknesses against me. Partners who didn't hold the space for me to be all of myself.

But I kept staying true to who I really am, trusting in my heart that I would attract other people who were right for me. I'm not just talking about a romantic partner, but friends, colleagues, the whole spectrum of people that come into my life.

The more I share my whole self, the more aligned my circles become.

And quite beautifully, through me being willing to go there and my partner, Kate, being willing to hold me through it, I've learned to love those shadowy parts within me. When you can express them and give them a voice and love them inside of you, you start to actually realise those shadows are part of who you are. They're part of what makes you, you.

Anger. Jealousy. Fear. Those things don't need to have a hold on you. When you acknowledge them and bring them to the light, they lose their power. When you shine a light on a shadow, what happens? It disappears.

But if you avoid that shit and push it down, it will stay there. And not only that, it will build.

Self-love isn't about loving the great parts of yourself; it's about loving all of you. Even the bits you don't like. Even the bits you're ashamed of. Even the bits that you feel you want to hide. It's all you.

And you are perfectly you.

What's more, ultimately, the love you're looking for right now, it's already in you. You're not going to find it in anyone else. Not your mother, your father, your partner, whoever. You will find love in them, but not the ultimate love you're spending your whole life trying to find. It's in you and through your heart's connection to its divine Source.

It starts in your relationship with yourself. If you can't love all of who you are, how can you ever expect anyone else to do that?

They're only going to reflect back to you the shit you're not willing to own yet.

If you feel insecure, the universe will provide experiences and situations that bring your insecurity out. If you feel jealousy, you'll attract experiences that bring it to light.

This world is so beautifully designed to squeeze us. It's because we are supposed to live in a place of unconditional love. A place of contribution and gratitude. A place of peace and calm.

Life will keep squeezing us to allow our shadows to come out, and either we can try to push them back down—which is ultimately impossible—or we can choose to transmute our shadows into light.

Be gentle with yourself. Be your best friend. Nurture the six-year-old within you.

Embrace *all* of who you are.

Even your ugly bits.

LEARNING YOUR LESSONS

Self-love is so much more than mantras or a gratitude journal. It's more than feeling great about yourself all the time. Self-love is when you can really hold yourself in the shit. When the stakes are high, and the odds are down, when you fuck up, when life gives you challenges, your self-love is the strength that drives you to get back up.

Challenges are going to come your way. Life's gonna throw stuff at you. So, you can approach life one of two ways: you can fight against yourself and bring yourself down. Or you can be your own biggest champion.

I've got a hint for you: if you go through life fighting yourself and bringing yourself down, it's just going to create more problems for you than you actually need. They're just going to keep compounding.

And remember, problems are not actually "bad." They're *gifts*. Because overcoming problems and challenges is what allows us to grow. They're essential for helping us become all of who we are meant to be.

In many ways, we create our own problems. We *choose* them. Because they're actually the *lessons*.

To get metaphysical with you for a minute, I honestly believe that we chose this life before we were even born. That on some level, our soul, essence, universal energy chose to reincarnate into the existence we are living now. And we did that because of the inherited lessons, problems, and challenges within it.

We chose this particular life with these particular experiences to help us to become who we ultimately are and the highest version of ourselves. Even the shit experiences. Even the terrible ones. I believe that on some level, we choose whatever we need to really find who we are inside.

You can choose to believe that or not. But no matter how you see it, one thing is true: whatever you've been through, and for whatever reason you experienced it, you *survived*.

As you're reading this right now, think of all the shit you've survived. Everything you've been through. Even if you do feel at this point like you've fucked up your life, actually, you're still here. You survived it all. That's not something to beat yourself up for—it's something to fucking celebrate!

And it's not too late to make your life into whatever you want it to be. Whether you're twenty, thirty, forty, fucking seventy, you've still got a life to live. You've still got time to experience life as your most authentic, vulnerable, beautiful, magnificent self.

For me, there have been many years of feeling lost. And many fuckups along the way. But the more I discover who I really am and live as such, the more amazing my life becomes.

Sure, it's a journey. You don't just go out and find the Nirvana you're looking for after two days. You've got to go through your journey. You've got to learn your lessons, overcome your challenges, get to know and love who you really are. You've got to put in the work.

But it's worth it.

Everything amazing that has happened to me came out of challenges and the lessons I learned from them. My amazing relationship right now came out of having so many others where I undervalued myself, where I didn't respect my boundaries, where I didn't love myself, where I stayed too long, where I allowed myself to be in a less than desirable outcome.

My financial success has come from me investing and losing so much money and learning some really hard lessons. I've failed so many times, bigger than many people can imagine.

Everything has come through experiencing the depths and the darkness of the other side, finally drawing my line in the sand and deciding "no more."

I invite you to do the same.

No more will I allow myself to be treated with less than I deserve.
No more will I allow myself to dim the light on my true self.
No more will I allow myself to keep giving in to my negative self-talk.
No more will I allow myself to neglect my own needs and self-care.
No more will I allow myself to give up on my dreams.

What is your heart telling you to decide right now?

What lessons have you been ignoring?

HOW TO START BUILDING SELF-LOVE

There are many ways to build and practice self-love. Just do a quick Google search and you'll find millions of pages on self-love mantras and activities.

It's easy enough to tell someone they should learn to love themselves. But how do you actually do it? Especially if you are harbouring deep resentments, fears, guilt, regrets? What if you actually don't like yourself much? Self-love might seem like an unachievable goal.

Here are a few ways to practice self-love starting today:

FORGIVE YOURSELF

Often what keeps us disconnected from self-love is guilt or shame around certain ways we've shown up or things we've done in the past.

But guess what? You're human. So you fucked up? We all do. It's how we learn. As we've already talked about in this book, failure is only feedback.

Stop emotionally whipping yourself to shreds for mistakes you have made. There is no ultimate martyr prize in it for you, only years of holding yourself back and wasting time feeling miserable.

Instead, take what you learned and do it better next time. Make amends and move forward. That's all anybody can do.

To start forgiving yourself, it can be as simple as standing in front of a mirror and saying, "I'm sorry, and I forgive me. I love you." It may sound a bit woo-woo, but there's something very powerful about expressing those words. If you don't feel comfortable doing it in front of a mirror, just find somewhere quiet and comfortable to repeat these words a few times each day.

Forgive yourself for being so hard on yourself. Forgive yourself for not being who you think you should be. Forgive yourself for feeling you need to have a life like the people you see on social media who seem to have it so much more together than you (they don't).

TALK TO YOURSELF KINDLY

How does your inner voice speak to you? Does it support you with the patience and love that you give others? Or is it like a bunch of mean girls from high school are camping in your brain?

Our inner voice can be kind of an asshole when you let the ego control it. Remember, the ego's number one priority is keeping you in your comfort zone. And it does that by keeping you small. How does it keep you small? By berating you. Bringing you down. Keeping you feeling weak or incapable. Making you drown in guilt.

Essentially, the ego keeps you stuck in the illusion that you are powerless.

Think about this—would you speak to your friends the way your inner voice speaks to you? If not, then it's time to change the track.

Here are a few ways to reframe negative self-talk into more empowering messages:

Why did I embarrass myself like that? I'm an idiot. Becomes…*Wow, that was a silly thing to do. It's going to be a great story to tell my friends.*

What's the point of trying? I'll never get there. Becomes…*This is just a temporary setback. I'll get there eventually if I just keep taking one step forward every day.*

I'm lonely, and nobody likes me. Becomes…*I'm going to keep working on myself, knowing that the more I show up as authentically me, the more I'll attract the right people into my life.*

As you can see, one version of self-talk is totally disempowering. The other builds you up.

MAKE HONORING YOURSELF
A DAILY PRACTICE

Everything you're learning in this book, when practised, builds up your self-respect, self-worth, and self-love. Protecting your boundaries. Showing up authentically. Embracing progress over perfection. Doing heart meditations. Daily rituals.

Incorporating all these practices into how you show up in the world adds up to a more holistically balanced and nourished *you*.

Self-love isn't just something you have; it's something you practice. It's something you work on and build. Honouring yourself this way makes you stronger, happier, and far more capable than you ever imagined you could be.

Ultimately, the only one who can make the decision to operate this way is *you*.

You can decide that you deserve love and start to behave in a way that cultivates that love within yourself. Or not. It's up to you.

But remember this—there's no prize at the end of your life for being the one that suffered the most guilt. There's no prize for being the one who sacrificed the most to others.

And as I've said before, the stronger, happier, and more fulfilled you are, the more you have to give to others. The truth is you can have a *far* greater impact on the people around you when you are operating with a full cup.

When you love yourself, you show up in relationships better. You show up in friendships better. With your family. At work. In your wider community. You have more to give, and what's more, how you show up influences others to do the same.

Showing up from a place of integrity and authenticity, respecting your boundaries and demonstrating self-love causes ripples as the people around you unconsciously reflect what you're putting out.

By loving yourself, you really can change the world.

But it begins with *you*.

CONCLUSION

Your Journey Is Just Beginning

WOW, WE'VE COME A LONG WAY. THANK YOU FOR ACCEPTING THE invitation to share my journey with you by reading this book.

I hope you have defined some dreams and made some decisions about what you want your life to be and how you're going to make it happen.

I've got some good news for you...

Since you've read this book to the end, you've already started creating this change in yourself.

Whether consciously or not, you chose to pick up and read this book because there's been a part of you longing to create change. You've been steered down this path to hear about my journey and to take from it what you will.

If you didn't crave change in your own life, you wouldn't be holding this book right now. You wouldn't have bought it at all. Or you would have bought it, read a chapter or two, then put it down.

But you got to the end. Thank you for journeying with me down memory lane and listening to the lessons I've picked up along the way. I hope they serve you as they've served me.

As I've said before, I'm not telling you this is the only way. This has been my way. I just hope that it has opened up something inside you, perhaps a path to your own heart's wisdom, so you can find your own path.

You've already taken the first steps. Congratulations!

Take a moment to recognise that. Breathe in deeply, and give yourself credit for following your heart to and through this book.

The journey doesn't end here. For you and for me, the journey continues.

If I can help you take at least one step towards loving yourself more and having the life of your dreams, this book and my time and investment into it have been worth it. If I can help you make two or three steps forward, then even more so.

So, keep doing your heart meditations. Commit to some daily rituals. Start keeping the promises you make to yourself and others. Speak up and maintain healthy boundaries in your relationships. Show up as your authentic self. And allow yourself to be more and more vulnerable.

With each step, you'll start to create the change you crave.

But be patient. We often overestimate what we can do in a short period of time, and we underestimate what we can do in a long period of time. By doing a little bit every day, over time, the effects will build into a tremendous impact.

WHERE TO NEXT?

Maybe, at this point, you are still making objections and assumptions as to why my advice wouldn't work for you. Why it's easier for me, harder for you, or whatever other justification your ego is shouting at you to keep you stuck in your status quo.

But I'm telling you...you've come this far. So, love yourself enough to take the next step and see what opens up. Commit to connecting to your heart. Understand the part your mind plays. And then start putting what you've learned into action. Remember, progress over perfection.

If you want to make faster progress, find someone who can help you explore these themes within yourself and keep you accountable to becoming the person you were born to be.

Now that I have followed the processes I've outlined for many years now, I can honestly say that I've made the most progress when working with coaches who are outside of my world and beliefs and can see my shit and call me on it.

A coach is able to see the beauty and the love and the greatness within you, far beyond what you can see in yourself right now. They will hold you accountable when you start to slip. Because you will—you're only human! They are your partner. Not your mother. Not your friend.

Whether you decide to hire a coach, go to workshops, or find a mentor, invest in yourself by actively expanding beyond your current comfort zone, seeking new ideas and ways to operate.

Life is short, and it truly is what you make it. The good news is that you have the power to make it whatever you desire.

So, start now. Take action. You deserve to start living a happier, more fulfilled, and balanced life. A life where you don't just survive … but *thrive*.

RESOURCES

American Psychological Association. "Stress Effects on the Body." *American Psychological Association*, November 1, 2018. https://www.apa.org/topics/stress/body.

Bisharat, Andrew. "Duo Completes First Free Climb of Yosemite's Dawn Wall, Making History." *National Geographic*, January 14, 2015. https://www.nationalgeographic.com/travel/article/150114-climbing-yosemite-caldwell-jorgeson-capitan.

Bryant, Ben. "A DMT Trip 'Feels Like Dying'—and Scientists Now Agree." *BBC*, September 14, 2018. https://www.bbc.co.uk/bbcthree/article/dd52796e-5935-414e-af0c-de9686d02afa.

Effendi, Irmansyah. *Smile to Your Heart Meditations: Simple Practices for Peace, Health and Spiritual Growth*. Berkeley: Ulysses Press, 2010.

Everything DiSC. "Research Report for Adaptive Testing Assessment." Resources to Learn More about Everything DiSC. Last modified November 17, 2020. https://www.everythingdisc.com/EverythingDiSC/media/SiteFiles/Assets/LeadGenAssets/Everything-DiSC-Research-Report-AT-Revised-20201117.pdf.

Hawkins, David R. *Power vs. Force: The Hidden Determinants of Human Behavior*. Carlsbad: Hay House, 1985.

Hormone Health Network. "What Is Adrenaline?" Hormone.org. Last modified November 2018. https://www.hormone.org/your-health-and-hormones/glands-and-hormones-a-to-z/hormones/adrenaline.

Koch, Christof. "What Near-Death Experiences Reveal about the Brain." *Scientific American*, June 1, 2020. https://www.scientificamerican.com/article/what-near-death-experiences-reveal-about-the-brain/.

Lally, Phillippa, Cornelia H. M. van Jaarsveld, Henry W. W. Potts, and Jane Wardle. "How Are Habits Formed: Modelling Habit Formation in the Real World." *European Journal of Social Psychology* 40, no. 6 (July 2009): 998–1009. https://doi.org/10.1002/ejsp.674.

Magliarditi, Barry Williame. *The Path to Freedom: The 9 Steps to Create a Highly Profitable Business That Runs without You.* Self-published, 2020.

Naftulin, Julia. "Here's How Many Times We Touch Our Phones Every Day." *Insider*, July 13, 2016. https://www.businessinsider.com/dscout-research-people-touch-cell-phones-2617-times-a-day-2016-7.

Neuro-Linguistic Programming. "What Is NLP?" NLP.com. Accessed September 30, 2021. https://www.nlp.com/what-is-nlp/.

Reichmann, Florian, and Peter Holzer. "Neuropeptide Y: A Stressful Review." *Neuropeptides* 55 (February 2016): 99–109. https://doi.org/10.1016/j.npep.2015.09.008.

Rosenberg, Marshall B. *Nonviolent Communication: A Language of Life.* Encinitas: PuddleDancer Press, 1999.

Russo, Andrew F. "Overview of Neuropeptides: Awakening the Senses?" *Headache: The Journal of Head and Face Pain* 57, no. S2 (May 2017): 37–46. https://www.ncbi.nlm.nih.gov/pmc/articles/PMC5424629/.

Stanborough, Rebecca Joy. "What Is Vibrational Energy?" *Healthline*, November 13, 2020. https://www.healthline.com/health/vibrational-energy.

Team Tony. "Stop Wasting Your Time! Harness the Power of N.E.T. Time." *The Tony Robbins Blog*, accessed August 28, 2021. https://www.tonyrobbins.com/productivity-performance/stop-wasting-your-time/.

The Game Changers. "Open Heart Meditation." *Open Heart Meditation Steps and Exercises*, 2020. SoundCloud audio, 5:32. https://soundcloud.com/user-865171340/sets/open-heart-meditation.

ABOUT THE AUTHOR

BARRY IS AN ENTREPRENEUR, BESTSELLING AUTHOR, SPEAKER, business coach, investor, philanthropist, and spiritual guide.

Since founding a global coaching enterprise, The Game Changers, in 2012, Barry has mentored thousands of business owners to scale to multiple seven figures (and beyond) while creating a life of more balance, freedom, and fulfilment.

Barry understands how our "inner game" dictates the quality of our experience of life and is dedicated to inspiring and guiding others to reach their fullest potential by upgrading their own internal beliefs, attitudes, and spiritual connection.

Today, he heads up several multimillion-dollar companies and is actively involved in facilitating the rapid growth of several additional business interests, all while working less than one day per week.

In addition to running his businesses, Barry also hosts *The Comeback Game* and *The Tradie Business School* podcasts, which have over two million downloads over the past eighteen months.

Barry spends his time living in Bali, surfing, writing, and seeking to create meaningful change in the world through his various professional channels and grassroots business initiatives.

Find out more at www.BarryMagliarditi.com